THE
UNIVERSITY EXPERIENCE
1945–1975

The Royal College of Science and Technology	The Scottish College of Commerce	The University of Strathclyde

THE
UNIVERSITY EXPERIENCE
1945–1975

An Oral History of the University of Strathclyde

CALLUM G. BROWN, ARTHUR J. MCIVOR
and
NEIL RAFEEK

EDINBURGH UNIVERSITY PRESS
in association with
THE UNIVERSITY OF STRATHCLYDE

© Callum G. Brown, Arthur J. McIvor and Neil Rafeek, 2004

Edinburgh University Press Ltd
22 George Square, Edinburgh

Typeset in Caslon
by Pioneer Associates, Perthshire, and
printed and bound in Malta by
Gutenberg Press

A CIP record for this book is available from the British Library

ISBN 0 7486 1932 1 (paperback)

Contents

List of Tables, Maps and Illustrations

Acknowledgements

This book explores one of the major experiences of British young people of the 1950s, 1960s and 1970s – going to university. It uses personal testimony from present and former staff and students, recorded on tape or disc, and transcribed. It was collected by the Scottish Oral History Centre at the Department of History, University of Strathclyde, during 2002 and 2003. The project has been a team effort, under the joint direction of Callum Brown and Arthur McIvor. The recruitment, interviewing, transcription and day-to-day management were undertaken by the research fellow, Neil Rafeek – a sizeable operation described in greater detail in the Appendix. The project was assisted by Hilary Young, an oral-history doctoral student in the Department of History, who undertook additional interviews and transcription. Some further transcription was undertaken by Sheena Rennie. The authors are very grateful to Hilary and Sheena for excellent assistance on the project. The project finances and administration were controlled by Arthur McIvor, who also edited the picture collection. Picture searching has been done by Rafeek and McIvor. The text has been compiled by Brown (chiefly Chapters 1, 4, 5, 6, and 7), and McIvor (chiefly Chapters 2, 3 and captions). Brown undertook overall editorial control.

This project would not have come to pass without our interviewees and correspondents who gave their time, their memories and their emotions to a project in which they felt the university they had either attended or worked for – in some cases for many decades – was deserving of commemoration. The authors hope they have conveyed faithfully those memories, and we trust that a just report has been made. The interviewers found great pleasure in these interviews, and received enormous help and extremely generous and friendly assistance with ideas for topics and contacts. To have received co-operation from so many people is something for which we are sincerely grateful, as it allowed us to acquire memorable interviews and create a large archive for the University of Strathclyde and posterity. We are also indebted to interviewees who lent or donated illustrations and memorabilia, and especially to those who gave permission for reproductions to be used.

Supported by the Principal's Fund, the project has attracted considerable assistance within the University community. The authors wish to thank the Principal for his generous and enthusiastic backing, for introducing us to a

THE UNIVERSITY EXPERIENCE 1945-1975

number of potential interviewees, and for obtaining administrative support from his staff and officers. Great assistance also came from emeritus professor David J. Tedford, the staff of the Alumni Office, the International Office, and of the University newsletter *PRISM*, and from the members of the Royal Tech Club – especially in tracing members of the university community who might wish to be interviewed. Map 1 was drawn by Gary Kerr of Estates Management, and Map 2 by Scott O'Donnell of Learning Services. Andrew Menzies of Learning Services undertook text graphics and reproduction of pictures. Most of the illustrations and documentary sources are from the Strathclyde University Archive, and we are grateful to the University Archivist Dr James McGrath and to Angela Seenan, Archives Assistant, for sterling help in the face or our demands. We also extend thanks to Grace Gough of *The Herald* Picture Library. We are also grateful to Dr McGrath for carefully reading through the entire book and for commenting on our text. All remaining errors are, as usual, the authors' responsibility.

As the book was going to press, news came of the death of two of our interviewees. Professor Noel Branton came to the University from the College of Commerce, and was the oldest and the first to be interviewed for the project. His enthusiasm and assistance were invaluable to us. Anonymous Interviewee 3 was the oldest Royal College student to provide recollections for this volume, entering vivid portraits of both the city and its Tech, and of the family circumstances of so many people during the economic trauma of the inter-war period. Both will be sadly missed.

Note on Oral History

All the oral testimony contained in this volume is published with the consent of the interviewees. Following legal and ethical guidelines, each extract of testimony is identified with the interviewee, except in a small number of cases where anonymity was requested and has been observed. Each interview is acknowledged and dated by footnote at first citation. The author of all quoted testimony is clearly identified either in the text or in a footnote at each citation. In the case of testimony from anonymous interviewees, a footnote provides reference corresponding to interviewees in the archived collection. Testimony is faithfully conveyed as spoken, following the procedures laid out in the appendix.

The authors have made every effort to ensure the accuracy of statements made by interviewees. However, the point of the book is to give primacy to the recollections, ordering of events and observations of the memories of those involved as management, academic staff, support staff and students in the formation of the University. Their testimony is not used in order to be empirically tested against other sources, but, in the best traditions of oral-history practice, is unveiled virtually stand-alone to allow their experiences, and their memories of them, to constitute an important and valid history. This is their story, and it is that which is privileged in this volume.

Notes on the Authors

Callum Brown lectured at Strathclyde from 1985 to 2004, latterly as professor of religious and cultural history. In 2004, he became a professor in the Department of History, University of Dundee. His most recent books are *Postmodernism for Historians* (Longman-Pearson, forthcoming), *The Death of Christian Britain: Understanding Secularisation 1800–2000* (Routledge, 2001), *Up-helly-aa: Custom, Culture and Community in Shetland* (Manchester University Press, 1998), and *Religion and Society in Scotland since 1707* (Edinburgh University Press, 1997).

Arthur McIvor is reader in history, and has taught at the University since 1984. His most recent books are *A History of Work in Britain, 1880–1950* (Palgrave, 2001), *Lethal Work: A History of the Asbestos Tragedy in Scotland* (Tuckwell, 2000) (with Ronald Johnston), *Organised Capital: Employers' Associations and Industrial Relations in Northern England, 1880–1939* (Cambridge University Press, 1996), and *Roots of Red Clydeside, 1910–1914?: Labour Unrest and Industrial Relations in the West of Scotland* (John Donald, 1996) (edited with William Kenefick).

Neil Rafeek is research fellow in the Scottish Oral History Centre, and completed both his BA History and doctoral degrees in the University's Department of History. His doctoral thesis, *'Against All the Odds'; Women in the Communist Party in Scotland 1920–91: An Oral History*, is to be published shortly by Tuckwell.

Preface by the Principal

Professor Andrew Hamnet MA DPhil CChem FRSC FRSE

The history of any great centre of learning, especially one such as the University of Strathclyde, which has been intertwined for generations with the lives of the people of its city, can be written from many viewpoints. A constitutional history would show the evolution of the systems of governance and the great men and women who had guided the institution since its inception. An academic history would celebrate the great discoveries made, the prizes won, and the sense of connection to the wider realm of scholarship. An architectural history would commemorate the buildings of the university, especially the Royal College Building with its magnificent Italianate design and marvellous (at least for the time) heating system. However, what I felt we lacked when I arrived in Strathclyde at the beginning of 2001 was a history that celebrated the people of the university: the staff and students who came through the doors of our buildings in George Street, Montrose Street and Pitt Street and whose legacy is the modern University of Strathclyde with its 14,000 full-time and its extraordinary 50,000 part-time students.

I was particularly anxious that the voices of that generation of staff and students that had seen the fusion of the Royal Technical College and the Scottish College of Commerce to form the original university in 1964 should be preserved before it was too late. In some ways, of course, we are too late: some voices have passed beyond the mortal plane and their reflections are only preserved in their writings and their papers. However, a remarkable number of staff and students have survived from that era; their voices could be captured and from that oral record we could distil a unique picture of an institution being born.

It is now forty years since those birth-pangs were felt in Glasgow: the lusty infant, as Charles Dickens memorably described one of our predecessor institutions, the Glasgow Athenæum, in 1849, has grown into a sizeable institution, rivalling the more ancient eponymous university in Glasgow in size and, in many areas, in reputation, but also working increasingly closely with it. To the Engineering and Science Schools of the Royal College of Science and Technology were added the strengths of the College of Commerce, which became the Strathclyde Business School, and Ross Hall, now the Scottish Hotel School. Compounding this mixture was the addition of a fledgling Arts and Social Science Faculty, initially with a 1,000 students but now doubled in size, and in recent years further expansion has taken place as the celebrated Jordanhill College, a major teaching training establishment, elected to join us.

John Anderson, Moses Provan, David Stowe and other of our founding fathers would, I suspect, now look on the size and complexity of the modern Strathclyde University with amazement: the breadth of subject matter taught; the national importance of the University within the modern Scottish economic framework; the fact that graduates of our institution are found in more than 150 countries, often in positions of considerable importance and influence; and the enormous space now occupied by our modern buildings, should not blind us to the vision that inspired these men: the realisation of the need to have a place devoted to useful learning, and to the provision of education in a wide range of professional spheres. Their legacy is our university, and we continue to carry forward their vision with pride.

Map 1 The development of the University of Strathclyde

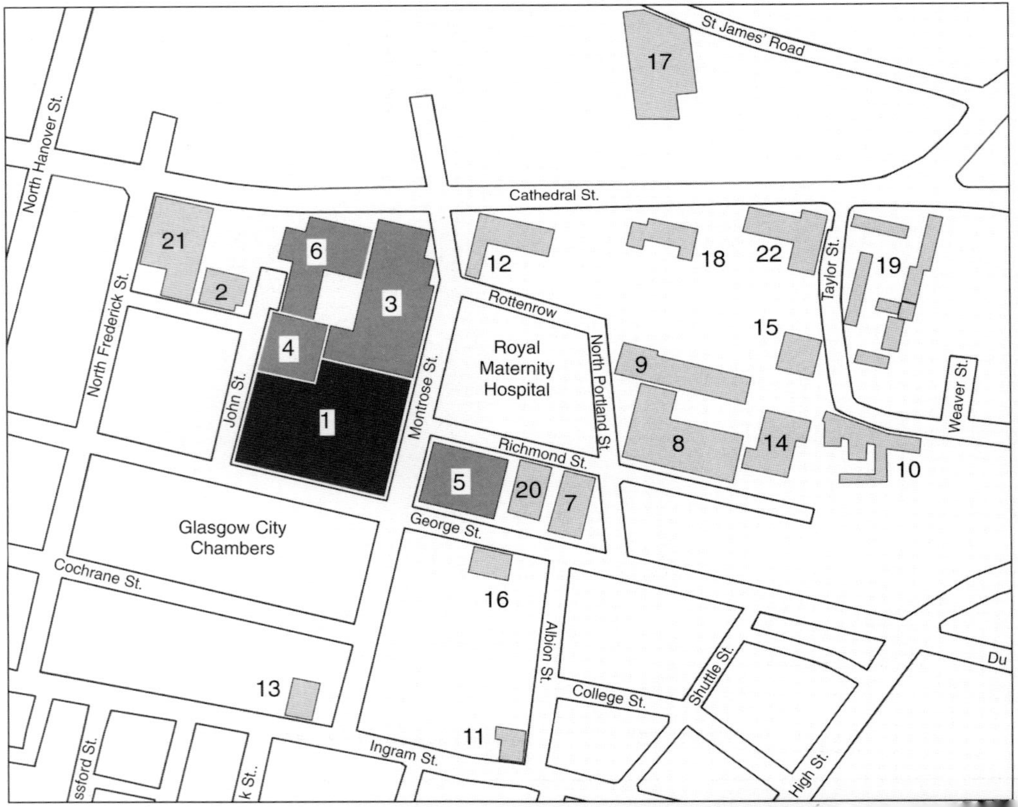

1945–1964

1. Royal College (1905)
2. St Paul's (1957)
3. James Weir (1958)
4. Students Union (1959)
5. McCance (1963)
6. Thomas Graham (1964)

1965–1975

7. Livingstone Tower (1965)
8. Colville Building (1967)
9. Architecture & Building Science (1967)
10. Balmanno Residence (1968)
11. James P. Todd (1969)
12. Centre for Industrial Innovation (1969)
13. 126 Ingram Street (1970)
14. John Anderson (1971)
15. Wolfson Centre (1971)
16. Turnbull Building (1971)
17. 181 St James Road (1972)
18. Stenhouse (1972)
19. Birkbeck Court (1972)
20. Collins Building (1973)
21. University Centre (1975)
22. The Todd Centre (1975)

Map 2 Glasgow: major industrial sites, c. 1950

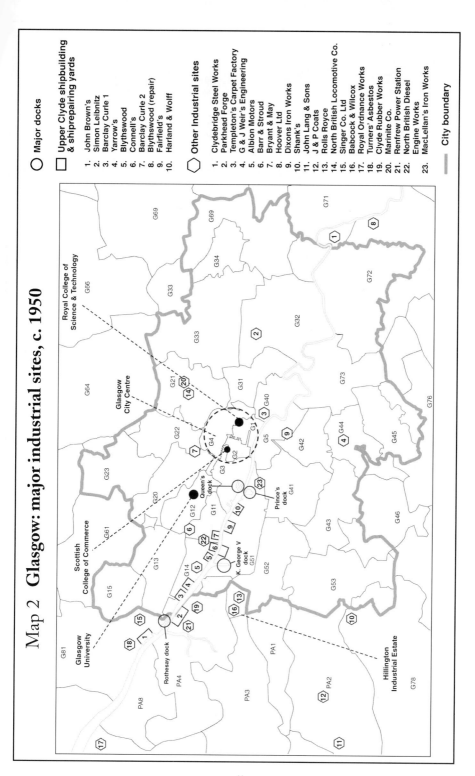

○ Major docks

☐ Upper Clyde shipbuilding & shiprepairing yards

1. John Brown's
2. Simon Leibnitz
3. Barclay Curle 1
4. Yarrow's
5. Blythswood
6. Connell's
7. Barclay Curle 2
8. Blythswood (repair)
9. Fairfield's
10. Harland & Wolff

⬡ Other industrial sites

1. Clydebridge Steel Works
2. Parkhead Forge
3. Templeton's Carpet Factory
4. G & J Weir's Engineering
5. Albion Motors
6. Barr & Stroud
7. Bryant & May
8. Hoover Ltd
9. Dixons Iron Works
10. Shank's
11. John Lang & Sons
12. J & P Coats
13. Rolls Royce
14. North British Locomotive Co.
15. Singer Co. Ltd
16. Babcock & Wilcox
17. Royal Ordnance Works
18. Turners' Asbestos
19. Clyde Rubber Works
20. Marinite Co.
21. Renfrew Power Station
22. North British Diesel Engine Works
23. MacLellan's Iron Works

—— City boundary

CHAPTER ONE

Introduction

In May 1964, the Royal College of Science and Technology and the Scottish College of Commerce merged, and three months later, in August, the Queen signed the charter erecting the University of Strathclyde. This was claimed as Britain's first technological university.[1] Its rise represents a larger story of British social, educational and economic history. In 1946, there were only 50,000 university students in Britain. By 1980, this number had grown to over 300,000.[2] This book is an oral history of some of those who experienced the formation of one university that contributed to that revolution. It is an account built almost solely on personal testimony – on the memories from lecturing staff, students and support staff who have come forward and recounted from their different perspectives the experience of being a member of a new university community from 1945 to 1975.

The experience of higher education in the second half of the twentieth century, as a piece of social history, has been largely ignored by historians. Until the 1960s, it was a history mostly of the male, white middle-class, with a few, usually exceptional, women, working classes and members of ethnic minorities being able to enter the elite bastions of Britain's older universities. But from the 1960s, being a student started to become not an exceptional but a common experience. University students in the whole of Britain numbered around 20,000 in 1900, still only 82,000 in 1954, but rose to 190,000 in 1966. There were more university students in Scotland alone (272,000) in 2001 than there were in the whole of Britain in 1970.[3] The target of more than half of all school leavers going on to university is now attainable, and with mature students returning to study as well, the university experience has become commonplace in British culture.

Universities in the early twenty-first century are part of British social heritage in a way unknown in 1950. The account in this book is determinedly a history of people's experiences, not an institutional history of the university. A plethora of university histories have appeared in recent years, including John Butt's detailed and unsurpassable institutional account, *John Anderson's Legacy: The University of Strathclyde and its Antecedents 1796–1996*.[4] The present account differs from them in its use of a large-scale oral-history project to provide a base of memory and recollection with which to understand the complex forces at work in the revolution of higher education in the middle of the twentieth century. The testimony is precious, each individual's story unique, but the material builds into a mosaic for the social historian to begin an experiential rather than institutional history of 'going to the uni'.

This introductory chapter sets the scene. It looks at the graduate world established during the late twentieth century, and the ways in which historians understand the cultural role of universities in Britain in the 1950s and 1960s. Oral-history inquiry is explained, as is the way in which the testimony was garnered for this book. Following a brief history of the origins of the University of Strathclyde, the chapter concludes by looking at the city of Glasgow and how our interviewees regarded it.

THE GRADUATE WORLD

Those who have been university students and staff during the last fifty years have lived through enormous change in educational and social history. Being a student in Britain has altered from being an experience of the few (mostly men) to being the standard preparation for life and work for most young people (of whom by the year 2002 a majority in Britain were women). The age since the end of the Second World War has witnessed great cultural upheavals, and it has been students who, more than any other single group, have fomented it and then, as graduates, crafted the new education-based economy. The proportion of eighteen-year-olds entering university has risen from 1.7 per cent in 1937, to 3.2 per cent in 1954, and to 4 per cent in 1960, but has since leapt to over 50 per cent in 2000.[5] Ours has rather quickly become a graduate world.

If students have re-fashioned much of our modern world, the staff of universities have been the instruments of change. They have taught, administered and researched, imparted skills and expanded the state of human knowledge. This conjunction of research with teaching has always been considered the distinctive feature of university learning. It is this that provides students with first-hand experience of how the learning of existing knowledge is linked to an emerging new knowledge, and how new ideas stretch into a future yet to be discovered. To facilitate this learning, library and technical staff have been vital, providing the lubrication for knowledge and the training facilities for skills. The wider university community is a complex one, and the administrative, security and estates staff have turned the modern campus into a major phenomenon of the built environment. Cities were once divided into business, industrial, retail and residential zones. Now, there is the educational zone – a vast area in most modern cities in which universities and colleges dominate entire swathes of the built environment, revitalising derelict quarters and transforming run-down city-centres.

2

Figure 1.1 Central Glasgow from the air, 1932
The Royal College is in the middle of this picture, behind the two blocks of the City Chambers (joined by the arches over John Street). To the left are George Square and the large roof of Queen Street railway station, through which generations of Tech and later Strathclyde students commuted to classes. To the top right are the white-tiled blocks of the Royal Maternity Hospital (demolished and purchased by the University in 2002). *Strathclyde University Archives.*

This book focuses on three key decades, from the end of the Second World War to the middle of the 1970s, as the period in which foundational changes to British universities were laid down. It was in this era that universities were set on the course of expansion, when the flummery of university life was overtaken by new traditions of democratic access, and when students emerged as ambassadors for youth as a whole – as innovators in style, protest, and new moral benchmarks.[6] In the 1950s, 1960s and 1970s, the traditional religious and moral conservatism of British society was undermined – nowhere more so than in Scotland where Victorian puritanism veined through every sinew of social activity, family custom and bye-law. Students became the new cultural leaders, regarded as never before as the highpoint of youth culture, challenging society's structures and rules, and challenging the leaderships of business and politics.

3

The history of universities is an area of scholarship that has been blossoming in Britain in recent years as their place in the cultural landscape has become more urgent to explore in the context of devolution, globalisation, and the altering construction of identity. Universities are now seen by social and intellectual historians as bodies that confer identity upon peoples and places. In the 1960s George Davie popularised the notion that Scotland's presbyterian heritage lay at the root of what he called 'the democratic intellect' which distinguished Scotland from England.[7] This intellect favoured a breadth of learning in distinction to English specialisation, and fed into a real democratic access to learning and opportunity (in parish schools and in universities) less apparent south of the Tweed. The 'lad o' pairts', the gifted boy (though not the girl), had been able – no matter the economic circumstances of his parents – to gain within the parish school of the presbyterian system the advanced schooling necessary for admission to one of Scotland's four 'democratic' and ancient universities. Despite the evidence of much empirical research that the Scottish educational system (including its church-controlled elements) was far from 'democratic' in its accessibility to all social classes and both sexes,[8] the 'egalitarian myth' has gained a strong foothold amongst Scottish intellectuals. Indeed, many of the virtues of (and perhaps even the necessity of) the Andersonian College were constituted by its providing for artisans, for working people and (in the early nineteenth century) for women those democratic opportunities denied these groups by the conventional universities. Still, the Davie thesis has developed into a widespread notion that universities in Scotland have been vital storehouses of national identity – in the form of a 'democratic intellect' – during the three centuries of parliamentary Union with England and Wales.[9] From another perspective, the rapidity of change and the increasing fluidity of the sense of belonging in modern European society have increased the desire of people to bear witness to their origins. But as race, ethnicity, religion and nationality become more complex formations, so people search for a broadening of the ways in which to understand their roots – including the University they attended. In post-imperial Britain, the weakening of the sense of national mission has led to a vague sense of unease with a fixed national, racial and religious patriotism, whilst the university where we learned our trades becomes a more benign, benevolent and morally-certain source of pride.

Whatever the reasons, university histories have mushroomed. The role of universities in the British economy and society as a whole, and their linkage to social and economic groupings have been studied by both economic and educational historians.[10] Most studies of individual universities have been institutional records, providing detailed narratives of the formation and advancement of the institution from a management perspective, and have been aimed at a graduate audience; as well as John Butt's 1996 book on Strathclyde, histories of the universities of Edinburgh, Glasgow, Aberdeen, and Glasgow Caledonian fall within this category.[11] Each of these has made significant contribution to the institutional side of the history of higher education in Great Britain. Somewhat different have been three books dealing with Aberdeen, Manchester and East Anglia universities. In a pioneering volume in 1988, Robert Anderson studied the demographic construction and transformations of the student community between 1860 and 1939 at the University of Aberdeen.[12] In one significant case, the history of a university has been researched and written by a leading historian of higher education: Michael Sanderson, the doyen of university, higher and technical-school history in Britain, has produced a benchmarking institutional history of the University of East Anglia, which was officially given the go-ahead in late 1960 and enrolled its first students in autumn 1963.[13] Meanwhile, Brian Pullan (with Michelle Abendstern) provided a detailed understanding of the development of Manchester University between 1951 and 1973, looking especially at the interaction between the institution and the society in which it was set. This involved a major oral-history project, interviewing sixty people, nearly all staff and administrators of the university, focusing on the development of university structures, student culture and the campus.[14]

The present volume draws on these examples, especially the work of Sanderson and Pullan. But this history differs in that it is based on the experience of the people at a university – not just the staff, as in Pullan's work, but also the students. This is, we think, new.

COLLEGES AND CULTURE IN BRITAIN IN THE MID-TWENTIETH CENTURY

The 1960s are becoming widely seen by historians of left and right as a defining period in the cultural history of Britain and Western Europe. The transitions in youth culture, of second-wave feminism (the first wave having led to women's suffrage in the 1910s, the second to equal opportunities legislation in the 1970s), and of sexual revolution and the undermining of authority, are widely acknowledged as the most fundamental and far-reaching for centuries, whilst some historians see the 1960s as marking the transition from modernity to postmodernity.[15] However intellectually constructed, there are few historians who fail to place the 1960s as the period of most rapid change in British society during the twentieth century.

Historians emphasise the discontinuities between the 1950s and the 1960s.

This can be seen in the literature on women's history, in which the 1950s are characterised as a decade – perhaps the last decade – of unchallenged constraint upon women's economic, educational, leisure and family roles. After the Second World War and some of the liberal changes of the 1930s, women in the late 1940s and 1950s felt the power of government policy and a national culture that demanded women's attention to home, hearth and family, to invigorate a depleted birth rate and reduced labour force, and a rather puritan culture of religious respectability that was especially felt by young girls in church and Sunday schools.[16] As the writer Angela Carter has been quoted as remarking, after the 1950s women deserved the 1960s. Discontinuity can also be seen in historians' understandings of the explosion of youth culture from its status as a sub-cultural, rebellious and 'beatnik' feature of the 1950s to its expansive, cross-class and transformative feature of 1960s and 1970s British culture as a whole. From sub-culture to dominant culture, this transition in youth was accompanied by a whole host of other things – amongst them, the liberalisation of sexual activity, the revolution in sexuality (specifically the movement for gay rights), the emergence of postcolonialism (the anti-apartheid movement and the rising awareness of racism), the end to formal British censorship, the rise of modern popular music, and the decline of organised religion.[17] With other changes in the significance and significations of fashion, media and the arts, followed by major demographic shifts (concerning marriage, the structure of the family, and the birth rate), the 1960s and early 1970s together constitute a period of most rapid change in cultural history.[18]

Historians have placed the colleges in the context of culture change in the 1950s and 1960s. An underground culture of the beat generation emerged in the 1950s' art colleges (including many of the leading figures of British popular music, art and fashion).[19] This gave way in the 1960s to a wider students' culture, fostered by the rapid growth of university access, new university campuses with few traditions, and a burgeoning youth. Women as well as men were seeking not merely skills and training but new lifestyles, values and ways of transforming the restraining world of parents and authority. The role of new graduates and drop-outs from universities in the frontline of the counter-culture is discernible in the oral-history work of Jonathan Green.[20] One of the themes from that work, as from others, is the way in which the university campus rapidly became between 1963 and 1973 both the site for developing student protest and the object of it. The attempts to overthrow the inherited traditions of autocracy and central management control in higher education were an issue for new and younger staff as well as for students. The student revolt in Paris in May 1968, especially at the Nanterre and Sorbonne campuses of the University of Paris, challenged the government of Charles de Gaulle. The revolt failed, but the consequences were great.[21] From these events emerged the European women's liberation movement, postcolonialism as a significant force within Europe, poststructuralism and postmodernism, and the emergence of what became known as Eurocommunism. In Britain, the student protest movement had gathered speed since 1965. Part of it was a revolt against college governance – especially at Essex, the LSE and Hornsea Art College, and at the University of Warwick where the Marxist historian Edward Thompson led a movement in 1969–70 of students and staff opposed to the close alliance between the university and business.[22] But partly it was about other issues – including white rule in Rhodesia, the Vietnam war, the war in Biafra, apartheid in South Africa, women's liberation and gay rights.[23]

In Scotland, the impact of radical student politics was felt more in the 1970s than in the 1960s. Despite a notorious incident of tomato-throwing at the Queen at Stirling University, the radicalism was centred mostly at Edinburgh University. The foundations were laid in 1968 after Malcolm Muggeridge, a famous Christian moralist and television religious pundit, felt compelled to resign as Rector of Edinburgh University after only two years in post because of the installation of a condom machine in the Men's Union.[24] Bizarre as this may sound today, it effectively highlights the puritan moral climate that still prevailed in Scotland at the time – Muggeridge having been, after all, initially elected by students. But there was a wider significance, as the historians of Edinburgh University make clear. The debacle showed how the student expectation that a rector would act to reflect majority student feeling might break down, leaving student opinion unrepresented on the university court. Student militancy rose with the support of the next rector Kenneth Allsop, and he was succeeded in 1972 by the first student rector in Scotland, Jonathan Wills. A year later Wills was succeeded by Gordon Brown (later Labour MP and Chancellor of the Exchequer) who completed the reformation of student power at Edinburgh University.[25]

The events at Edinburgh were the nearest that Scottish universities came to confrontational student revolt on the scale of Essex or even the LSE. But the events were nowhere near the level of student radicalism in Europe in the late 1960s. Yet, its greatest effect was probably not in protest against university but in protest by university students – notably at Murrayfield in the 1970s in the so-called apartheid tour of the Springboks rugby team, when effectively half the stadium was taken over by protesters, most of whom were students. There were other causes too. Apart from party-political causes (which involved not just socialists, communists but also the Young Liberals, led at the time by the later Labour MP and minister Peter Hain), there were other new pressure-group political issues. These included Shelter, the campaign for the homeless; environmental campaigns that led to the Friends of the Earth and Greenpeace movements of the early 1970s; and Christian-inspired postcolonial campaigns like Third World First and Oxfam. It is worth remembering, then, that student radicalism was not just from the far left, the libertines and the underground, but included young people of religious and non-religious backgrounds who helped to pioneer items in the emerging new moral order of the late twentieth century.

ORAL HISTORY

The oral-history project upon which this book is based involved in-depth interviews with nearly fifty staff and students of the University, with additional recollections submitted to us in written form. The material has focused on a diversity of reactions and themes, and the archive amounts to more than 360,000 words of transcribed testimony. No more than a fraction is quoted here.[26]

The development of oral history has revolutionised the way in which we look upon the nature of the past and our relationship to it. In both academic and popular modes, oral history has developed since the 1970s into the major method for accessing the history of the twentieth century.[27] In so doing, institutional, official and what has sometimes been referred to as 'top-down history' has been turned around by 'history from the bottom up'. More recently still, from the 1980s onwards, new methods of study have taken the memory as the basis of culture, and the examination of the way in which people narrate their own lives is theorised in modern historical studies as the basis of understanding cultural values, cultural change and the construction of identities in an increasingly multi-cultural world.[28] In some senses, oral history has provided vigour to the history of the neglected – the history of workers, women, the peoples of imperial colonies, of ethnic minorities. It has also been the basis for histories of the elites – be they low-profile bankers or high-profile politicians. In another way, it has provided new evidence on neglected fields, or those inaccessible in any other way – such as the experience and impact of asbestos-related diseases upon workers and their families in Glasgow in the last fifty years.[29] But in another sense, oral history has transformed the agenda of research and understanding of the past, shifting our focus to moments and experiences which not only reveal forgotten history, little regarded in the official record, but also the perspective of the less powerful or the minority.[30] In these various ways, oral history has provided the historian with an investigative tool of great empirical and conceptual potency.

In constructing an experiential history, context is important. In drawing the background of the city and its social problems, its built environment and cultural forms, there is the opportunity to draw on a vast reservoir of oral-history, autobiographic and related testimony that has been generated especially in the 1980s and 1990s. This material is rich and profuse, and capable of drawing the reader to a deeper understanding of particular themes, issues, incidents and places in which the story of the book is set.[31] But the authors have eschewed this, for a number of reasons. Firstly, we have sought to exploit our interviewers themselves in contextualising the city and the University's place in it. There is richness enough there, we feel, to provide that sense of place and time. Secondly, in calling upon testimony from hundreds of different sources beyond the university we felt that the sense of the umbilical chords to the University community would become broken, that the testimony would be emerging from those with less or even no links to the University or its precursor colleges. That linkage we felt endows the testimony with a special quality. And third, following on from that, we felt that by concentrating on the same interviewees for different aspects of the story brings out a sense of individuals' lives and their overall links to the University. What we think develops, as one runs through the material from the 1950s to the 1970s, is a sense of individuals from diverse backgrounds, coming to a university as teacher, student or support worker, and finding interaction between the institution and their own lives and identities, and with destinies in life. The interviewee thus in this book is no mere passive observer or chronicler of an institution, but is part of the chain of human beings breathing air into it. It is as a community that a university exists, not as a building. Indeed, we use the word 'campus' less in its spatial and material sense than in its communitarian and collective sense as a university people.

In this regard, the book relates the experiences of the individuals to their contexts – their families, community groups, places, and to other institutions to which they belonged. What comes through is the sense of the role of the institution as a focus for learning in the midst of a society of rapid and sometimes chaotic social and cultural change. The bulk of the interviewees were born or brought up in Scotland, and it is to that society of the 1950s, 1960s and 1970s that the experience of educational revolution is related. Many of those who entered the university as students in the 1960s and 1970s would not have gained that opportunity even a decade or two decades earlier. Indeed, most of them came from families in which they were the first to go to a university, though some had fathers (rarely mothers) who had attended the technical or commercial colleges before. Coming to Strathclyde is a personal journey, sometimes a frightening one. Yet the testimony gives a sense of a golden age gone. For staff of the institution, there is the sense of a mission in the 1950s and 1960s. Many staff came to education in the post-war years on the tide of a labourist agenda of 'education for all', and the University of Strathclyde, because of its very rapid expansion, was soon to have more than an average number of lecturers and professors for whom teaching was a calling, and one that would and should change society from old grooves of social exclusivity to one of social action and change. Writing in 1972, the historian of university expansion, A. H. Halsey, noted that 'the older class conceptions of education have been eroded rapidly in the post-war years. Statistics of inequality of educational opportunity have become popular knowledge and have turned access to universities into an almost commonplace criterion of distributive justice.'[32] The 1960s were an era of profound liberal values and liberalising legislation, and part of the process was of opening up education to allow the working classes and women access to the fruits of learning deprived them in higher education before.

At the same time, there is a sense of the golden age as a simpler life. People were self-driven in the 1950s and 1960s, the small tokens of esteem and grace and human values encouraging all in a united mission. For staff, there was practically no form-filling compared to today, and the drive of the Research Assessment Exercise (by which every British academic's life is now perpetually ruled to the production of four research items every five or six years) was absent. The tea trolley, as we see at one point, brought the university academic down to the scale of the rest of the society. This was no ivory tower where the ordinary and the mundane did not enter. On the contrary, this was a period and a place where the very heart of British life and culture was embedded in the post-war years, in the baby boom. It was a time of prosperity but not much materiality. Rationing was still underway in Britain until the mid-1950s, cars were a luxury for the few, and the opportunities for leisure and recreation were, for many, limited by cost. Television was only starting to arrive in the late 1950s and 1960s, and for most students the work of the college came first. But there are issues raised by oral interviewees that counter the sense of the golden age gone. As Britain lost its empire, immigrants and home students alike lost roles, and a new multicultural society had to be forged, giving rise to the challenge posed by racism.

Higher education funnelled the values, hopes and aspirations of the modern world in the midst of incredible global change. The sense of sanctuary from the outside is there in the memories. At the same time, there is the sense of training to change that outside world, bettering its economics and its values. The testimony has a freshness and a vibrancy, and we hope

Figure 1.2 The Royal College, c. 1962
Built 1903–5, this was the main college building, seen from the east, looking along George Street. Note the new James Weir Building, completed in 1959 (up the hill to the north) and the site in the foreground cleared for the construction of the McCance building (which was opened in 1963). *Strathclyde University Archives.*

that we have been able to capture that in this book. The testimony appears as the people speak – as raw, straight from the lips, often without the grammatical signposting and punctuation we know of from the written word. This is the spoken word, and with it come the unfinished sentences, the pauses, and the laughter heard in interview. The interviews were recorded on tape or minidisk, and transcribed to a word-processing package as honest reflections of the way things were said, complete with dialect. This is standard policy in oral-history work, because tampering with people's memories – even for the best of motives – sullies and distorts. In this way, the oral historian keeps faith with his or her source, and with the past that is being recalled.

THE UNIVERSITY

The University of Strathclyde in Glasgow is both new and old. It was born as a chartered British university in 1964, making it quite young, emerging at the time of tremendous university growth in Britain in the 1960s. Yet, its significance was not so much in its *newness* as in its *transformation*. The Anderson College was born in 1796 in the midst of the chaotic commercial and industrial expansion triggered by the emergence of the cotton industry. It became Anderson's University in 1828, then the Glasgow and West of Scotland Technical College in 1887, 'Royal' in 1912, and the Royal College of Science and Technology in 1956 (but was colloquially referred to as the Royal College or the 'Tech'). In 1964 the Royal College and the Scottish College of Commerce merged, and the new institution was chartered as the University of Strathclyde. Each college brought to the new university distinctive skills, different students and diverging traditions in learning. They tapped on older educational traditions in Glasgow dating back to the very beginnings of the Scottish Enlightenment and the Industrial Revolution.

Glasgow's educational base stretched back to the first University of Glasgow, founded in 1454, to serve what remained a relatively small market town. Even at the time of the Treaty of Union between Scotland and England in 1707, Glasgow had a population of no more than 12,000 people which, in European terms, was a small centre compared to the great regional capitals of continental nations. The University of Glasgow also remained small, but was part of a distinctive Scottish tradition of town colleges that placed higher education at the forefront of religious life, teaching and learning. During the Scottish Enlightenment of the eighteenth century, the city attracted some of the greatest minds of the age – including Adam Smith and James Watt – to work and to study. The spirit of science and discovery was being boosted, of course, by the expansion of trade and empire as Scots became part of the greatest enterprise of imperial expansion the world has witnessed.[33] And it was in this atmosphere of renewal, expansion of the globe and of the mind, that the birth of Glasgow's second university occurred.

John Anderson (1726–96) was successively professor of oriental languages (1754) and of natural philosophy (1757) of the University of Glasgow.[34] He was a physicist with an interest in the practical, or experimental physics as he called it. He mixed with men of science, politics and learning (ranging from his fellow scholar Adam Smith to entertaining Benjamin Franklin when he visited Glasgow). Yet, he also sought out skilled workmen and their masters in an 'anti-toga' evening class, and he was fascinated with practical instruments of science that could improve life and work. He lived in an era of excitement and change. The son and grandson of the manse, as a young man he had carried a firearm to defend Stirling Castle from the Jacobites in 1745, published an early manual on field guns used by French Revolutionaries, designed an artillery piece, and was made an honorary citizen of the French Republic.[35] As John Butt has noted, Anderson became more radical in his views the older he became. He 'began his adult life as part of the modern Enlightenment consensus within Glasgow, modified only marginally by his devout Presbyterianism'.[36] But he became ever more separated from his university colleagues and more drawn to mercantile men, pious Calvinism and practical science. In his will of 7 May 1795 he gave most of his wealth 'to the Public for the good of Mankind and the Improvement of Science', by which he founded a university. He stipulated this institution in great detail, with its four faculties (Arts, Medicine, Law, and Theology), thirty-six professors, a ruling body of eighty-one trustees of tradesmen, artists, 'medeciners', clergy, lawyers and other professions (to be watched over by a committee of 'Visitors' composed of the Lord Provost and senior bailies of Glasgow Corporation, leading churchmen, lawyers, physicians and surgeons), together with a school. Anybody connected to the University of Glasgow, as he put it in his will, because of 'their Acts of Vanity, or Power, Inflamed by a Collegiate life, will be kept out of Anderson's University'.[37]

Anderson's College (or University or Institution as it became variously referred to) sprang into life in the late 1790s, and was the pioneer model of degree-grade classes in both science and arts subjects for artisans and, uniquely, for women. Indeed, the college was a pioneer of women's higher education, and it attracted as its early lecturers other pioneers – including George Birkbeck and Thomas Garnett who each went on to major academic positions in London. Anderson's College has recently been re-evaluated as constituting a significant milestone in the world development of higher education for women. Historian Sarah Smith, herself a double graduate of the University, has described how the distinctive Scottish system of class tickets, which became a substitute form of pre-graduation qualification, encouraged attendance by non-graduating workers and women. The result was that the student body of Anderson's was the first in which mature students, employed men and women formed the majority of the student body.[38] Though it lost students to a new Mechanics Institute that split from the College in 1823, it became reinvigorated by growth in technical education, especially in the later nineteenth century when paper qualifications, signalled by completion of a course by examination, became predominant. From 972 students in 1796–7, there were over 2,000 by the 1850s, with the majority in sciences and technical subjects. Students who passed through its classes learned practical physics (natural philosophy), chemistry and all its specialisms, mechanical engineering and also medicine, and many went on to run or found businesses in the west of Scotland. Anderson's became the practical college of the industrial economy – including the sciences of metallurgy, naval architecture, mining, public health and agriculture. New classes – plumbing, bakery, automobile manufacturing – followed, as did new means of delivery (including sandwich classes and close relationships with west of Scotland firms).

The work of the Anderson's College lay at the heart of the adaptation of education to the needs of the economy. By the late 1880s the needs of the educational base of Great Britain were being seen in the context of the second, steam-based industrial revolution, and its call for highly-skilled artisans and engineers. These were needed to staff and develop the sophisticated economy with its constantly evolving technology – the shipbuilding and railways industries, the pharmacy industry, as well as chemicals and dyes. There were growing educational needs, and the responsiveness of traditional universities could be a little slow, and it was in this context that the 'Tech' provided the city with its heart.

The role of the Tech in the city's industrial landscape was critical, especially its training role in engineering and shipbuilding. It had a distinctive character. As one of the interviewees, James Laurie,[39] who came to study pharmacology in 1952, recalls: 'We tended to look upon the Glasgow University as "the other place" where people with academic ambitions studied. The Tech was very much a college of practical hands-on science and technology.' Whole families passed through the Tech and the University. John MacLaren, who was later to become professor of bio-engineering at the University, recalled how his family first made connection with 'the Tech':

My grandfather was manager of the Baltic shipyard in St Petersburg. He died in 1896 with the family, which included eight boys, one of whom was my father and settled in Dumbarton a number of them were students at the Tech, including my father in the early years of the century and set up a boat-building business in Dumbarton, well known locally as MacLaren Brothers. Various brothers dropped off one at a time to become engineers and ship designers and boat designers in other parts of the country leaving my father eventually on his own in the boatyard known as Sandpoint Yard in Dumbarton. He attended classes at the Tech about the time that the Royal College building was being opened, or built, but had no connection from then until the war years when the luxury motor-yacht business failed six months before World War Two

Figure 1.3 The Scottish College of Commerce, c. 1960
Built in 1934 in Pitt St, Charing Cross, this was the main site of the Scottish
College of Commerce until 1972 when it was sold and became the headquarters of Strathclyde Police. *Strathclyde University Archives.*

broke out, partly because of the Depression. He became an inspector in
Barr & Stroud's in Glasgow about the time that Sir James French, managing director of Barr and Stroud, was chairman of the governors of the
Tech. During the war years he became an instructor in wartime courses
training inspectors in the basement of the Royal College. He was very
active in the various affairs both at the college and Barr & Stroud's at that
time.

This intimate interaction between education and industry was characteristic
of the higher education in which the Andersonian came to specialise.

Joining the old Andersonian in the union of 1964 that created the
University of Strathclyde was the Scottish College of Commerce.[40] Its
origins dated from 1845 and the formation of the Glasgow Educational
Association, which gave birth in December of that year to the Glasgow
Commercial College led by twenty-five-year-old Moses Provan. It was
designed to fill the gap between the University of Glasgow and the

Mechanics Institute. Opening in 1847 in converted Assembly Rooms in Ingram Street (two streets away from the current University campus), it quickly established itself as a literary as well as commercial institution. Its opening meeting was chaired by Charles Dickens with a full house of civic dignitaries. Dickens said: 'It is a great satisfaction to me to occupy the place I do, on behalf of an infant institution: a remarkably fine child enough, of a vigorous institution, but an infant still.'[41] The institution became the Athenæum, which asserted a high-cultural function in civic affairs, attracting large-scale donations and – on one occasion – the patronage of Queen Victoria to a fund-raising bazaar. In many ways it was a curious body, with shareholders, a newsroom for commercial research and newspapers (including an early electric telegraph in 1854), and it elected Prince Albert as its President in the 1850s. It was responsible for bringing many prominent figures to the city. Ralph Waldo Emerson gave two lectures in 1848, William Makepeace Thackeray gave four lectures in 1856, Thomas Hughes (author of *Tom Brown's Schooldays*) gave two lectures, and Dickens spoke again in 1851. The institution moved to the purpose-built and very grand Athenæum Building in St George's Place (still standing in what is now Nelson Mandela Square) in 1888, and this became the home of the music and arts departments and later of the Royal Scottish Academy of Music and Drama. At other premises, different subjects were taught. The students increased and the topics expanded – from modern languages to elocution and music, and by the late nineteenth century the list included political economy, mercantile law, and commercial geography. In 1901 the College was reconstituted as a 'central institution' funded by the Scottish Education Department. It was renamed frequently: in 1903 it became the Central Institution for Commercial Education in Glasgow and the West of Scotland, in 1913 the Glasgow and West of Scotland Commercial College, and later the Scottish College of Commerce. It was aimed at the school-leaver and the pre-university entrant. By 1913 there were 1,419 students in cramped conditions, but after some fifteen years of fund-raising a new central building opened in Pitt Street close to the city's main shopping area in late 1932. By then, the College was strong in languages, economics and commercial subjects. It had a thriving student culture and students' union, 46 per cent of its 1,821 students were women (1939 figures), and it could boast one prime minister (Bonar Law) as an alumnus. Discussions on university connections with Glasgow had taken place between the wars, but it was under Dr Eric Thompson, the Principal from 1946, that reorganisation and expansion to 3,000 students prepared the way for integration with the Technical College. It brought to the new University distinctive expertise in a variety of disciplines – including arts and history subjects, half of the Glasgow School

16

of Management, the Scottish School of Librarianship (set up in 1946 as only the second in the whole of Britain), and the Scottish Hotel School (founded 1944), and its strong reputation in economics. Though sections of the College (notably secretarial courses) were eventually to end at the merged institution, the College of Commerce became the basis for many of the disciplines of the new University – the humanities, social sciences and several non-science vocational technical subjects (as well as large numbers of women students).

In a leader comment in September 1963, the *Glasgow Herald* reported on the news that a charter for the University had been agreed in draft form: 'The new university had to be recognisably Scottish, but the machinery of government in the existing Scottish universities, based on a medieval concept enshrined in a Victorian constitution, could be adapted only with difficulty to the new foundation.' The distancing from the management set-ups of the four old universities of Scotland – those of St Andrews, Glasgow, Aberdeen and Edinburgh – was a deliberate move (though the University Court would include teaching representatives that Anderson had excluded in his 1796 will). The stronger base in the humanities and social sciences, as the *Glasgow Herald* concluded, was vital: 'the system of government for Strathclyde had to be consistent with the advancement of science and the provision of liberal education in a twentieth-century atmosphere.'[42] In this regard, Strathclyde was the first Scottish university not to be subject to the provisions of the Universities (Scotland) Acts of 1858 and 1889, excluding it from the need to have a rector or a general council (of graduates), excluding the necessity of discussing ordinances with other universities, and not requiring Privy Council approval for its regulations. The university could also select its own students (thus opting out of the requirements of the Scottish Universities Entrance Board of the early 1960s). As the first Principal, Samuel Curran, was quoted as saying, the constitution of Strathclyde bore some strong similarities to that of many new English universities, and he wished to allow three-year honours degrees and an increased flow of students from England.[43] However, Strathclyde sustained the strong Scottish-university tradition of broad education, as it adopted a careful balance between the technological and the arts-based institution.

The decision to create Strathclyde, as also a number of other new universities, preceded the Robbins Report of October 1963 that is widely held to have signalled the policy of rapid university expansion in Britain.[44] Strathclyde expanded its students and built new buildings at astonishing speed, and colonised an ever-increasing area of central Glasgow (see Map 1). With the Nobel-prize-winning Lord Todd of Trumpington as the first Chancellor of the University (1965–91), and Dr (later Sir) Samuel Curran its first Principal and Vice-Chancellor (1964–80), the University switched from Scottish Education Department funding in April 1965 and became wholly reliant on the London-based University Grants Committee. 'Uniformity' became the watchword of the Robbins Report which explicitly criticised how in Scotland 'conditions of entry vary unnecessarily between institution and institution'.[45] Education started to be seen less as the basis of economic advancement and more as the basis for a modern democratic society that allowed individuals free access to economic and social advancement through widening educational opportunity.

GLASGOW

Such opportunity was much needed by Glasgow. It was a city that in the 1950s still buzzed with the excitement of engineering, shipbuilding and the making of things. It was a city where engineers could feel proud and useful, and where identity as a man often rested on prowess in wrestling with practical engineering problems and machines. Yet, by the mid-1970s, it was a city in the throes of serious structural readjustment in its own economy and to that of the region that it served. The staple heavy industries upon which the whole of the west of Scotland had depended since the middle decades of the nineteenth century were in sharp decline, causing massive unemployment that was to contribute to the national recession of the late 1970s and early 1980s. It was this disappearing economy that the Royal College had been specifically developed to serve. So, unlike most of the new universities of the 1960s, which were created in green-field sites adjacent to smaller regional centres and market towns,[46] the period in which the University of Strathclyde was formed was not a 'golden age' for its locale but, indeed, a period of rising depression in economy and society.

Glasgow grew as an imperial city making imperial products. It attracted workers from very poor backgrounds to live in a city full of poverty and poor housing. One of the University's recent professors described his family background:

We come from a long line of Irish farm labourers (*laughs*) and my great-great-great-grandfather emigrated from Ireland to Manchester in the 1840s, during the potato famine, and he took some of his family with him, and my great-grandfather became apprenticed and eventually became a blacksmith and round about . . . the 1870s, possibly, he married down in Manchester and he had fourteen children, believe it or not (*laughs*)! And some of the younger ones he took up to Glasgow and they became domiciled in Springburn and the reason being – during that time

Glasgow was becoming a big engineering centre – heavy engineering was the thing in Glasgow, shipbuilding, locomotive building, sugar machinery, all sorts of things, and he got a job with the eh . . . – the locomotive company up in Springburn . . . He got a job there as a blacksmith and my grandfather became an employee, I think it was the NB Locomotive Company, and he became an employee and became a tradesman-grinder, which was a trade in those days . . . Very well paid in those days, actually. I mean a tradesman-grinder in those days would be paid as much as a medical man.[47]

But things changed for the skilled worker. The 1920s and 1930s had brought world recession to the city, with the effect, as the city's historian Irene Maver (and double alumnus of the Strathclyde History Department) has said, of 'leaving a searing impact on the industrial workforce'.[48] At the height of the inter-war recession, in May 1933, over 121,000 Glaswegians were dependent on public assistance. Rearmament, late 1930s' economic recovery and the Second World War brought relief from the unremitting decline, but the impact was transitory. Shipbuilding returned to the Clyde on a large scale (400,000 tons of ships being launched each year in the early 1950s), with 15 per cent of the city's total workforce in 1951 being in shipbuilding, engineering and metal manufacture. Table 1.1 shows the composition of the workforce on Clydeside in 1951, and indicates not just the continuing dominance of the traditional staple industries but also the male dominance of waged work. But the shift from heavy industry was unstoppable, and even in the midst of the recovery of the post-war years, in December 1951, there were 17,500 people registered unemployed in the city.[49]

Professor John Paul recalls the River Clyde in the post-war years:

It had about six shipbuilding companies between the centre of Glasgow and Dalmuir [in Clydebank to the west], but *one by one* they closed down . . . Well, the biggest warning was North British Locomotive Company [at Springburn, two miles to the north of the Royal Technical College] which had a magnificent business, building massive steam locomotives which were exported all over the world. And they didn't see the move to diesel coming, and – *too late*, they jumped into it and they had some not very good designs, *and folded*. And I think shipbuilding on the Clyde was a little bit like that. They stuck to boilers and steam turbines too long, some of the companies went into internal combustion, but late, and they did quite well but it was the other countries like South

Korea with a cheaper labour force that went in and took the market away for big ships.

Table 1. 1 Employment in main industries on Clydeside, 1951

	Workers (thousands)	Percentage male
Mining	37.5	98.4
Shipbuilding	58.2	95.4
Construction	71.8	95.3
Metals	44.2	94.1
Vehicles	29.4	92.9
Mechanical engineering	81.7	84.6
Transport & communications	94.5	83.0
Public administration	53.6	82.2
Timber	18.4	79.9
Miscellaneous metals	19.3	77.7
Chemicals	21.1	73.0
Instrument engineering	6.6	62.1
Electrical engineering	11.4	58.8
Paper	21.8	57.8
Food and drink	47.1	56.1
Textiles	55.7	33.9
Clothing	30.9	21.7

Source: B.P.P., Census of Scotland, 1951

In the face of fundamental industrial decline, government policy became intensely interventionist, encouraging international companies in new economic sectors to come to the west of Scotland – including IBM and Honeywell in electronics and computing. New industries were bolted on to the traditional heavy industries – car-making at Linwood from 1963 (making the Hillman Imp) and the Ravenscraig steel mill at Motherwell (which was modernised as a symbol of regional economic regeneration). The care of the city was now secondary to that of the region, with economic development, enterprise and population itself being 'overspilled' to new towns and peripheral housing schemes. The result was that the population of the city, which had stood at just over one million since 1911, started for the first time to contract from its peak of 1,089,767 in 1951 to 897, 483 in 1971.[50] Thirty years later, in 2001, this figure had fallen still further to 577,869.[51] The workers sought fair treatment in the midst of this massive economic change, leading to the workers' work-in at Upper Clyde

Figure 1.4 The site of the future Livingstone Tower
Photographed in 1962, just prior to their demolition to make way for
University expansion, these tenement buildings in George Street show the
type of overcrowded housing that was being slum-cleared in much of central
Glasgow in the 1960s. The nearby Gorbals was also undergoing re-development
in these years. *Strathclyde University Archives.*

Shipbuilders in 1971 in which hundreds of thousands of other workers supported industrial action to save the closure of a major shipyard at Govan in
the south-west of the city. The 1970s became a period of heightened industrial militancy in the city. At the same time as the economic problems deep-
ened, social problems mushroomed. The state of Glasgow housing was the
worst in the Western industrial nations; in 1951 the county of
Lanarkshire, containing Glasgow, had a housing overcrowding figure in
excess of 1.25 persons per room, the highest in Britain, compared to 0.74
for England and Wales as a whole.[52] The 1950s and 1960s witnessed mass
re-housing, with hundreds of thousands of new houses erected to decant
population from slum areas in the centre to the outskirts and to new towns
of East Kilbride, Livingston, Cumbernauld and Irvine. In the city itself the
new houses became tower blocks from 1958 to 1970, resulting in new

21

problems of disrupted communities, isolated families, and the integrated social problems of drugs, drink, violence, and rising unemployment. With other problems (such as organised crime, smog, and low civic self-esteem), Glasgow intensified its long-standing reputation as the worst city in Western Europe.

Add to all of that the traditional image of Glasgow as a seat of religious bigotry. The sectarian confrontations between Catholic and Protestant were given a wider signification by Rangers and Celtic football clubs – the Old Firm.[53] The rise of the Troubles in Northern Ireland from 1969 always threatened, but never quite, spilled over to Glasgow and the west of Scotland.[54] Glasgow was still a place where religion mattered: on Easter Sunday 1955, reputedly 120,000 people came to hear Dr Billy Graham preach at Hampden Park after a six-week crusade of nightly meetings of up to 10,000 people in the Kelvin Hall in the city's west end.[55] Graham also preached in the Royal College's own Assembly Hall. More broadly, the culture of puritan religion, reflected in the presbyterian heritage of Scotland, was still prevalent in daily life. Cinemas and public houses did not open on Sundays, public houses had very short opening hours, sexual life was circumscribed, and Sunday activities were still regulated – in part by law and in large part by community pressure to conform. Scotland in the 1950s had an air of moral oppression and cultural claustrophobia; to be a libertarian was to be a rebel, to court being labelled 'unrespectable' and 'rough'. Yet, for all that, Glasgow in the 1950s and 1960s was still not an especially religious city: little more than 10 per cent of the population went to church on a Sunday in the mid-1950s.[56]

In truth, there were in the 1950s, 1960s and 1970s many Glasgows. The city was portrayed in a series of stock representations – images developed as ways of comprehending the city and exporting it to other places. In the 1960s, John Davies,[57] professor of psychology, recalls how the media in England conveyed a violent image of the city – and especially of certain parts of it. He recalls that 'the Gorbals had a *terrible reputation*. It was a working-class English stereotype of what Scotland was like I suppose, or what Glasgow was like.' Sociologist Sean Damer has shown how there has been a long struggle between images of the city, and how in the 1980s the images became transformed by a campaign to sell the city as one of modernity – of new industries, high culture, scenic location and wine bars. The result, he argues, has been 'a workers' city whose rulers resolutely pretend that it is something else'. Image and reality were not the same thing, he says: 'Historically, Glasgow's bad image was largely created south of the border'. The city's people were being punished for 'their radicalism' and were having their attentions diverted from appalling housing conditions.

Figure 1.5 Cathedral Street and beyond, 1962
A striking picture of the northern edge of the Royal College site. Note the Thomas Graham building under construction (middle right) and the site cleared for the construction of the new Allan Glen's school further east along Cathedral Street. In the background one of the earliest-built blocks of high-rise flats in Glasgow can be seen (Royston Road), as well as the Royal Infirmary and Cathedral (top right-hand corner). *Courtesy of* The Herald.

'Nowadays,' he concludes, 'it is to do with marketing the place, in selling it as a good location for government offices and outlets for the Next fashion chain'.[58] The marketing of Glasgow has intensified in the 1990s and 2000s. The city has been constantly pushed to the forefront of urban chic in British culture, being re-branded more violently than almost any other city on the planet. There were many different Glasgows to experience.

Professor Noel Branton[59] recalls that in 1946, on his appointment as a lecturer in economics to the Scottish College of Commerce, his colleagues in Cardiff Technical College regarded Glasgow as a dangerous place. 'People down there, they said "that's where the throat-cutters are", you know, but anyway I haven't seen any of them (*laughs*).' Indeed, his impression was very different from the image: 'I thought it was quite a pleasant place (*laughs*),' he recalls. But Glasgow was a complex place, and image was always grounded in some form of reality or other. Roger Sandilands[60] came at the beginning of October 1963 to study in the first year of the Arts and Social Studies undergraduate programme, drawn in large part by the place:

> I loved being in the big city, from being in the sticks. I was brought up in the Home Counties in what was at that time a very rural area . . . My father was Scottish and my mother half Scottish, so I had lots of relations up here, and I just loved being in the big city where there were theatres and cinemas and bars, and two big universities, the Mitchell Library and a big Victorian city that had *fantastic character* even though it was dirty and poor and drunken (*laughs*). There were the Barras, all these things were quite fascinating to me, and I felt for someone who's interested in doing Economics it seemed a living laboratory of economics in action in terms at least of the kinds of *real problems* that economists should be interested in; unemployment, inequality, poverty, poor housing, social problems in general. So to come up to Scotland and do a degree in social studies, *in a place like Glasgow*, in the heart of Glasgow which was being ripped apart right to slums of Townhead as it was then, was quite an *eye opener* and I thought really exciting.

Universities and big industrial cities with social problems came together in a very important way in the 1960s. The intellectual ferment of the social conscience, the use of social science and new technology to solve social problems, confronting the deprivation as well as the boredom of the post-war world of reconstruction and empty bombsites – all this brought to the universities of a city like Glasgow those who wanted intellectual pursuits to be socially relevant, not ivory-tower segregation. And for those universities being born in the midst of this collision of radical intellect with social-science reality, there was a special sense of mission and occasion. This in a sense separated the likes of the Strathclyde-to-be from the 'country-campus' universities like Stirling, Lancaster or Essex. Strathclyde was literally situated at the heart of a city with massive social and economic problems, immediately adjacent to a maternity home specifically established in the late nineteenth century to attack the poor mortality rates of mothers and children of central-city poverty. Strathclyde represented for many that sense of academy and society in benevolent collision.

Roger Sandilands' experience left him in no doubt that the city's reputation

24

Figure 1.6 A Glasgow home
In 1951, 44 per cent of Glasgow people lived in homes of one or two rooms –
house-types called the 'single-end' and the 'room-and-kitchen'. Overcrowding
had diminished only a little in fifty years, and placed the city as one of the worst
in the industrial western world. *Courtesy of* The Herald.

for grime, poverty and violence was not a myth. In his second year at
Strathclyde, 1964, he recalls the images with clarity:

Oh yes you saw it, I mean you saw people fighting, you saw people
smashing windows just wantonly, a lot of vandalism, and a lot of kids
fighting each other. I think there was quite a lot of trouble at these dance
halls which were very popular in those days ... I don't think I saw
anything desperately frightening but you did see a lot of fracas, and
drunkenness. I was aware of gangs, and there were graffiti on the
walls – 'Townhead Tongs', the Maryhill gangs and so on – and you were
aware of them, *but the police were very* strong and they didn't mess
around. There was a big police [presence] keeping a lid on the violence I
think ... one day I must have been staying with Mrs Bremner, it must

have been Elmbank Street, and I heard music one Sunday, flute music, went out to see what it was all about, and ended up at Blythswood Square and there were all these flute bands massing around Blythswood Square playing their various tunes, and I thought 'this is *wonderful*' and I thought 'This is *really nice*'. I thought 'God, this is Glasgow culture' you know, 'they've got a real sense of folk tradition and communal *spirit* and isn't this just great, what lovely tunes'. It was only much later that in my naïvety I learned what was behind it all and what they were celebrating and the sectarian conflict and the Rangers/Celtic syndrome. But it didn't really affect me very much, the friends I had, most of these runners and the running crowd, they were quite enlightened and just good fun and I enjoyed that very much.

Diana Henderson came to the city as a student in 1966 from the Scottish Borders, and found the contrast stark: 'I really was a small-town country girl and never having lived in a city before I was very taken aback by Glasgow. It was like another world. My memories are of endless rain, of dereliction and demolition, people begging in the streets and sleeping under cars and people selling things on the pavement. I saw my first Orange March which was an extraordinary sight.'[61] To some extent, the culture of Glasgow today still has resonance with 'Orange' and 'Green'. Richard Rose,[62] professor in politics from the late 1960s to the early twenty-first century, recalls his journey to the city from Northern Ireland in the mid-1960s: 'If you didn't care for football you were alright, the crack wasn't as fast as in Belfast, but then the pistols weren't so fast either.' John Davies arrived in the Department of Psychology in 1969:

> I was terrified because Glasgow had a bad reputation at that time. That was the time of the Easterhouse problems, Clive Noble was running the Easterhouse project and Frankie Vaughan [the pop singer], when I was here, . . . he went round and asked [gangs] to disarm and all the kids were handing in pick axes and things that they'd stolen from the local building sites and handing these in to Frankie Vaughan. And I thought it was going to be terrible, I thought I would be knifed if I walked down the street, and I had a perception of 'the Jocks', you know. But now I understand the Scots paranoia, I feel, quite, quite at home with it, after I've been here thirty years.

Dr Brian Furman,[63] reader in the Department of Pharmacology and Dean of Science, came to the city in the same year, 1969, as a lecturer in pharmacy. His recollections are grim:

It was a fairly *bleak place* in 1969. It was – the first impressions of Glasgow then were a black city because it was, all the buildings were *black* and you got the impression that the buildings had been *built* black but in fact it was all the industrial *soot* and Glasgow the –, it really had a poor reputation in 1969. It had a reputation as being a violent city, of being a city with a lot of poverty associated with it and it was with some trepidation that my wife came to Glasgow (*laughs*).

Professor Peter Robson of the Law School came to Strathclyde in late 1969, and despite his experience of innovative store-front law facilities for the poor in east-of Scotland communities, Glasgow was different:

I'd lived in Scotland for a number of years, I'd lived in Edinburgh, but Glasgow was, *reasonably depressing*. It was very, very dirty (*laughs*) . . . I remember somebody taking a colleague and I for a drive up to one of these housing developments up in Maryhill where he was doing a programme about the problems of redevelopment in Maryhill, and my colleague and I were giving advice and he was a planning lawyer and I was a housing lawyer by that time. And I remember this man saying 'Glasgow doesn't have any decent restaurants'.[64]

But street culture has changed in the intervening four decades, especially since the mid-1980s. Dr Furman again: 'But of course Glasgow pulled itself up by its boot straps in the '70s onwards and is now *unrecognisable* compared to what it was in 1969. And it's now a very, very attractive city which I defend very strongly against all critics when I meet people.' With Glasgow elevated in 1990 to the status of European City of Culture, there ensued a dramatic improvement in the infrastructure of leisure and city-centre decoration, a growth in cultural facilities of all sorts, a liberalisation of licensing laws, and a diversification in the types of entertainment available (especially at night). There was a maturation of a much more vigorous and diverse spectrum of arts, drama and literature in the city. This in great measure eroded the extreme polarisation between high and low culture, between 'rough' and 'respectable', that used to characterise Scottish society in the 1960s and early 1970s.

One of the University's careers advisors has eloquently said that 'the students who come to Strathclyde, both then and now, have not really ever been people who can afford not to get a job when they finish, you know. We're not talking about "Oh well I'll just bomb around in Daddy's yacht".'[65] The students of the Tech and the University of Strathclyde included those who grew up in a city of poverty, depression and social problems. For many, the social problems were within their own experiences, their own families, and their entry to the university and success in it seems remarkable. One anonymous interviewee, a student and lecturer at the College, recalled of his father and mother:

> I mean, he ended up smoking forty cigarettes a day and he was an alcoholic to boot – and so it made life very difficult for my mother when we were all young, obviously, because he spent most of his so-called wages on drink and mother had six children. I was the eldest, the second was a boy who died when he was eighteen months old with pneumonia which was a killer disease in the early '20s for infants . . . We hit a bad financial patch in the 1929 crash in America which was a worldwide depression, you know it started the worldwide depression and Scotland didn't escape and of course we were in very poor circumstances, I can tell you, when we came down to Mosspark – and I mean, I can remember –. Well, my youngest brother, he was an infant so he was still on milk – the bottle – but I can remember my mother dividing a fried egg between four of us and we had a half a slice of toast and a cup of tea and that was your breakfast, you know? And I mean people talk about being poverty-stricken today, *they don't know the meaning of the word.*[66]

It was the interviewee's mother who got him to the Tech College:

> She was very keen on education and she felt that for the rest of us there was only one way forward and that was to become educated, so she struggled to keep me at school and I left school at, I was sixteen and a half when I got my higher leaving certificate. And I started in the college in September 1938, so I was sixteen and nine months (*laughs*) when I started in the College. And because of the family circumstances – we were so poverty-stricken – that the local Glasgow Council paid my fees. Now it was all of £36 in those days, and I also got a bursary from the Carnegie Trust and it was £18 a year and this was supposed to buy your books and all the rest of it, but I had to use the £18 to eke out my fares to the college and in those days everybody lived at home, you know, there was none of this *nonsense* of going away to the bloody ends of the earth to go to college! . . . I started at the college in 1938, September 1938, and I graduated in June 1942.[67]

The city's heritage was a complex one. Malcolm Allan,[68] a former senior member of the library staff, recalls another aspect of the 1960s: 'you still had the rolled-up umbrellas and the bowler hats on the gentlemen-of-the-city

Figure 1.7 Dixon's Blazes
This was the local name for Dixon's Ironworks in the Gorbals (see Map 2). The flames could be seen for miles around, and it was said that a newspaper could be read at night by the glare from the twenty-four-hour furnaces. *Courtesy of* The Herald.

as it were, from Newlands, who travelled from Langside Station on the Cathcart circle.' It was a case of different strokes for different blokes. An Edinburgh mature student, Noel Cochrane,[69] at the age of thirty in 1969, with a wife and young family in the Scottish capital, came daily by train to study in the Arts Faculty at Strathclyde. He explained that he had 'worked and lived in London so I'd enjoyed that experience but actually to be in Glasgow to commute to Glasgow to get the opportunity, limited *although it was*, to go to Glasgow pubs, listen to Glasgow craic, just walk the street and see the architecture, that was all good experience.' For all its sense of liveliness in politics and street life, its cultural kudos was not always of the highest. In the late 1960s, eating out was a bit of a torture for a couple in search of culinary excitement, and there was little for the respectable folk of the university to do. Hamish Fraser,[70] formerly of the Department of History, recalls:

> When I was in Glasgow as a postgraduate student [in the mid-1960s] there was absolutely nowhere to eat after six o'clock in the evening. You had to go to hotels but there were no eating places. Pubs didn't have any food. There was a self-service restaurant somewhere beside Charing Cross and that shut at 6pm or 6.30pm, and that was it.

Of course, the attractions of the city included the more predictable. Located less than forty-five minutes' drive from the Scottish Highlands, the city was a paradise for those with city jobs and country pursuits. Barrie Walters,[71] appointed as a lecturer in French in 1967, says:

> I felt the *great thing* about here was not just it's a big city with lot of things going on in the city but within half an hour you're in fantastic countryside and I remember when we first moved up here my wife and I used to go off every Sunday morning, take our breakfast and go out to Lake of Menteith or Loch Lomond or the Trossachs and have breakfast and see a bit of the countryside and learned later that the neighbours suspected that we were Catholics and we were getting up early to go to Mass (*laughs*).

John Davies did not find the urban west of Scotland especially edifying in the 1970s, but with his background in music he found that the city was convenient for accessing a suitable landscape for his moods:

> I've always had a, something to do with the music, I don't know how they're connected, but classical music and the hills and stuff always seemed to –. I always had a love for the hills and I still *climb a bit*, you know, and I have a motorbike and so I can jump on the bike on a Sunday morning, I can be at Glencoe in an hour and a half and in among it. *Fabulous countryside* and further north, up in Sutherland, I, on a couple of occasions, have quite literally just *run away* for three or four days, just 'I'm sorry I've had enough', and I stick a tent in the back in the car and I just take off and wander around Quinag and Suilven and those places, camp and (*laughs*), crazy about Scotland, it's my favourite country. This countryside's just marvellous.

New arrivals in Glasgow in the mid-twentieth century found a city that though founded on empire and the making of imperial products was

Figure 1.8 Glasgow in the smog, c. 1960
This shot of Jamaica Bridge, looking north over the river Clyde towards Central Railway Station and the city centre, evokes something of the grime, smoke and environmental pollution of the industrial city of this era. Many students and staff commented on this – one recalling that a white shirt could only be worn for two hours. *Courtesy of* The Herald.

culturally incredibly insular. Bashir Maan[72] first came to the city from Pakistan in 1953. He felt that he had in some measure been misled about the nature of the city and its society:

> My impression was not what I was looking for over there. Under the empire we were told 'Oh such a beautiful country', the people would be all like those who were ruling us there and this and that, but when I came here I saw people shabbily dressed, poor people, drunk people standing at every corner. I became kind of disappointed with the whole atmosphere here; the streets dirty, the houses dirty, people living in – eight to ten members of the family in one room. At that time there were a lot of *slums* and *poverty*, deprivation was quite a lot, which, to a person who had

been brought up under a kind of, shall we say, thinking that 'Oh well there the streets are all paved with gold and it's all clean like gardens' and things like that. When you come and see all the mess and poverty and deprivation, well, naturally you feel disappointed.

For those coming from closer to home, Glasgow could still be exotic. The sense of the local was still very strong in Scottish society. Bill Speirs,[73] Strathclyde student and now General Secretary of the Scottish Trades Union Congress, was brought up in the 1950s and 1960s in Renfrew, some fifteen miles to the west of Glasgow. He puts the city in the geographical context of the time:

I mean you didn't go to, not the way things would happen now, you didn't go to clubs in Glasgow. You might go to a rock concert at the Apollo or Green's Playhouse as it was then, there might be a couple of clubs that brave people would go to, but basically people stayed within their own community. And that's why, again, when I went as a student, you know, just getting the bus to Glasgow; in those days you would get it in Renfrew and it would drop you off on the Clyde [river] front, that's where the buses left from at that time. It was before even Blythswood Bus Station, which has now shut down, (*laughs*) had been built. It was while there was still all warehouses *right along* the Clyde, you still had boats stopping there, and you would get off the bus there and then walk up through the centre of the town. This was completely new territory to me, I mean despite the fact that Renfrew's just next door and, now, nobody would think twice about going back and forwards, Glasgow was another world, and it was for a lot of people and not just from Renfrew but from lots of places round about Glasgow.

This sense of distance, of daring, of unknown territory, was an important dimension to growing up in Britain in the mid-twentieth century. So, Glasgow in the 1950s could be as much an unknown place for a lad from Renfrew as for a young lad from Pakistan or a newly-appointed professor from America.

NOTES

1. Samuel Curran, first Principal, writing in *The Times*, 11 February 1969.
2. G. Walford, *Restructuring Universities: Politics and Power in the Management of Change* (London, Croom Helm, 1987), p. 10.
3. Figures from Census 2001, accessed at www.scrol.gro.gov.uk on 7 January 2004.

4. J. Butt, *John Anderson's Legacy: The University of Strathclyde and its Antecedents 1796–1996* (East Linton, Tuckwell, 1996).

5. Data from A. H. Halsey (ed.), *Trends in British Society since 1900* (London, Macmillan, 1972), p. 206.

6. Robert Anderson notes of Aberdeen University that global changes in the 1960s marked the likely end to patterns of student life instituted in the nineteenth century. R. D. Anderson, *The Student Community in Aberdeen 1860–1939* (Aberdeen, Aberdeen University Press, 1988), p. 118.

7. G. Davie, *The Democratic Intellect: Scotland and her Universities in the Nineteenth Century* (Edinburgh, Edinburgh University Press, 1961).

8. See R. D. Anderson, 'In search of the "lad of parts": the mythical history of Scottish education', *History Workshop* vol. 19 (1985); R. D. Anderson, *Education and Opportunity in Victorian Scotland: Schools and Universities* (Oxford, Clarendon Press, 1983), esp. pp 24–6, 343–4.

9. See also D. McCrone, *Understanding Scotland: The Sociology of a Stateless Nation* (London, Routledge, 1992), pp. 36, 99.

10. Much of this literature is critically reviewed in R. D. Anderson, *Universities and Elites in Britain since 1800* (Basingstoke, Macmillan, 1992).

11. R. D. Anderson, M. Lynch and N. Phillipson, *The University of Edinburgh: An Illustrated History* (Edinburgh, Edinburgh University Press, 2003); W. Thompson and C. McCallum, *Glasgow Caledonian University: Its Origins and Evolution* (East Linton, Tuckwell, 1998); J. C. Holt, *The University of Reading: The First Fifty Years* (Reading, Reading University Press, 1977); M. Moss, J. F. Munro and R. H. Trainor, *University, City and State: The University of Glasgow since 1870* (Edinburgh, Edinburgh University Press, 2000).

12. Anderson, *Student Community*.

13. M. Sanderson, *The History of the University of East Anglia Norwich* (London, Hambledon and London, 2002).

14. B. Pullan with M. Abendstern, *A History of the University of Manchester 1951–73* (Manchester, Manchester University Press, 2000).

15. A. Marwick, *The Sixties: Cultural Revolution in Britain, France, Italy and the United States c. 1958–c. 1974* (Oxford, Oxford University Press, 1998), pp. 3–16; C. G. Brown, *Focus on Postmodernism for Historians* (forthcoming, Longman-Pearson).

16. P. Summerfield, *Reconstructing Women's Wartime Lives: Discourse and Subjectivity in Oral Histories of the Second World War* (Manchester, Manchester University Press, 1998); P. Tinkler, *Constructing Girlhood: Popular Magazines for Girls Growing Up in England 1920–1950* (London, Taylor and Francis, 1995); L. Heron (ed.), *Truth, Dare or Promise: Girls Growing up in the Fifties* (London, Virago, 1985).

17. Marwick, *The Sixties*, esp. pp. 41–246; I. Macdonald, *Revolution in the Head: The Beatles' Records and the Sixties* (London, Pimlico, 1995), pp. 1–34; B. Osgerby, *Youth in Britain since 1945* (Oxford, Blackwell, 1998), esp. pp. 82–154; C. G. Brown, *The Death of Christian Britain: Understanding Secularisation 1800–2000* (London, Routledge, 2001), pp. 170–92.

18. For the Scottish context, see M. Anderson, 'Population and family life', A. J. McIvor, 'Women and work in twentieth-century Scotland', and T. C. Smout,

'Patterns of culture', all in A. Dickson and J. H. Treble (eds), *People and Society in Scotland vol. III 1914–1990* (Edinburgh, John Donald, 1992).

19. Macdonald, *Revolution*, p. 13; Marwick, *The Sixties*, pp. 57–9; B. Miles, *Paul McCartney: Many Years from Now* (London, Vintage, 1998), such as p. 40.

20. J. Green, *Days in the Life: Voices from the English Underground 1961–1971* (London, Pimlico, 1998); J. Green, *All Dressed Up* (London, Pimlico, 1999).

21. K. A Reader, *The May 1968 Events in France: Reproductions and Interpretations* (New York, St Martin's Press, 1993); T. Ali, *1968 and After: Inside the Revolution* (London, Blond and Briggs, 1978).

22. E. P. Thomson et al., *Warwick University Ltd* (Harmondsworth, Penguin, 1970).

23. For a detailed LSE-centred account, see C. Crouch, *The Student Revolt* (London, Bodley Head, 1970).

24. An almost identical stushie over a condom machine, and their unreliability when 'used by uninstructed parties', occurred at Manchester University in 1967–8; Pullan, *University of Manchester*, p. 168.

25. Anderson, Lynch and Phillipson, *University of Edinburgh*, pp. 201–5.

26. For details of the project and the archive, see the Appendix.

27. The most accessible guides to oral-history method from the academic stand-point are P. Thompson, *The Voice of the Past: Oral History*, third edition (Oxford, Oxford University Press, 2000); and T. Lummis, *Listening to History: The Authenticity of Oral Evidence* (London, Hutchison, 1987).

28. For a guide to the literature, with extracts from key texts in the field, see R. Perks and A. Thomson (eds), *The Oral History Reader* (London, Routledge, 1998).

29. R. Johnston and A. McIvor, *Lethal Work* (Edinburgh, John Donald, 2000).

30. See the techniques explored in Summerfield, *Reconstructing*.

31. For instance, the oral-history collection at Springburn Museum, and that collected in many doctoral and undergraduate dissertations at Strathclyde and Glasgow universities.

32. A. H. Halsey, 'Higher education', in A. H. Halsey (ed.), *Trends in British Society since 1900* (London, Macmillan, 1972), p. 196.

33. For the context of Scottish commercial and industrial expansion in the eighteenth and nineteenth centuries, see S. G. E. Lythe and J. Butt, *An Economic History of Scotland 1100–1939* (Glasgow and London, Blackie, 1975), pp. 136–200.

34. Butt, *John Anderson's Legacy*, pp. 3–5.

35. Ibid., pp. 8–10.

36. Ibid., p. 11.

37. Quoted in ibid., p. 20.

38. Sarah Smith, 'Retaking the register: women's higher education in Glasgow and beyond, c. 1796–1845', *Gender & History* vol. 12 (2000), pp. 310–35. This even applied to Oxford and Cambridge. See ibid., pp. 311–12

39. Testimony of James Laurie, interviewed 30 October 2002.

40. This paragraph is based on J. Graham, *One Hundred and Twenty-Five Years: The Evolution of Commercial Education in Glasgow* (Glasgow, n. pub., 1964).

41. Quoted in ibid., p. 11.

42. *Glasgow Herald*, 12 September 1963.

43. Ibid.; see also Butt, *Anderson's Legacy*, pp. 164–7.

44. Sanderson, *University of East Anglia*, pp. 73–4.

45. BPP 1963, Cmnd. 2154, Robbins Report on Higher Education, pp. 82–3.
46. As well as UEA, there were the out-of-town campus universities of Essex, Lancaster, Stirling, Sussex, Warwick and York created between 1962 and 1968. Other universities (such as Heriot-Watt) were initially city-centre based and subsequently moved.
47. Testimony of Anonymous Interviewee 3, interviewed 17 December 2002.
48. I. Maver, *Glasgow* (Edinburgh, Edinburgh University Press, 2000), pp. 203, 207.
49. Ibid., p. 212.
50. D. Daiches, *Glasgow* (London, Grafton, 1982), p. 245.
51. Figure for Glasgow City; from Census 2001, accessed online at www.scrol.gov.uk on 7 January 2004.
52. C. G. Brown, 'Urbanization and living conditions', in R. Pope (ed.), *Atlas of British Social and Economic History since c. 1700* (London, Routledge, 1989), pp. 178–9.
53. T. Gallagher, *Glasgow: The Uneasy Peace: Religious Tension in Modern Scotland* (Manchester, Manchester University Press, 1987).
54. S. Bruce, *No Pope of Rome: Anti-Catholicism in Modern Scotland* (Edinburgh, Mainstream, 1985).
55. C. G. Brown, *Religion and Society in Scotland since 1707* (Edinburgh, Edinburgh University Press, 1997), pp. 162–4.
56. Figure calculated from censuses of churchgoing in Glasgow, organised by Dr John Highet of the University of Glasgow, and analysed in C. G. Brown, 'Religion and secularisation', in A. Dickson and J. H. Treble (eds), *People and Society in Scotland, vol. III 1914–1990* (Edinburgh, John Donald, 1992).
57. Testimony of Professor John B. Davies, interviewed 30 May 2003.
58. S. Damer, *Glasgow: Going for A Song* (London, Lawrence & Wishart, 1990), pp. 209–10.
59. Testimony of Professor Noel Branton, interviewed 4 September 2002.
60. Testimony of Roger Sandilands, interviewed 1 November 2002.
61. Written testimony of Diana Henderson.
62. Testimony of Professor Richard Rose, interviewed 18 October 2002.
63. Testimony of Dr Brian L. Furman, interviewed 2 June 2003.
64. Testimony of Professor Peter Robson, interviewed 18 December 2003.
65. Testimony of Barbara Graham, interviewed 15 August 2003.
66. Testimony of Anonymous Interviewee 3.
67. Ibid.
68. Testimony of Malcolm Allan, interviewed 6 December 2002.
69. Testimony of Noel Cochrane, interviewed 24 February 2003.
70. Testimony of emeritus professor Hamish Fraser, interviewed 15 October 2002.
71. Testimony of Barrie Walters, interviewed 16 April 2003.
72. Testimony of Bashir Maan, interviewed 12 May 2003.
73. Testimony of Bill Speirs, interviewed 17 July 2003.

CHAPTER TWO

College Learning and Teaching after the Second World War

The students of the post-war period were invariably committed and determined people. Many had served in the war, either in the armed forces or on the home front, and there was a tremendous sense of purpose in the role of education. Education was the bulwark of a new society, a society with a renewed sense of justice, a sense of the immorality of poverty and want, a society educated in war on Beveridge's five fundamental social needs and how the nation was to address them. This was no airy-fairy intellectualism, nor merely political sloganising. Wartime information films resonated with people's sense of a new Britain to be born, and those feelings came to college in the decade that followed.

EDUCATIONAL HIERARCHIES AND THE
TRANSITION TO COLLEGE

No university is an island, entire of itself. It exists in a society with its distinctive culture or cultures, and the interaction between the two is often intimate and compelling. This does not mean that the university is a mere mirror of its social context, reflecting back and regenerating the same structures, ideas, values and thoughts. A university may do this to some extent, and for some members of the university community. But for many, the university is a challenge to its context, providing not just excellence in knowledge and learning, but also disrupting accepted ways of doing things. A university must confront.

School life in the 1940s and 1950s was hierarchical. As well as private schools, there were fee-paying state schools, and the divide between junior and senior secondary schools. The junior was ostensibly for vocational training and the senior was for the gifted child headed for academic training and possible university entry. In reality, it was a system that at eleven or twelve years of age carved out an elite, and caused bitterness and resentment. Thomas M. Devine,[1] who was later to become professor of Scottish history and Deputy Principal of the University, recalled the impact of attendance at senior secondary in Motherwell.

There were some tensions, there's no doubt about that. And you would get the odd difficulty with the *vast mass* who had gone to the so-called junior secondary and who could only stay on for three years and then had to leave . . . They probably, by very definition, thought we were a shower of snobs, but I think because, especially in some parts, the individuals going on to senior secondary it was called, they would be *so few* it would be a bit like people going to private school in Lanarkshire today. You're not talking about very, very many so I don't think, so I don't think, you know, it was ever thought as a serious issue.

In particular, he recalls the wastage of young potential – those who never got the opportunity to complete school leaving certificates, let alone get a place at university. Tom Devine again:

It was a single-sex male school which was quite incredible because remember the comprehensive-isation only came in after I left school, so it was based on the Eleven-Plus, which I think, two primary school classes aged eleven or twelve classes in the primary school I attended, I think there was about, first there was sixty-five to seventy, you know, if you take the two classes together, male and female pupils, three of us went to university. Only three. *No women, no girls*, just three boys. Two of them finished and I was the only one that was still there in fifth year, and this is why I have *absolute contempt* for those who praise the traditional Scottish educational system. It was a disaster area before the comprehensive school came in. What a, you know, a *terrible wastage*, and of course they *could* get away with it in those days. The nature of the economy still demanded a lot of semi-skilled and unskilled labour, but of course that age has now passed. So I went to Our Lady's High School in Motherwell which at that time was the premier Catholic senior secondary in Lanarkshire, drawing boys from as far away as Shotts in the one hand and Baillieston on the other. And it was an incredible, almost a cosmopolitan situation, 'cos there was peculiar accents all over place, strange country folk and sophisticated *urban dwellers*, all caught up in the same, the same cauldron.

British education had a reputation of being highly structured. Its heritage was one of being layered in ways that reflected the class, ethnic, gender and racial structures of the nation. And then, of course, in Scotland there was the divide between the non-denominational schools (in essence Protestant) and the Catholic schools, both fully-funded by the state, but sitting within most west of Scotland communities as separate educational structures. All those structures were amply reflected in the students who came to Strath-clyde and its predecessor colleges. New students came from backgrounds that had been under-represented in Scottish higher education until then. Scottish university admissions had tended to be dominated by men, by seventeen and eighteen-year-olds, by children from middle-class back-grounds, by those who were Scots-born and raised, by the Protestant, and by the white. These were the characteristics of the overwhelming majority of students in Scottish universities, as to a great extent in Britain as a whole. It left women, working-class, Catholic and black students grossly under-represented. But things were to change. Going to university meant for many students in the 1950s and 1960s their first contact with different groups of strangers. For many, their first encounters with people of different religion came at university. For many, too, it was the first encounter in the education system with people of the opposite sex. There were so many structures exerting power over individuals that a culture of resistance was marbled in the minds of those whose families had no heritage, nor even any thought, of gaining access to higher education.

The Glasgow (later Scottish) College of Commerce offered a wide vari-ety of higher education courses in the period after the Second World War. These ranged from part-time evening classes, through the Diploma-level classes in commercial and secretarial subjects (frequently undertaken at night classes by secondary school teachers), to the top end of London University validated B.Sc. degree courses in economics, which compared to the best offered in other universities in the country. Tom Carbery,[2] who lectured at the College in this period, acutely observed the diverse back-grounds of students:

It might be useful at this point to say something about the students. The Scottish College was getting, was, for its degree course, it was putting people in for the B.Sc. Econ., for the B.A. and for the B.Sc. in sociology as well as an Associateship of the College itself. And the Associateship courses *mirrored* the London degree courses very substantially. So far as the London degrees were concerned, the students came from two or three different streams. The first cadre I was inclined to refer to as 'export rejects'. That was an unfortunate term and it wasn't very clever either *but it was young people who'd already been to university* but who had been misdirected or who had been subjected to too much domestic pressure, or *just had chosen badly*. So, you've got the young man who had thought he would be a Church of Scotland minister and had been studying divinity. You got the boy who had been doing dentistry because 'Uncle John's a dentist and Uncle John will take you into the practice and Uncle

John's not married and you'll take over the practice'. It was the boy or the girl who had been doing Medicine 'because Dad was a doctor and medicine runs in the family you know', and the boy who was doing accountancy for much the same reason or the girl who had been doing law for much the same reason, *and they were miserable*. And as often as not *they were seen as failures* . . . And he came to us and he said 'I'll do the B.Sc. Econ., or I'll do the B.A. or I'll do the B. Sc. Sociology and I'll see where it takes me'.

Tom Carbery reckoned this group represented 40 per cent of the degree-level students. On top of that group, he adds, there was a second large group of students:

Then there was another 30 to 40 per cent, and this was a group which I dubbed 'the Motherwell Mafia'. This was a crowd *heavily* from Catholic secondary schools. Very working class in background, and the rest of that group would be made up with their counterparts from non-Catholic schools, but in a much wider geographic spread. But the common denominator for all of this group was the working-class background and a family with no academic tradition, which was a big distinguishing feature from the first big group because of course they were mainly, if not exclusively, from families that contained graduates or professional graduates. But this second lot consisted of young people, mainly boys, who had been doing *really well* around the age of fifteen/sixteen, and who by normal standards would have left and scrambled into a job somewhere. And the school had sent for their parents and said 'Oh don't take him away, he's doing well, we believe he can get to university, wouldn't that be nice?' and the parents said 'Yes'. So they allowed the child to stay on 'til he was seventeen or eighteen and to the lad's credit, he obtained the three Highers and two lowers or the four Highers or whatever, which was the minimum entrance requirements for the University of Glasgow. But then they would go up to Glasgow for interview and they would have thick working-class accents, they were not always as grammatical as they might have been and maybe, who am I to say, there was a certain amount of religious discrimination in some instances, but anyway, whatever the reason, and whether they were at St John's or John Street, they were rejected. And then all hell broke loose, because the parents went storming into the school and said '*You said if he stayed on he would get to university, and now he's been rejected!*' and careers masters said '*Ah well now*, he may not be able to do a Glasgow degree but he could do a London degree without going to London'. 'Why, don't we have him apply to . . .' and they applied to us and we took them and God help us and bless us, we turned them into graduates every bit as readily as Glasgow would have done.

The final group of Scottish College students that Tom Carbery identified in his profile of the pre-university student body at the Scottish College were the students from other parts of Scotland or from overseas (mostly the African countries of the British Commonwealth). Eric Furness noted that African students rose from fifty-three in 1955–6 to double that number in two years, and he took a special interest in them, inviting every one in the course of a session to his home, and establishing an International Student Society.[3] Carbery commented of new students:

What I do recall is that we had fascinating experiences when we opened the doors to take in a new intake. Until University status descended on us, we did things that academic staff here *would never have dreamt of doing*. We had to do our own registration, we had to welcome the students in, we had to do that which is done by admin staff, we had to do the clerical work. We had to 'man' the desks. And I always had a tendency to arrange little sweepstakes and little gambles and so on. So one of the things we used to gamble on, have a wee sweepstake on was 'Who would get the first young person, who had seen a train for the first time the day before', and you got them. There were either from Orkney or Shetland or from one of the Outer Isles. They had seen planes, they had seen boats, they, some of them had seen submarines, they had seen photographs of trains *but they had never seen a train* until they had come on to the mainland.

The Royal College attracted students from a similarly-wide background in the 1940s and 1950s, though the core originated from affluent middle-class families in the west of Scotland, many of whom had a heritage in engineering. Nonetheless, even in this period there was a significant cohort of overseas students, from Norway, India, North America and elsewhere – about 450 by the late 1950s, constituting around 20 per cent of the total student population.[4] The first Royal College Freshers' Day in October 1959 was designed for the seventy-five or so new overseas students: 'to initiate the strangers into the Scottish way of life'.[5] The reputation of the Tech and advice from experienced contacts were important in attracting such students to Glasgow. Kjell Sandberg, a Norwegian electrical engineering student at the Royal College during 1960–3, commented that he came because 'of discussion with friends also with the same ambitions, the opportunity given

Figure 2.1 Examination hall, College of Commerce, c. 1946–7
Note the preponderance of female students, one of the features of the Scottish
College of Commerce's commercial subjects in contrast to the male dominance
of science and engineering at the Royal College. *Strathclyde University Archives.*

by the College to start in second year and the reasonable cost of living in
Scotland'.[6] Amongst home students in full-time degree courses at either
the Tech or the Scottish College, probably only a minority were from the
working class, and fewer still were women. The reasons for this were not
merely exclusion and elitism, but the result of the culture of resistance to
university education. This started within the family, often the working-class
family, and extended into friends and community, and it could eat into
the minds of potential students who had toyed with the idea of college
applications. This resistance remained strong and widespread in the two
decades after the Second World War. David Paterson's[7] father was a leading

member of the Labour Party in Clydebank, and later became Provost of that burgh. The family were typical of many with great pressure upon sons and daughters to earn a wage and contribute to the family economy. He recalled:

> You know working-class families, you were the son you'd to go out get a job, make money, get a steady job, get married have a kid . . . or two, have a council house and that was your life. So when I said I was going to university, there was a lot of resistance to it. My father had successfully stopped my elder sister from going to university on the grounds that that wasn't what women did. And for all that he was a Labour Party man trying to change the world that took no account of women's rights or education, which was really for other people.

Even those attending the top state schools (the high schools), did not always understand the higher-education system. David Paterson had good qualifications that should have ensured easy entry to the course of his choice:

> Well my background is that, I came from Clydebank, studied at Clydebank High School, and in my latter year I was the school captain there and had decided at that stage that I was going to read law at Glasgow University and had been provisionally, I think, accepted for a place and irrationally was put off it by the deputy head master . . . at Clydebank High School, who asked me if I was intending to take *silk*. And I had no idea what that meant, and I was very embarrassed by it and somehow it put me off the whole business. So instead of doing law at Glasgow I looked around for something else to do. *Should* have gone to Glasgow University, didn't.

So, many careers were dramatically altered through misunderstandings and momentary off-putting words and phrases. 'There shouldn't have been any doubt about it because I had the entrance qualifications but I really don't know,' David Paterson recalled. 'I came from a non-, an uneducated family who had no appreciation of universities or colleges, there was no career guidance, there's no real advice given as to what might be the better, you know, productive course to take . . .' In consequence, his career changed because of the perception of the friendlier, more accessible tone of another Glasgow college: 'I was interested in economics, saw this thing at the Commercial College advertised with an external degree at London, and so I went to the Scottish College of Commerce to be a student in economics

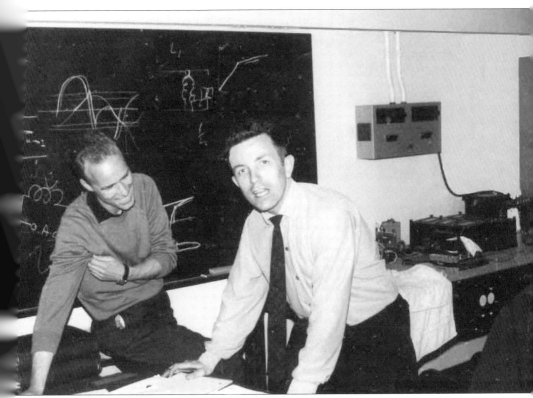

Figure 2.2 The Norwegian connection, c. 1962–3
Kjell Sandberg (left), an electrical engineering student at Royal College with a
lecturer, Dr Ian McAllister. The Royal College attracted large numbers of
Norwegian students, mostly engineers – a connection that is still sustained
today. *Courtesy of Kjell Sandberg.*

and that's what I did,' he reports. 'I liked the sound of what was on offer at
Commercial College and for no better reason than that, that is where I
ended up'.

With entry to university still so limited in the 1940s and 1950s, it was
not merely working-class families that struggled to understand the educational system and gain entry for a child. In many ways, the pressures in
middle-class families could be even greater, with expectations set higher. Yet,
the entry standards were still a big hurdle. With university admission male-
dominated, the pressures upon girls could be particularly immense. Doris
recalled how the school-leaving results were announced to all at her school:

We had an assembly every morning where some of the teachers played
cellos and violins, and we all sang a hymn. And the day our Higher

results came out the Principal said that the girls in fifth year would be delighted to know that the Higher results were out and only one girl had failed. And everybody thought it was them. I thought that was the *cruellest possible thing* she could have done.[8]

Elizabeth McCudden[9] reflected on the situation of the female at school and in science classes in the 1950s – in each of which there were somewhat different experiences:

I came from a senior secondary and I was the only one that did something other than teaching. Girls were encouraged to do that kind of thing. The difference I think going to a girl's school I think was, you weren't competing with boys. Boys were kind of, it was assumed they would be the best at maths and science. I was the only girl in my science class. I was the only girl. And it was actually very difficult to be the only girl, because it was in the days when you got belted if you hadn't done your homework. It wasn't easy to be different from everyone else. But the vast majority of girls did languages, became teachers. And actually not all that many went on to university. And it, in senior secondary, in the top classes you had people who were very capable of going on but they came from maybe a working-class background where the attitude might have been 'The sooner you get out the better the job'. Getting a good job was more important than getting a degree. My brothers was encouraged into trades because that was a good job. And I think because I was the youngest in the family they didn't bother too much about me and I said I wanted to do this.

Scholastic secondary-school education was strong in certain parts and echelons of Scottish society. John Paul's memories of Aberdeen Grammar School recall a type of Scottish education, centred on 'the classics', that was perhaps more resonant of eastern and rural Scotland than its western and industrial part:

It was a *very good school* indeed. The teachers were of high quality and knowledgeable and (*laughs*), the senior group in any year had to take Latin, and for one year I had to take Greek also, Ancient Greek, so it was very much a classical school, but it had a very strong mathematics department and an adequate science department. So I don't regret *any of the time* I spent there except I was a child of age twelve when I went to stay with an aunt and, divorced from the family for quite a period and not having had the acquaintance of the younger ones at school, I was a

Figure 2.3 School of Pharmacy, Dispensing Laboratory, Royal College c. 1950 Nan Nuttall, pharmacy student (third from left) and the lecturer Mr Macintyre (second from right). One interviewee commented that change in the pharmacy profession was limited between the 1920s and 1970s. *Courtesy of Agnes Nuttall.*

bit of a loner . . . I was a studious boy at that time and it wasn't much of a shock really except I never had so many chilblains on my feet as I had during those four years. Aberdeen was a very cold city.

Others made the transition to higher education directly through industry. A common route was through evening classes as an apprentice, or the sandwich course, sponsored by employers in the region. One of Strathclyde's engineering professors came through to the Tech to do his Associateship in mechanical engineering, sponsored by Stewart and Lloyds, the steel manufacturers. After graduation in 1958, he completed a Masters degree at Sheffield, then left Stewart's for six years in a research laboratory in the nuclear industry before being enticed back to the new Strathclyde

University in the mid-1960s to lecture.[10] That experience was a common and distinctive one in the Andersonian, a heritage that the planners of the new university were to be keen to sustain.

THE ALLAN GLEN'S CONNECTION

One of the key routes for students into the Technical College was through Allan Glen's School, described by one Glasgow councillor in 1965 as 'the only school of its kind in Britain – a high school of science'.[11] This secondary school, located in central Glasgow virtually adjacent to the Royal College, had been founded almost uniquely in mid-nineteenth-century Britain outwith the main educational ethos of the time.[12] Rather than fostering an academic approach to learning, Allan Glen's was a school dedicated to science and engineering skills. A unique link between the school and the Royal Technical College had developed in the Victorian and Edwardian periods (with common Boards of Governors), giving many students a straight route from the secondary into the further and tertiary sector, and making for a striking continuity of experience. University thus did not always represent a breakaway from family, and educational background, but could be a stage on an educational staircase from home to career. That career could go all the way to the top. Lord Todd of Trumpington, first Chancellor of Strathclyde University, was a former pupil of Allan Glen's School.

Emeritus professors John T. Webster from Design Manufacture and Engineering Management and John Paul from Bioengineering both came through the Allan Glen's School *en route* for long connections with the University. John Webster recalled winning a scholarship to gain entry to Allan Glen's as a pivotal moment in his life: 'that was the sort of the opening of the door into science technology and eventually the Royal Tech. I suppose I regard the going to Allan Glen's as [a] very formative event in my life. As it was for many people at that time'. He went on to comment on the attributes of the school:

> Well the accent on, well, applied learning, applied science and the accent on being disciplined and learning to discipline yourself. And it was a school where you were conscious of the fact that there was an element of privilege in getting there, whether one likes privilege in education or not, there was an element of privilege in getting there and it was up to you to benefit from that.

The school also had excellent contacts with local industry, and these were instrumental in getting John Webster placed during the Second World War in an apprenticeship with the London Midland Scottish railway works at St Rollox to the north of the city centre. The LMS then insisted that he take evening classes at the Royal College, which in turn qualified him for entry after the war to the full-time civil and mechanical engineering degree course at the Tech. In the case of John Paul, he was a natural for the engineering profession: 'My father was an engineering draughtsman, my elder brother did an engineering degree at the Royal College and it was natural therefore that I came to the Royal Technical College for a Bachelor's Degree in mechanical engineering commencing in 1945.' He recalls that it was an 'excellent school' with a very strong bias towards technical subjects, science and mathematics:

> The headmaster at that time, a man by the name of Steele, was quite a forward thinking man in education and he, I can't say exactly what he did, but he had a name for having an unusual structure in the school. So in Allan Glen's I studied the usual English, French, maths, physics, chemistry, but they had technical subjects which involved a little woodwork but also engineering drawing, so that was a start to coming into the classes here. Also, I took the fifth and sixth year there and it was amazing how much the first year course was covered by the sixth year at school, so that gave me a flying start in a College.

Engineering and the sciences were socially-cosmopolitan subjects, attracting the middle-class and working-class boy alike in Glasgow and the west of Scotland. However, there were significant differences in where pupils ended up, depending upon the school attended. John Paul recalls that 'Glasgow was thought as the middle-class man's university and, well, people came there from Hutchie[13] and the fee-paying schools. I think from the fee-paying schools you tended more to go to Glasgow [University], but Allan Glen's was *strongly feeding* all departments of the [Royal Technical] College, a few going to university.'

Allan Glen's School not only crafted engineers in embryo for the College, but it also attracted them. One former student[14] had engineering in his blood. He chose engineering as a career quite simply because 'my grandfather was head foreman in John Brown's Heavy Turning, [and] my father was an pipe arrangement draughtsman, an engineering pipe arrangement draughtsman in John Brown's.' He recalls of his grandfather working at John Brown's shipyard in Clydebank early in the century:

> Well they were regarded as the 'hat men', and these were the guys that walked round with the bowler hats, and I think above him there would

be, I really couldn't guess, but not a hell of a many people between him and the managing director. He was not director level let's be quite clear but the head foreman had below him other foreman and that was the whole heavy turning shop at John Brown's and that was the place where they turned the turbines, the shafts, the propeller shafts, all that kind of stuff, so it was a pretty big workshop so I would say it was a *fairly important* job, not a director or anything fancy like that. And he was in the head foremen's row of houses in Abercromby Street which John Brown's built for the head foremen.

His own father followed the tradition and sent him to Allan Glen's:

Well my father principally had me going to Allan Glen's. And Allan Glen's School, with some connection through the governor's or something, I can't really spell it out with you because I don't really know, *with* the 'Tech'. And the bulk of the people from Allan Glen's who were in engineering *went to* the 'Tech'.

The interviewee describes how Allan Glen's fitted into a distinctive pattern of life in the city in the 1950s:

I lived in Knightswood and the buses from Knightswood had quite a large percentage of Allan Glen's people, High School people, Hillhead High School, all going into town, so there was no . . . you mean kind of like 'You shouldn't go to a good school like that or something or you went to not a very good, good school?', no, nothing like that at all. We just regarded it as normal. I mean in the Scouts I was in, there was several from Allan Glen's, in the Bible class at the church there was, again, quite a few from Glen's, so you were always in company, you were never sort of on your own.[15]

And from Allan Glen's to the Tech, the transition seemed to follow with logic and with family pride. Like many others, the interviewee took classes at the Royal College whilst taking his degree extra-mural from Glasgow University. 'And that's why I was in the Tech', he concludes, since 'from an early age we built machines and engines around my grandfather's people, and I just never really thought of anything else but engineering, whether that's brainwashing or not I don't know.'

THE COLLEGES AND CAREERS

The fate of a young person's career can be decided in a number of ways. The choice of subject of study, and thus the determination of entire career, can result from awareness of the almost transcendental sublime in the person's subject of choice – or it can be awesomely accidental. One anonymous interviewee's interest in engineering and science falls within the first category:

> I was very interested in it, if that's the question, yeah I was fascinated by it in the sense of some of the labs we did were quite instructive and you weren't, things that you thought you knew but didn't really. I mean such simple things as what some of these guys, what would they have invented or they discovered. Faraday for example, we did his experiments and that was quite fascinating, finding out how it was done and also the Wimshurst's machines[16] that stick in your mind, that's where you work a handle and it generates static electricity and you've got a ball and you can take a spark that long (describes) on to your finger which has got a voltage of, I don't know, is it 10,000 volts a centimetre or something? It's some figure like that, you can take thousands of volts on to your finger because there's no current behind it. And things of that nature, you know I found it fascinating, *yes*. I'm trying to find some way to separate off fascination and interest from plain enjoyment, it's difficult to say.[17]

As we saw earlier, David Paterson was put off law by a chance comment at his school, illustrating how the smallest of remarks, most innocently made, can turn a career destiny. This was perhaps especially so in the middle decades of the twentieth century when knowledge of the educational and other systems of society – structures, hierarchies, and the rights and opportunities of the individual – were not nearly so clearly demarcated as they are now.

Yet, the divisions between Glasgow University and the Royal College were well known. James Laurie, who came to the Tech in 1952, contrasted students there and those at Glasgow University: 'We considered ourselves the workers, the others were dreamers.' Amongst other things, this perception in Glasgow and the west of Scotland had by the 1950s boosted the Royal College's strong tradition of mature students. Its courses were clearly targeted to the market, and by providing a combination of technical with managerial training, plus an externally-awarded degree, the College was able to steal some of the finest students from under the noses of the University of Glasgow. James Brown[18] recalled:

> Yes, I joined Singers Sewing Machine Company, the Singer Manufacturing Company in Clydebank, who were sponsoring students through

university. I had to do one year of practical work in training school, apprentice training school, during the working week and three nights a week night school to keep in touch with the academic side for the year. I got talking to the students who were one year ahead of me and learned that by going to Strathclyde, the old Royal College, instead of Glasgow, I could matriculate at Glasgow University and sit all my degree exams at Glasgow University whilst taking the courses at the Royal College. The advantage of that was that at the end of my degree in addition to my practical training in the factory, I would have done an industrial administration course which would give me an exemption from part three of the Institution of Mechanical Engineer's exams so that on graduation I would only need a few years in a responsible position to become a chartered engineer.

James Brown recalls the first-year curriculum in mechanical engineering:

In the first year everyone did the same course: maths, physics, chemistry and engineering drawing. In second year we did maths, applied mechanics, engineering drawing, metallurgy, material science, metallurgy was part of that. We all had to do electrical engineering for a year, thermodynamics, structures, dynamics and control.

His decision about which subjects to study was made precisely and without deviation: 'I made a conscious choice to choose the subjects I regarded as most useful for the rest of my working career and I've *no regrets*.'

Women's subject choices, like their careers, were shaped by much more restricted structures. Pat Fraser,[19] a pharmacy student in the late 1950s, recalls after having been at a girl's school: 'I was thrilled to be in classes with boys! To be in class with boys! I was a wee bit ill at ease to start with in fact. I'd gone to a girls' school in Glasgow, Notre Dame, and so I mean you kind of clung to those who you knew.' Women students were rather a rare commodity in the post-war Tech College, in the recollection of one female student, Doris: 'Women, there was only – there was one engineer, one metallurgist, about six or seven of us doing pharmacy, and that was it.'[20] Prospective women students were surrounded by certain expectations. Doris recalls: 'My friend and I went up to the Royal Technical College, she wanted to do metallurgy, so we both went up to Tech. And it was suggested metallurgy was not a very good career, would we not like to try pharmacy? And we said "Sure!" So that's why we became pharmacists.' Yet, though women students might be rare, even unique, on a given College course, there seemed to be little of the ideological impulse for feminist change that

Figure 2.4 Scottish College of Commerce Librarianship class, c. 1946–7
Looking very much like a schoolroom, this shows the importance of women in
the pioneering Librarianship course at the College. The lecturer is a Mr Paton.
Strathclyde University Archives.

was to surface in the later 1960s and 1970s. Asked how she felt as a young
woman going into higher education, Doris replies: '*Didn't mean a thing* –
I – it was strange going from an all-girls' school to this male-dominated
society (*laughs*), but you know, I really didn't give it much of a thought.' Yet,
the curriculum at the College, as in so much of the technical-education
sector in Britain, was highly gendered. Doris again: 'Well they didn't teach
us nat. phil.[21] – *we did botany*. Nat. phil. wasn't a suitable subject for a girl!
You know it was *an odd* upbringing for that period of time, whether it was
because it was during the war or not, I don't know, might have been.' This
last comment fits closely with an interpretation of many recent historians
that Britain became more conservative in the 1950s than in the period of
the war years or of the preceding 1930s – especially as related to gendered
roles and the supposedly 'suitable' careers for women.[22] The return to
'hearth and home' in the ten years after the Second World War, as it is put,
deprived many women of educational and career opportunities, but may

also have hardened ideas of suitable subjects once a woman got to college. The numbers of women at the Royal College were still very limited in the 1950s and early 1960s, but the Scottish College of Commerce at Pitt Street taught subjects in which there was a stronger heritage of female participation.

Situated a mile or so to the west of the Royal Technical College (see Map 2), the College of Commerce had almost entirely different subjects and a different ethos. Malcolm Allan, later to be a member of the senior staff of the Andersonian Library, was himself a student there in the 1950s:

> I was an evening-class student there in Scottish College in 1956–7 and then I was a full-time student for one session at Scottish School of Librarianship '57–8 and it was just after I finished, no just before I did that, that the library was re-done at Scottish College – a single reading room that took 105 people.

Tom Carbery studied at Glasgow University (where he obtained the Diploma in Public Administration) and then part-time during 1952–6 at the College of Commerce for the B.Sc. Economics (validated by London University) whilst working full-time as a civil servant. This was an unusual achievement at that time, as he explained:

> The College had a full-time cadre of students who entered the B.Sc. Econ. exams every year but they had a small group of students who worked in the evenings with a view to taking the degree. The fallout rate of the part-timers was *horrendous*. I subsequently inquired from London themselves and whereas no one was certain, the belief of the staff was that on the external degree there was a 90 per cent wastage rate for the B. Sc. Econ. In other words, for every ten ambitious young people who embarked on the B.Sc. Econ, only one finished it and most of them ended with a pass degree.

This distinctive problem caused much deliberation, including at London University where they felt that students 'found it was harder-going than they had thought it would be'. But there were other possible causes:

> Sometimes career progress intervened. Domestic considerations intervened; people had children, marriages became dicey and ropey, things of that nature. And whereas it was, it was probably easier to get tuition either from a college or a correspondence course for the foothills of the B.Sc. Econ., there were very few places offered tuition for the final year.

Even the Pitt Street College, even the West of Scotland which became the Scottish College, *had never had* part-time students taking the Part Two final. They had some people through as far as the Part One final but had never, prior to myself and two or three others, had folk wanting a Part Two final course. I was fortunate in that there was this group of three or four of us who managed to get through the Part One in 1955, then approached the college and persuaded them to make some extraordinary arrangements for us to obtain tuition for the Part Two, and in 1956 we sat the finals and I managed to get a 2:1 and my friend got a 2:2, and I would then again digress here to say that, I think I'm right in saying that, somewhat commendably, London is far from, or was far from, profligate in its distribution of 'Firsts'. The only 'First' with a B.Sc. Econ. I ever knew was Sir Kenneth Alexander.[23]

This moulded Tom Carbery's career choices in quite a fundamental way. He went on to teach part-time at the Scottish College for several years, and in 1961 was appointed to a permanent teaching post. This was only after being passed over earlier because of a dispute with the College Principal over wages. He recalled the incident vividly:

I had applied for a full-time post in 1957 but argued with the then Principal of the College, Dr Eric Thompson, as to my starting salary. The figure he quoted was about £20 or £30 a year higher than my civil service salary, but I pointed out that as an established civil servant I was superannuated without paying the 6 per cent superannuation, whereas I would have to pay 6 per cent into the superannuation scheme at the college and therefore to that extent would be out of pocket. Eric Thompson suggested that if I had a zeal for teaching, I should not be interested in the salary. So I suggested to Dr Thompson that that led me to infer that he and the other people who argued that higher salaries were needed to be paid throughout the educational world in order to *attract* more applicants and better-qualified applicants, was a fallacious argument if that they should have been coming out of a zeal for teaching. So the result was I didn't get the job . . .

However, in 1961 another vacancy arose which suited him better, and at the interview he was asked: "*I have only one question to put to you . . .*" And that is, Dr Thompson?" "*Are you and I going to argue about money?*" And I said "No Sir'," and he said "*How very wise. When can you start?*'"

The two colleges were vital to new careers for other students who, in the 1950s, were in rather different circumstances. Bashir Maan, now a leading figure in the Glasgow Asian community and one of the early wave of post-Second World War immigrants, attended courses in textile chemistry at the Tech and subsequently accountancy at the College of Commerce in the early–mid-1950s. His memories of the Colleges are positive. He emphasised the strong reputation of both institutions, the existence of small but significant pockets of overseas students, and the marked lack of racism within the Colleges, in marked contrast to what he had been accustomed to in Pakistan and what he saw in Glasgow in this period:

> The Royal College culture at that time was very kind of, how should say, *exclusive*. A small place, a college with a *great reputation* all over the world, you know and I think the staff was very friendly. I didn't find any, shall we say, kind of racism in the students or in the class. Everybody was quite fair and fine, so I actually liked the place, it had its own culture, its own atmosphere which was *very good* at that particular time . . . I never found any difficulty with the staff or the local students, and we had quite a few students from abroad, other countries, in that class also. I remember there was one from Greece, one from India, from Pakistan. I was from Pakistan and there other people also from other countries, so it was kind of an international class.[24]

About the College of Commerce he is also complimentary:

> Oh that was *very good also*. I didn't find any difficulty in that College with either the staff or the students. I mean this is one thing I was *amazed at*. There was no *obvious* discrimination or even any kind of sign of it, you know. Everything was fine in these colleges. Perhaps we were moving in about the students at that time, that and not seeing anything of the colonial past, and that was one reason because these students we were sixteen, eighteen, nineteen, twenty, twenty-one [years old], and the Partition had come in '47,[25] the Raj had ended in '47. So they were *very young* when the Empire ended, so perhaps they did not have those, shall we say, *ideas* of being the superiors or the rulers or things like that, but I found in that atmosphere, the College atmosphere, both College atmospheres, things were *really fine*. No problem.

The students' careers started mostly at the point of graduation. According to one student who experienced a graduation at both the College and at the University – for first and second degrees – this was a ceremony at the old Royal College which, even in the early 1960s, was not up to the pomp and grandeur of most universities, and which the new University of Strathclyde

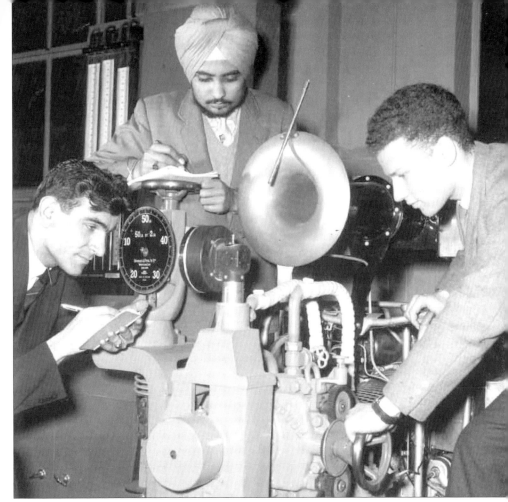

Figure 2.5 Overseas students at Royal College, 1958
A group of mechanical and electrical engineering students studying a gas tur-
bine engine in a laboratory. Left to right: K. Krikovian (from Iraq), K. Jawanda
(India) and T. Komoly (Hungary). *Strathclyde University Archives.*

was to develop. But in the mid-1940s, there was another, ancillary ceremony
that occurred for students of the Royal College – one that was more curious
and perhaps to modern ears wholly unlikely:

> when I graduated, it was quite funny, actually, the recruiters used to
> assemble in the foyer of the old College building, down at, you know,
> where you come in the door. And we would be down there and they
> would have their clipboards and they would say 'Are you a chemist?',
> 'Yes', 'Sign here', and I'd say 'Oh, wait a minute'. And it got such a bloody
> pest that we used to slip out through the boilerhouse side entrance, it's
> still there, yes, to escape these buggers . . . 'Just sign there' and that was

it. I mean, that was the way it was – you know, there was a half a dozen jobs you could have got, just by signing on the dotted line ... And we were so naïve ... But when you're young like that you never think of these things, you see, and anyway I had other ideas. I could've got a job with ICI, which I eventually ended up with. I was a bit stupid. I should've gone to them right away, but I didn't because I was wanting a job that would be at home because, you know, getting my first professional salary, it made a hell of a difference to our living conditions. So that was the situation and I sort of – I went to ICI eventually and if I'd gone immediately I graduated of course I would have had twice the pension I have at the moment, but these things happen. And so I got a job with Beattie's Bakeries ... in Dennistoun.[26]

The job market in the 1940s and for the next twenty years was still remarkably good for most graduates. Students got jobs all over the world, especially in the parts where the British Empire was in retreat and new industries were being established in the wake of the withdrawal of west of Scotland firms.

TEACHING AND THE CLASSROOM REGIME

The higher-education classroom of the late 1940s and 1950s marks a stark contrast to that of today. The hours were long, the studies unrelenting, and the regimes in class sometimes curiously out of place. Studying was labour-intensive, with few of the technological aids enjoyed by today's students. Coursework had to be laboriously hand-written, and sources had to be located using the library card indexes, without any electronic bibliographic aids. Attendance at lectures was generally compulsory and absences were not tolerated. One former engineering student recalls that students invariably became friendly with those sitting next to you in classes – but that was not a matter of choice:

> The way the thing was laid out of course, the ones you became friendly with usually were the people whose names started with the same letter as you did, because in the class you sat in alphabetical order so that the people I knew were either Ms or Macs or something like that. I'm not saying you didn't know anybody else, don't misunderstand me, but the people that you mixed with in your few months at the college were the people with alphabetical names, similar names.[27]

Elizabeth McCudden in pharmacy recalled the same structured learning environment and its impact on friendships:

Figure 2.6   Royal College lecture, c. 1963–4
Attendance at most lectures was compulsory until the late 1960s. Note the formality of the student dress code, with sports jackets and ties in abundance, and some blazers. *Strathclyde University Archives.*

I think when you are in that small group situation as we were in labs, a bit like medicine I suppose, when you working in labs with people all the time, you are arranged alphabetically you just, you know, get quite friendly with people that you're with.

In general lectures, women stood out in other ways. Pat Fraser and Elizabeth McCudden recalled their memories in conversation with each other:

PF   Our first-year classes we were in for physics with engineers and architects, so it was a huge class with few girls. So you daren't be late. If you came in late and you came in the bottom of the lecture hall, you never did, you went up another storey so you were at the back, because you would get shouted and whistled at! It was great! In the sense because you were a girl rather than you were late.

EM We always sat at the front.

PF And we went for lunch to the refectory. This other lady reminded me of this. When we went to the ref the girls went to the front of the queue, to be served and what you were served was a choice of sausage rolls, beans and bridies.

Inevitably, perhaps, teaching methods and quality varied within and across the colleges. David Paterson recalled the mixed quality of teaching at the College of Commerce:

Well you get some lecturers who had prepared handouts, for example explanatory notes maybe if we were considering, say if you were doing price theory in Economics and I remember one lecturer had prepared a series of diagrams with supply, demand, and . . . things of this nature with explanatory notes done in his own style which reflected his style of teaching. And when you went back home to study, this rang bells with you and helped you to understand. But others came in and sort of delivered a lecture in quite a different impersonal, impersonal style is the word I would use and then walk out at the end. And you know you're left hoping you've written down the correct stuff and so forth, there wasn't very much support and you didn't get very much from these people when you went to speak to them. But others were very good, they were prepared to talk to [you] *ad nauseam* or debate issues with you and they were quite stimulating but the Scottish College of Commerce was not (*laughs*) was not one of the nation's prime academic institutions. It was not Glasgow University or Edinburgh University or Cambridge or Oxford, it was nothing like that. But there were some very bright students there, there were some very good lecturers and I think some students went on to achieve, you know, quite good careers.

Similarly, Stanley Tweddle[28] noted of the pre-1939 evening classes at the Tech:

At that time, I think they were *reasonably good*, there was a heck of a lot of cribbing that went on – you had to do experiments etc. etc. and I think the same experiments had been passed on since 1908 (*laughs*). And then,

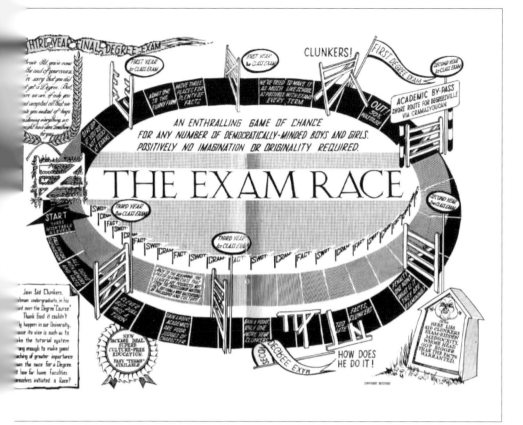

Figure 2.7 'The Exam Race', mid-1950s
A Royal College student's critical review of teaching methods, published in the student magazine *Mask*. It caricatures learning as over-dependent upon absorbing facts, and assessment as using excessive closed examinations. *Strathclyde University Archives*.

of course, you had exams at the end of the year, which was important to pass otherwise you had to pay for yourself the next year!

Doris, a pharmacy student, commented on the mixed standard of teaching in the Royal College:

Yes, some of them were very good, some of them were middling, and some of them were terrible ... *Oh yes*. There was a chemistry lecturer who wrote up things on the board and as soon as she wrote them up she rubbed them out – I mean she wrote with one hand and rubbed out with the other, she wasn't good, she was pretty poor. But there were some lovely lecturers. Dr Hopper was *a lovely man*, he was Irish, and he was a good lecturer, he was funny, he was nice. He was, as I said, they were all nice to the girls. I don't know what they were like as far as the boys were concerned, but they were all, they were all very nice.[29]

Such comments reflect a broad range of experience – good, indifferent and bad. Though innovation in teaching was evident, especially in engineering and the externally-validated degrees, the testimony of the interviewees suggests a relatively-slow pace of change in course structures, content and teaching methods compared to what followed from the mid-1960s. One pharmacy student, for example, commented that the course he did in the 1950s was practically the same as that undertaken by his father thirty years before.[30]

With the benefit of both a student's and teacher's perspective, James Brown recalls the highly-motivated classroom atmosphere:

Well there was a very high standard at Strathclyde of maths lecturers and engineering lecturers, people doing research work at a pretty high standard and the students were of a high standard, there was quite a lot of intercommunication between us and the students and the lecturers over problems. Ph.D. students were treated almost like members of staff and treated as equals, undergraduates were treated less like school children. Well there was a big jump from school to university, there was only something like a 30 per cent pass rate in first year, for instance in the first exam in Chemistry, because people who had gone straight from fifth year to university rather than doing sixth year hadn't learned to be self-motivated. I've subsequently advised school pupils to do a six-year to give themselves a chance to mature and think out what they want. I don't think anyone I've advised has regretted it.

He recalls that the engineering course was 'a very difficult course, a very intensive course.' Leisure time was limited, snatched in between lessons and other work:

We spent virtually no time in the Students' Union, we had three hours of lectures every morning except a Thursday when we had one hour free. We would go round to the Students' Union in John Street on a Thursday and have a coffee and we would see the same students round there every Thursday, usually pharmacy students or from some less demanding course. Occasionally we would have a lecturer off sick and no one able to stand in for them, so we would go down to the Union for an odd hour randomly. The same students still seemed to be there drinking coffee and playing cards.

One former student also recalled the rigour of the engineering degree at the College: 'Well it was quite, using an non-emotive word, quite difficult. I mean we started off with about 200 in the class and by the second year that had been whittled back to just over 100.'[31] Similarly Robert Orr[32] (who won a prestigious Caird Scholarship to the Royal College, which he attended from 1955–8) recalled the strict regime that he imposed upon himself in order to succeed. He was a direct-entry to year two, and found himself struggling with the high level of maths:

> It was a bit difficult for me, because these people had done one year of applied maths and I had gone in there and the lecturer said 'this is the complex conjugate'. I'd never heard of the complex conjugate! I'd never heard of the complex conjugate (*laughs*). So it was very tough for me in the first year, well the second year. Third year wasn't too bad because I was on a level footing then.

His self-discipline extended to only allowing himself two periods free from study – Wednesday evenings and Sundays – when he travelled home to Dundee to see his family. Douglas Logan[33] exhibited a similar degree of hard graft in first-year mechanical engineering: 'I was mad enough and got into the habit very early on, i.e. right at the beginning, to go home and, sorry, I'd just scribble down *vehemently* during the lecture and fortunately I could work it out still within six hours and I actually re-wrote my notes every night. So I was exceedingly boring and worked till midnight virtually from the first year, but I had a good set of notes.' In the testimony of our interviewees, this powerful work ethic was more frequently and fervently referred to by students from the 1940s and 1950s than from those later. As Robert Orr noted: 'I just worked hard and put my nose to the grindstone (*laughs*)'.

Ronnie Simpson,[34] who came to the Royal College from Fife to study engineering after working in Rosyth Naval Dockyard, reported:

> I came through with one or two friends who had also served their apprenticeship, and there were four or five of us came to Glasgow at the same time. So we had company for each other and I think fitting into the Royal College, you were *working* and I think it was at that time students worked harder than they do nowadays. So that you worked hard but you also enjoyed life as well.

Then as now, much depended upon the quality of the teaching and the capacity of individual lecturers to inspire their students and bring their subjects to life. John Webster in Engineering was asked about the quality of staff and the capability of teachers to motivate both students and fellow staff members:

Q How do you think the standards of the Royal College compared on a British level?

A Oh the Royal College standards were very high and as it developed in engineering these standards were maintained. I'm a bit out of touch with things now obviously, quite deliberately but the standards in engineering were very high. Part of that was the degree to which they had been fortunate in the people who were there at the sort of start of the big expansion, Adam Thomson and Alex Scott and people like that. There were a number of them you know about, a cadre I would have said of about ten, fifteen people who were of *excellent* quality, excellent quality. And who were very accomplished in motivating people and stimulating them. Sometimes the stimulation was a boot, sometimes the stimulation was a clap (*laughs*), but they stimulated you.

Royal College students were aided from the mid-1950s by a much-improved library, developed significantly under the College's first professional librarian Charles Wood.[35] These and other developments increased the standing of the institution. Stanley Tweddle commented that the Royal College was on a par with any British engineering faculty, and was recognised as such by both British and US employers. He claimed: 'Well, pretty well the employers in those days, I mean the first place that they came to look for employees was here, it was recognised as such'. Others noted the inspirational qualities of particular teachers. For one Strathclyde engineering professor, this was the vital factor that drew him back to teach at Strathclyde from a promising and dynamic career at the cutting edge of nuclear research in industry in the early–mid-1960s:

I guess the only reason I would have wanted to teach was having seen Bobby Kenedi[36] teach because he was a *tremendous* teacher. A very effective teacher and I just admired the way he taught, so I guess he had a big influence in more ways than one as to why I came back.

Q Could you go into that: his teaching method and why he was good for students?

Figure 2.8 Andersonian Library, 1957
Located in the Royal College on George Street (later removed to the McCance
Building and later still to the current Curran Building). Note the preponderance
of male students. *Strathclyde University Archives.*

A   He had a very polished style. I think he must have prepared exceed-
     ingly well, he had a very polished style and just captivated the students.
     You know, there was almost a fight to get in the front seats in his
     class whereas normally you sit at the back and not pay too much
     attention but he was very, very good with students, very *clear* in his
     exposition of things, so he inspired the students and he certainly
     inspired me.[37]

In creating an environment conducive to quality teaching and research in
engineering, John Webster emphasised the close links which existed
between Glasgow University and the Royal College, where joint degrees
had been in existence since 1919, and an intimate relationship existed
between local industry and the academy:

There was a culture of acquaintanceship with the engineering *infrastructure* in the whole area . . . I was LMS railway, that was my background, but so many of my others – colleagues and contemporaries – were from different organisations, you know. Colvilles was the great steel company, *so many* of the metallurgy people had a Colvilles' acquaintanceship. There was MacFarlane engineering, was an electrical engineering firm on the Southside of Glasgow, and some of my colleagues had been with MacFarlane engineering and related back to them. And . . . there was a *very close* relationship between members of staff and Weirs . . . It wasn't representational, it just *happened,* that so many of the people were contacts, or had contacts, or had been involved with organisations. And there *was some,* shall we say, *engagement* backwards and forward whereby someone would come in and be working as a lecturer and then would go back out to industry and work in, then come back in sometimes or not . . . I can think of quite a number of instances of that. People *had* come in, been in this system of teaching and research, and then went back out.

John MacLaren (later professor of thermo-dynamics) was in a unique position to comment on the learning and teaching experience at the Tech because his involvement with the institution stretched back to the 1930s. He initially worked as an apprentice marine engine fitter in a Clydeside foundry and attended evening classes in 1936 before going full-time:

> I transferred to the revered 'sandwich' scheme at 'the Tech', which was more a degree course, jointly with Glasgow University. The course was *very highly regarded* in that it was intensive in the sense that you had six months in the summer *in industry* of which there was much in mechanical engineering in the west of Scotland and six months at the College reading for either the diploma course, or the Associateship – three years or four years – or the Glasgow B.Sc. course, run jointly with Glasgow University. They were intensive in the sense that you spent six months on the College course up until Easter. You stopped your studies on the Friday night and started in the workshop on the Monday morning. So you had six months' academic work and six months' industrial experience.

Against the advice of the Tech Principal, John MacLaren rejected the offer to stay and work in the Tech, building marine engines, and instead joined the army in 1939. Amongst his traumatic war experiences was a long spell after the fall of Singapore as a Japanese POW, which included surviving the forced construction of the Burma railroad. He returned at the end of 1945 to complete the final two years of his degree:

Figure 2.9 Royal College mining engineering students, 1952
Undertaking practical work in a Scottish coalmine. The College had a close
relationship with industry, and a large number of workers were involved in
evening classes and sandwich courses. *Strathclyde University Archives.*

I'd been there for two years in 1937–9, I had my class tickets and I went
back in and after six years in the jungle. The professor of mathematics
knew as well as I did that I was not qualified to go into the third year of
mathematics, but he could do nothing about it! He didn't like it, but he
could do nothing about it, I had my class ticket from the second year. So
seven years later I was back into the third year of mathematics, knowing
no mathematics, straight back out of the jungle of Thailand. The point
was I was struggling, I was struggling with my background.

We were back to catch up with lost time. *Which is worth mentioning*,
because the staff at that time, like Dr Peter Caldwell, dated back to the
end of the First World War when the returned service people came back

and rightly or wrongly established a reputation for themselves of making mayhem – *a wild lot!* – our coming back as students caused fear and trepidation about these wild soldiers coming back but *it didn't work out that way*. As I say six of the seven first-class honours people were people that had been away for five or six years; they hadn't heard, or didn't heed, Sir David Anderson's call to stay and finish their degree.

John recalled how difficult it was to return to full-time study and how tough the exam diet was in that period:

> So we had a very busy time of it at that time, but that's not an excuse for me – upper-second – *it was very hard-going* and I was in with some very good people. A trivial example of that is being an engines man, we had six honours papers to sit in five days – which is different from nowadays when they're complaining if they don't have a day off in between the two exams! A the heat-engines paper I got stuck at – I couldn't do a question – and I went 'God, where am I going if I can't do this question? Heat-engines, my strongest subject.' My good friend, who got a first, and went on to become the innovator of refrigeration in fishing boats at sea, in the North Sea, he couldn't do this question. He said to himself 'The question can't be done' – and moved on. I wasn't of his calibre. If I cannae do the question, there's something wrong with me! And I didn't do well in that paper.

Others recalled this tough exam regime. John Webster singled out the London externally-validated degrees in civil and mechanical engineering as particularly taxing:

> Now the University of London, you sat eight papers in four days... Morning, afternoon, morning, afternoon, morning, afternoon, morning, afternoon. And I confess that on the fourth day in the middle of the afternoon paper I fell asleep. I must have lost an hour, an hour and a half.

Shortly after graduating John MacLaren applied for and got a job at the Tech as a lecturer in engineering. He recalled being told at the interview that he was being offered a job 'for life', should he want it. However, in the late 1940s and 1950s, the working conditions could be poor and the hours long:

> Well, the teaching, we were in room that was called 13A that had no daylight, I can take you to it, it's not a staff room now, it wouldn't be

tolerated (*laughs*). And in that big cupboard there were . . . one . . . two, three, four, five, six, seven, eight of us (*laughs*) crammed in there. It was a heavy teaching load and on top of that you had one night a week, unpaid, evening classes. I did twenty years, unpaid evening-class work. Two points about that. The year I stopped doing evening classes, they started *paying for evening classes*, but the other point was that you had no sympathy whatsoever, from the older permanent staff that – all us youngsters came in 1947 – had to do two nights' unpaid evening-class work up until the end of the war when we came in – and considered we were lucky only having to do one night.

For some lecturers there was also something of a sense of inferiority to overcome when you were plunged into teaching mature students who had been through the war. Stanley Tweddle recalled:

And even Professor Kenedi whom I knew afterwards he started at the same time – or round about that time – we were his first class – and I met him socially afterwards and we were talking about it , 'I was scared to death', he said 'All these blokes, I'd never done anything except be at school and been a lecturer . . . blokes with a lot of experience and I'm talking to them and telling them what to do!'

Perceptions are refracted through context and experience. Much, however, depended upon where you were coming from. One of our interviewees commented on the transition from a dynamic research engineering department in industry to working at the university in the mid-1960s, recalling how 'dull' university teaching was to him initially. To add insult to injury, he experienced not only a diminution in job satisfaction but also took a 20 per cent wage cut. Such negative experiences were, however, relatively rare, and even in this case was transitory. Despite being tempted to leave the institution after being offered his old job back, he stayed, finding more stimulation after he began work on his own Ph.D. whilst working as a lecturer.[38]

What is clear is that then, as now, trying to cope with a heavy teaching load, marking, and doing research was a very difficult juggling act – especially for those like John MacLaren who were working on their doctorate whilst in full-time employment (he got his Ph.D. in 1955):

I can't quote the hours now, you had . . . twenty-three hours' class contact and then the evening class on top of that – buy your tea downstairs, pie and chips, before your evening class – eh, and the other aspect of it is that, if you had any ambition at all in your chosen field, or the field you'd landed up in, you were going to try and do a Ph.D. and that was not an essential part and parcel of the job. This is where it's relevant, you were there to teach. There was a fellow did a Ph.D. in aeronautics and was on the staff and he was considered a wee bit odd. Very good, you know, but that's not what you're here *to do*. You weren't stopped from doing it, but he had got on with. So that when the classes *stopped* at Christmas time, for example, you had two things to do. You had a pile of marking . . . and what to do for your Ph.D., and there were little in the way of facilities. There were people like Professor Alex Scott who were encouraging you, he was number two to Professor Adam Thomson, who was head of department. But Alex Scott would come along and talk you into doing a line of work and then leave you to it, so you were encouraged in that sense, but very little facilities and very little time, because you couldn't get home for Christmas until this marking was done, great piles of marking.

A significant element of the teaching in the 1940s and 1950s that John and others recalled was the heavy commitment to part-time, evening teaching. In mechanical engineering in the 1950s three times as many students were taught in the evening than in the daytime. This required a small army of teaching assistants – at peak John MacLaren recruited seventy in mechanical engineering alone. Some, such as John Webster, obtained permanent posts, whilst others went on to teaching jobs at the local colleges such as Stow, Falkirk and Kilmarnock as those institutions in turn expanded from ONC into HNC and HND programmes.

At the Scottish College of Commerce in Pitt Street, workloads were similarly severe, especially for new lecturers. Eric Furness, appointed lecturer in economics in 1948, taught twenty-one and a half hours of daytime teaching and two hours of evening teaching each week. 'The only real problem,' he recalls, 'was industrial administration which was given to works managers. I was terrified at first, never having been in a factory in my life. But, by using a good textbook I managed to keep one lecture ahead of my experienced students.'[39] Appointed a lecturer in the same college over ten years later, Tom Carbery recalls even greater pressure:

> When I did start in '61, my timetable was that I had to teach for twenty-eight hours a week over eight different subjects.
> Q Could you say what the subjects were?
> A *Well*, there was a good end and the bad end. The good end was that I had to take a class in American government at final Honours year level, I had to take a class in British government at final Honours

year level. I had to take a comparative government class at third-year level and I had to take government classes in the first two years, an introduction to British politics and then a subsequent class, and I also did the applied economics which I'd been teaching for five years anyway and a first-year class in economics. Now that was the *better of it*. The stuff that was not so easy was that I had to take a class in international trade, notwithstanding the fact that I had managed to *avoid* questions in international trade while a student, and there were one or two other things of that sort of nature that I found difficult.

As with the Royal College, the teaching at the Scottish College was mixed in quality. Tom Carbery again:

Some of the teaching was *extremely good*; a lot of it was acceptable double plus. Another block of it was acceptable and there was a rump of about 10 per cent which ran from indifferent to atrocious. That said, it seemed to me that the great strength of the Eric Thompson, Noel Branton administration of the place was that they did strive to recruit people who, first of all, were enthusiastic and secondly who held out some promise of being better than average teachers. And so what I noticed *through the '50s and through the '60s* was that gradual improvement in the teaching, and some of the people that were recruited were quite *outstanding* teachers. The best teacher I had during my four years there was the late Alex Smith, who ended as reader in politics here. Moreover Alex Smith was, from the students' point of view, *a magnificent teacher*, in that his lectures were extremely well prepared, they were very well structured. He taught you well, he pointed you towards good reading material, and over the piece he helped one over stiles as you encountered them.

Carbery and Smith went on to form a formidable team, teaching B.Sc. Economics so well that their results were better than those achieved at the London School of Economics in the early to mid-1960s. He explained how this was achieved:

I think it came about in two ways. First of all because we had small classes and were able to develop a rapport with the students, and I know that in my own case, although I generally had pretty good relations with a wide variety of students, and that kept on throughout the years, it was the relationships in those early years that have been the more numerous and the deeper. But the second I think was that Alex and I were, well maybe we were crafty. Remember, LSE in theory had an advantage over us; they set the papers. We had no idea what was coming up. But what we did was, we said 'Let us learn when LSE calls for the papers and we'll get the learned journals for the three months or four months *prior to when they set the papers*, because these are the articles the guys are reading when they're asked to set the papers.' So we could identify likely questions coming up and give lectures round them and say to students 'Well, were I to be in your shoes I would be thinking that one might care to think of preparing for a question on – or be prepared for – and *it was amazing* how often this would happen. Time and again we would have sent these young people into the exam room with three or four 'bankers', and two or three of them would come up in the exam paper.

The teaching of the 1940s and 1950s was as effective as any in the modern era. New technology does not displace the effective communicator. But some systems were a little slack. Whilst classroom teaching was very regimented in most ways, it was much less ordered in other ways than would be the case today. Take the danger of mercury poisoning in the pharmacy lab. Pat Fraser recalls, in conversation to her friend Elizabeth McCudden, the absence of accident reports:

[Elizabeth] got this in her hands and her hands went to her mouth. So I said 'Oh we need to take you over to Mary Dawson', Dr Dawson. Oh it was a very poisonous substance. Anyway, there was no fuss, nobody did anything. 'Pat, you take her up to the Royal Infirmary'. End of story. There was no writing . . . accident reports or anything like that. And I'd to take her to the Royal Infirmary and . . . she said to me, Mary Dawson said to me, Dr Dawson, 'Just you take her up Pat.' . . . And so in we went to Royal Infirmary, and when we were taken eventually into the casualty, you got your glass of milk and they discussed the whole chemistry with both of us. It would be precipitated as an albuminate. Remember that. Don't worry. You were like 'Och that was all I got', you wanted a bit more fuss.

Such slackness in procedure would be much less likely today. But then, classes were smaller. A new lecturer in textile physics in 1959 recalled being surprised by the scale:

I was a little surprised at the smallness of the number of people who were . . . actually taking the ARCST at that time, the Associateship, and . . . we also were doing a Diploma which had rather more students on it. I shouldn't think we had a dozen in any year, anyhow, and also we did night classes in those days. I used to lecture to a night class on some-thing that I had not had much to do with which was 'mill engineering', steam engines and electric motors and all sorts of things like that and how you ran them in textile mills. Those classes were for City and Guilds students, I think it was, in those days and we had, I suppose there'd be about, maybe, a dozen or fifteen in the evening class . . . [who] were older, usually, and for what they were, they were very good. I used to get on with them quite well, and as far as I know they got reasonable results in their examinations, which was the important thing. But they were, clearly, of course, people who were actually in the industry and looking for City and Guilds and I think also Textile Institute qualifications, so they could advance in the textile trade.[40]

GROWTH

The education sector in Britain grew with enormous speed after the Second World War. The Royal College was no exception, as John Webster recalled:

Well the department to which I was appointed was the one which bore the name, and this was a name which was very carefully fitted to what it did − the Department of Civil and Mechanical Engineering and Applied Mechanics. That was a joint activity. Civil and mechanical engineering and applied mechanics. And there were eight professors, and there was the professor of mechanical engineering who at that time was Adam Thomson. And there was also a professor of chemical engineering who was Alex Scott, and civil engineering was headed by a reader, who was Dr Hunter and after Dr Hunter retired there was a chair created and it was . . . Bill Fraser who became the professor of civil engineering.

The increase in the professoriate was a consequence of swift post-war expansion − an expansion that proceeded with essentially-minimal reorgan-isation, as John Webster recalls:

And all this was against the background of a *big expansion* in the depart-ment, because there was a big expansion taking place in technology, and education for technology, nationally and internationally. So if one looks at the numbers in that department, possibly in the latter days of the war, it was running on a shoestring with maybe about ten people total. But of course when the student numbers began to appear, people who were now able to get to university, people who had come back from the forces, there was a very big forces element. In some of the classes, there'd be fifty in a lecture class and forty of them were ex-servicemen. Very big numbers. The fiscal, or the financial arrangements were, nationally, were worked out to allow that. People coming back from the forces, having been able to show that there was an interruption of their education because of their service in the forces, were able to get a grant and quite a generous grant for the time, to study at university. Applied not only to engineering but applied to all disciplines but we did have a very big increase in student numbers and therefore there was a big increase in staff was required to deal with it.

One consequence was overcrowding. Buildings designed for relatively small numbers of students, and without the needs for laboratory and workshop training facilities that emerged in the mid-twentieth century, became quickly strained. John Paul recalls the effect in engineering in the Royal College:

We had a well-respected Engineering Department from the '40s through to university status and beyond, and it was recruiting students from home and overseas, a lot from Norway, a lot from India, a few from North America, we got a few from North America to bioengineering too in due course. And it was doing well and it was doing *so well* it was getting packed and the Royal College was getting crowded and hence money came first of all for the James Weir building in Montrose Street. Mechanical Engineering moved up there and Civil and Chemical with it and I sometimes go back to the old rooms and laboratories we had in the Royal College building. Some of the laboratories were in the basement, the machine shop was in the basement, Electronics was halfway up and Thermodynamics was partly in the basement there.

Noel Branton came to the Scottish College of Commerce in 1946 as lecturer in commerce and economics after seven years at Cardiff Technical College. He came to an interview where he was clearly the favoured candidate:

I got this interview (*laughs*), it was a farce because very clearly I was going to be appointed anyway you see. In fact I was told afterwards that the chairman of the meeting that interviewed me when I'd withdrawn to get the verdict, said 'We're offering him £700. If he goes back to Cardiff and says he has accepted it and they make a bigger offer . . .' So, they raised it to £800.

The fifteen years before the creation of the University involved some major readjustments to rising expectations of what the constituent colleges should be. Professor Noel Branton recalls both the premises and some of the courses at the College of Commerce as less than perfect. Asked how he found the College set-up on his arrival in 1946, he replied:

At Pitt Street? Oh deplorable! *Deplorable.* There's no other word for it. In fact I believe that they were a centre for the training of teachers. And I think, I haven't any evidence or anything, I am pretty certain that they were in grave danger of *losing that* because the Scottish Education Department was fed up with them, you see. And of course the Scottish Education Department directly controlled the college as it did with the Technical College before the university.

Some of the courses were post-sixteen, but not higher-education status, what Branton described as 'youngsters, who were beyond the school-leaving age but below sixteen'. One of the areas that were dropped was teacher training, but some ruthless decisions had to be made about the nature of the institution, its identity in terms of subjects taught, and the strengths of the teaching systems compared to other institutions. Some of the changes took time, and the external degree-awarding bodies (ranging from Glasgow University to London University) could sometimes restrain change rather than push it forward. Under the Principal, Eric Thompson, a rolling five-year plan meant, as Noel Branton recalls, 'we were doing something new all the time, that's what it really came down to'. A myriad of changes were introduced as classes became separated, many becoming more specialised, whilst some classes were split as they mushroomed in size.

On the eve of merger and chartering as a university, the Scottish College and the Royal College of Technology were still physically quite small places, employing around 100 and 300 teachers respectively. But each had a certain status and established reputation in academic terms. The original 1905 Royal College building on George Street, stark and solid in its red sandstone, gave it a *gravitas*, as Karen Morrison[41] recalls, when she arrived in 1963: 'I liked the Royal College, I've always liked the Royal College because to me it looked like a university should look and that's where Admin was of course when I came, the Principal was there, the Registrar, the Academic Registrar, and all the great and the good were based in the Royal College.' But central administration was soon to move out to the McCance Building in Richmond Street, the flatted concrete-and-glass style of office block and lecture theatre that graced many expanding universities of the period. Karen voiced the feeling of many others – that the McCance couldn't match the stature of the Royal College building:

To me the McCance doesn't look like a university. I know it's stupid, but it doesn't look like a university, but somehow the Royal College always had a bit of presence. If you were coming in there you were coming into somewhere. But of course they built on so many little nooks and crannies to accommodate expansion in departments and stuff. There has been quite a bit of change there I think from the original.

Somehow, the small move of the university administration across the width of Montrose Street to the McCance Building was a symbol of the new university age: 'it's just a wee white building, it doesn't inspire great emotion, I would think, whereas the Royal College *looks like* a university.'

Of the 'wee white building', great things were going to be expected.

CONCLUSION

Before merger and elevation to university status, the learning and teaching experience and the environment in the two Colleges were very different in the mid-1950s to what they were to become within a decade. These were relatively small, still in many ways elite colleges, catering for a mixture of degree and sub-degree qualifications, but lacking the prestige of degree-awarding powers and university constitutions. However, the learning experience was intimate and personal. Inevitably, the quality of teaching varied widely. The pace of change in methods and course structures was relatively slow before the 1960s, and classroom regimes were quite regimented, in common with other centres of higher education. Nonetheless, the testimony is on balance very positive and nostalgic, with a sense of some kind of bygone 'golden era' permeating the recollections of staff and, more especially, many of the students. It is noteworthy that so many Royal College and Scottish College teachers in this period were singled out for praise and remembered with affection by their students. The Scottish College was offering top-standard economics degrees, whilst the Tech was providing first-rate engineering degrees, both comparable to anywhere in the UK. The Tech had a worldwide reputation for excellence, especially in engineering. To be sure, the students tended to be more utilitarian in their approach to their studies, and invariably had a stronger work ethic, seeing study as a route to better careers and as a way to 'get on' and improve prospects for themselves and their families. The study and examination regimes were also tough.

Something of the austerity and prim, ordered world of the post-war decades comes through in the testimony. In this environment, college students matured and developed as individuals, and went on to careers, mostly in the

Figure 2.10 Young science student at Royal College, 1952
An evocative image of the engrossed student. *Strathclyde University Archive.*

commercial and industrial fields in the second half of the twentieth century. What the oral testimony indicates is a wide range of experience and attitudes. What also consistently comes through in these voices of students and teachers of this era is a belief in the emancipatory potential of education. At the same time, clearly and unequivocally articulated is the joy attained through the intellectual challenge and stimulation derived from study and teaching, and from absorbing and creating knowledge.

NOTES

1. Testimony of Professor Thomas M. Devine, interviewed 2 May 2003.
2. Testimony of emeritus professor Thomas F. Carbery, interviewed 7 February 2003.
3. Written testimony of emeritus professor Eric L. Furness.

4. Testimony of emeritus professor John Paul, interviewed 9 May 2003; testimony of emeritus professor John T. Webster, interviewed 30 April 2003.
5. Reported in the *Evening Citizen*, 29 June 1959.
6. Testimony of Kjell Sandberg, by email to Neil Rafeek, July 2003.
7. Testimony of David Paterson, interviewed 8 May 2003.
8. Testimony of Anonymous Interviewee 4, interviewed 18 December 2002.
9. Testimony of Elizabeth McCudden, interviewed 4 December 2002.
10. Testimony of Anonymous Interviewee 2, interviewed 27 November 2002.
11. *Glasgow Herald*, 4 February 1965.
12. J. A. Rae (ed.), *The History of Allan Glen's School, 1853–1953* (Glasgow, Aird and Coghill, 1953), pp. 124–5, 131.
13. Hutcheson's Grammar School.
14. Testimony of Anonymous Interviewee 6, interviewed 26 November 2002.
15. Ibid.
16. The British scientist James Wimshurst in the early nineteenth century invented an advanced induction static machine, which by the late nineteenth century was indispensable for generating the high-voltage current for experimentation using high-voltage vacuum tubes (www.arcsandsparks.com, accessed 5 January 2004).
17. Testimony of Anonymous Interviewee 6.
18. Testimony of James Brown, interviewed 30 October 2002.
19. Testimony of Pat Fraser, interviewed 4 December 2002.
20. Testimony of Anonymous Interviewee 4.
21. Natural philosophy was the name given until the late 1960s (and in some places the 1970s) for physics.
22. L. Heron (ed.), *Truth, Dare or Promise: Girls Growing up in the Fifties* (London, Virago, 1985), p. 5; C. L. White, *Women's Magazines 1693-1968* (London, Michael Joseph, 1970), chapter 6; S. Rowbotham, *A Century of Women: The History of Women in Britain and the United States* (London, Viking, 1997), pp. 242–9, 280–4.
23. Sir Kenneth Alexander was the University of Strathclyde's first professor of economics, and went on to be Principal of the University of Stirling. He was regarded as one of the most prominent Scottish economists of his generation.
24. Testimony of Bashir Maan, interviewed 12 May 2003. See Chapter 5 for further comments on racism in Glasgow at this time.
25. The Partition of the Indian sub-continent into Pakistan (at that time Eastern and Western) and India at the time of British withdrawal.
26. Testimony of Anonymous Interviewee 3.
27. Testimony of Anonymous Interviewee 6.
28. Testimony of Stanley Tweddle, interviewed 2 December 2002.
29. Testimony of Anonymous Interviewee 4.
30. Testimony of James Laurie.
31. Testimony of Anonymous Interviewee 6.
32. Testimony of Robert Orr, interviewed 10 March 2003.
33. Testimony of Douglas Logan, interviewed 1 August 2003.
34. Testimony of Dr Ronnie Simpson, interviewed 9 September 2003.
35. Testimony of Malcolm Allan.

36. Professor Robert Kenedi, appointed professor of bioengineering at the Royal College in 1963, and then professor of bioengineering at the University of Strathclyde until 1980.
37. Testimony of Anonymous Interviewee 2.
38. Ibid.
39. Written testimony of emeritus professor Eric L. Furness.
40. Testimony of Anonymous Interviewee 5, interviewed 17 July 2003.
41. Testimony of Karen Morrison, interviewed 25 November 2002.

CHAPTER THREE

Student Life, 1945–1963

In popular consciousness, the 1950s were not so much a calculation of the calendar as a stretch of cultural time. They constituted the period from 1945 to 1963 – considerably more than a decade in number of years, and something of a marker in the cultural heritage of the twentieth century. The first year marked the end of the war, and the beginning of reconstruction under a victorious Labour Party slogan of 'Never Again' – a slogan referring only tangentially to the war, but more consciously to the depression years of the inter-war period. The slogan marked the beginning of a new sense of justice, equality and opportunity, and an end to the hardships of life. At the other end of the period, 1963 marked a lot of beginnings. It was the year that The Beatles issued *She Loves You*, the single that was to mark out both them and the music revolution. It was the year in which popular satire peaked on the television screens in *That Was the Week That Was*. It was the year in which the Bishop of Woolwich caused Christian furore by proclaiming the death of God, and the year in which John F. Kennedy was assassinated.[1] And it was also the year that the Royal College of Science and Technology planned its merger with the Scottish College of Commerce, and the first students were admitted to what were to become the degrees of the University of Strathclyde.

THE ERA OF AUSTERITY

Historians have developed a twin fascination with the 1950s on the one hand and the 1960s on the other. They are seen as ying and yang. If the 1960s is seen (rightly or wrongly) as having been the decade of hippies, youth culture, colour (television, clothes, record sleeves), carefree sexuality, the generation gap and overturning humbug, then the 1950s is seen as having been staid, puritan, black-and-white and hypocritical. They are perceived as cultural opposites, with the 1950s playing the part of the dark, suppressed grime of post-war puritanism, closed pubs, barren Sundays, and a cruel and dark culture as represented in Alexander Trocchi's *Young Adam* (released in 2003 as a film starring Ewan McGregor). However, such over-generalisations mask a complex reality.

During the Second World War, and for some time thereafter, socialising

Figure 3.1 College of Commerce Women's Common Room, 1946–7
The marked lack of amenities (note the absence of lampshades) evokes post-war austerity and furniture rationing. The students are doing their best to look studious in their free time. *Strathclyde University Archives.*

amongst the College and Tech students was proscribed for a number of reasons, not least long working hours and fatigue. This was especially the case amongst those combining work and study, and a large proportion of students at night classes were in this category. For many, study was a chore, a vehicle to facilitate promotion, and improve career prospects and qualify for better wages. Many came to the colleges to study and then left, and thus the sense of 'attachment' to the institution was more muted. Stanley Tweddle commented:

> When the war started in '39, we were working twelve-hour shifts in the Albion [works], and then every month you changed from night-shift to day-shift and that was the only time you had off was a Saturday when there was a change in between – you changed seven o'clock in the morning, you'd finish, if you were finishing the night

shift, and you wouldn't start off then until the Sunday at seven o'clock which was twenty-four hours later. So you had a whole twenty-four hours and that was time off, but as apprentices we got let off if we were coming to the classes, we finished early, but we had very little time left, quite tired in those days, to try and do home-work. I was quite happy to join up and get out of it (*laughs*).

Q How did you manage with the work at the college?

A I got through it all right.

Q And would you and your colleagues socialise much?

A Ah, no, to begin with I was a stranger completely coming here, and it took a year or more – a year – maybe longer than that, but I got into a gang of folks, a few girls and what-not at eighteen, reasonably soon. So, but you mainly came in to classes and went back again. There were another couple of people that I knew that came with me and went back, we didn't linger at all after night school (*laughs*). And then when the war had actually started we were working long, long hours and there was just no time for socialising.

David Paterson's description of his arrival as a student at the College of Commerce, still in his school uniform, gives a flavour of a bygone age of the cultural 1950s:

I was very disappointed. When I went it was kind of, it was almost like a prison kind of a building, Pitt Street. Famous place, but it looked a bit bare and concrete and steel frame windows, and I didn't much like it to be honest. Just the physical environment of it, it was I think, it was quite a warm intimate place when you got to know it, small classes, small classrooms, lecture rooms. Fairly academic staff and quite a mix of students and I got to like the place but, as I think I said before, my initial impressions of the people were strongly coloured when I went up to the cafeteria more or less on the first day that I was there and having been at Clydebank High School I was still wearing my chocolate and gold Clydebank High School tie and sat down at a table and a young lady immediately engaged me in conversation and agreed that we had both been at the High School. And we compared notes and I knew no one that she knew, and it then transpired that she was of course talking about Glasgow High which would have been a fee-paying school and when it was discovered that I had been at Clydebank High which was very much a working-class school, I had a polite smile and she disappeared. That rather set the pattern for, in a way for me because it was really quite a middle-class institution, university or college in these days. And there

80

Figure 3.2 On location with Scottish miners, 1949
Royal College mining engineering lecturer Dr William Burnett (centre front) enjoys a beer on an outing with a group of coal miners in the Lothians. *Strathclyde University Archives.*

were very few of us who were actually from what you would call recognisably working-class west-of-Scotland backgrounds. There were one or two of us, but my abiding impression of it is of a middle-class student body and quite snobbish and quite discriminating in their attitudes towards those of us who came from humble backgrounds. Didn't find that amongst the lecturers there was none of that at all. But amongst the student body that was very much the case.

The Colleges seemed to reflect the ranks of a highly-structured society. For instance, the Royal College had a blazer. As James Laurie remembers from the start of his student days in 1952, the blazer carried the Technical College badge on it: "'*Mente et Manu*" or "By Mind and by Hand", motto for a technical college. The colloquial translation among the boys at the Tech was "Mind your Haun".' Such emblems positioned the Colleges in a society in which most citizens knew their position in terms of social class. Consciously and unconsciously, one 'read' the way people clothed or cut their hair.

A former student considered the social configurations at the Royal College and Glasgow University:

It was the Royal College or the University, it wasn't as widespread as it is now. So the people you were mixing with were the ones who had either been to schools like Allan Glen's or good-quality comprehensive schools like Hyndland, if you know Glasgow at all. Hyndland was a good school, and there's quite a few like that. So all the people at the Royal College or University came from, not a similar background, but from the pupils' point or the students' point of view, they were sort of similar. Okay, my father was just a draughtsman, another guy in the class, his father, I think he was a bus driver or something, so that in that sense there was a mixture. But it was overlaid with the five years/six years of education in what you would say was *either* a selective school or a semi-selective. To me in these days also we'd junior secondary schools, and if you weren't very good you went to junior secondary school and the betters-off, not better-off, the better-qualified people are more intelligent if you want to put it that way … I believe some people went to the junior secondary were just lazy but not probably intelligent enough, and so there was a slight difference there.[2]

Despite the exclusive nature of the colleges, and despite only 10 per cent of Scottish eighteen-year-olds going into higher education in 1950, coming to college meant for many students the first real face-to-face encounter with structures of society. They met the members of other sections of society, and this contact could be enriching and enlightening. For some this encouraged conformity, whilst for others this clash of social worlds charged their political commitment. Robert Orr came from a relatively-poor working-class background in Dundee and made a conscious decision to absorb middle-class values in an attempt to fit in, even to the point of taking up tennis and squash. David Paterson found the experience of coming to the College of Commerce endowed his political life:

Well it just, it really reaffirmed all my prejudices that the middle class and above were useless parasites on society. And it really just reinforced all my, at that time, pretty strong left-wing political views and I was coming up against living evidence what the 'movement' in inverted commas was up against. So really it reaffirmed a lot of my political opinions and views and on the other hand I found some of it quite entrancing because I met people who had had experiences that were totally beyond the comprehension of somebody from Clydebank. So that the person with whom I became most friendly and whose best man I became, very middle-class chap, just back from crossing the Atlantic on the *Queen* [*Mary?*] and had spent a holiday touring in a motor car the

United States, other people had foreign holidays in places like Switzerland and France, and that seemed to me to be just like something from another planet. I couldn't comprehend this. Other people lived in very large houses and the experience of going to one or two of these places for parties and so forth I just found absolutely amazing. So that whilst it reaffirmed some of my old prejudices and opinions it also opened my eyes to another part of the world I hadn't seen before.

One former student recalled that in the years after the Second World War, political debate was lively between students:

Oh yes, this was just after the war with the Labour government just having taken over and there were feelings on both sides. And, oh, we obviously weren't at hammer and tongs, but we had great discussions. I don't mean debating society, just in the classroom and, yeah, very friendly... We didn't have Scot Nats, Liberals I don't remember, it was Conservative and Labour and there was equal, I would reckon about equal numbers of both.[3]

Yet, the colleges were remarkably peaceable places for politics in the 1950s. Most political campaigning was frowned-upon on site, and most students were there for one thing only – to learn.

This was perhaps particularly the case for the older students who returned to resume their studies after war service, many of whom were married and had children. Stanley Tweddle had undertaken night classes at the Tech before war broke out, and had started his mechanical engineering degree course before joining up. He returned to study after demobilisation and working for a short spell, eventually graduating in 1952 with the College's Associateship. He noted:

The thing was that we seemed to fall into two classes when I came back then. There was those who had been in the forces and had come back again and those who were just coming through in the normal course as students and they seemed so young and immature to we older ones. We were only what? I suppose we were only six, eight, ten years older, but it did seem . . .

Q Did you find – did you stay in separate [student] camps, between those who had been in the war and those who hadn't?

A Yes, I mean, I wouldn't say it was a rigid thing or anything like that, you'd speak to the rest etc. – but there was a feeling of difference, you know.

83

Q Why do you think that was?

A Well, because we were different. I mean if you were only six years older, you were at least thirty years older than they were in what had happened.

Some, like Stanley Tweddle, had to cope not only with the difficulties of resuming studies after five or six years, but also with the pressures of a dependent wife and children. This seriously curtailed his social life as a student:

> I found it difficult to come back again after a six-year gap and start learning again, particularly as there was all kinds of other distractions. I mean I was married by that time, I had two children, or I had one and the other was just – no I think Alison was actually born before I started, we couldn't find anywhere to stay, you know – there just weren't any places for people coming back from – they were putting up what-do-you-call-it the temporary housing.

Stanley Tweddle and his family ended up living in Largs in a rented house. This was a period when supplies were difficult to obtain for the civil population, and evenings in winter were spent in hunting for fuel:

> You always had to beg coal from the, or coke, gas works, pick up bits of wood along the foreshore and fill the pram with it – oh aye, it was a desperate time just after the war... I was married and had two kids and it makes it difficult even to study when you've got kids crying, you know... Oh well, you just studied whenever you got the chance or a few minutes' peace or when you weren't out looking for extra rations somewhere.

A keen sense of duty and responsibility curtailed Stanley Tweddle's social life as a married mature student at this time:

> Maybe, as a married man, one of the things I would have liked to have done would be to have played rugby, which I'd done *a lot of* in my youth, but there just wasn't the time with everything that had to be done. You couldn't join in any other things that went on. I mean, they used to have the Rag Day and whatnot, well I never joined that, far too busy studying. It was *so important* that you finished up with a good pass because, whereas originally and for the kids that are there now, it was their own future that we were tying up in it. I had a wife and a family to support and they

84

were more important than yourself, like you know, to get a good degree to get a good job.

Again, evident here is the sense of the utility in higher education; this was a means to an end. For such students, social life was heavily curtailed.

Before the war, student experience had in many ways been quite comfortable. At the very least, the College facilities reflected the relative prosperity, privileged position and reasonable affluence of the vast majority of students. This contrasted sharply with the experience of most working-class families in Glasgow in the 1920s and 1930s, where high levels of unemployment and job insecurity meant endemic poverty, malnutrition, deficiency-related diseases, low life-expectancy and the dearth of even basic amenities such as light and warmth. The war, however, brought some changes, as one chemistry student at the Tech recalled:

When we started in 1938 *I had a full year in the College* under peace-time conditions and the College, it was a very pleasant place to work in because it had air-conditioning, heating, *even in the corridors*. So you could sit in the corridors, there was seats in the corridors and you could sit in the corridors and do you your homework quite comfortably. But after, when the war started, they started cutting down on the heating so the corridors were no longer heated, but the lecture rooms were still heated and the laboratories, of course, it was simple, you just turned all the Bunsen burners on (*laughs*) and put a gauze on top of the tripod and in five minutes flat you were, you'd plenty of heat, so that was the thing (*laughs*). And I, *I enjoyed, in fact I enjoyed all my college years, even during the war*. During the war, of course, we had to do what was called 'Fire-watching' and all that that meant was you had to spend maybe about three days a week in the college, but then it ran forward so that you were not always on the same days, you know, sometimes you were at the weekends and it would run forward and the big advantage of this was that you got special rations, see? So that you had a good tea in the College and in the morning you have a very good breakfast, bacon and egg and porridge and toast and marmalade and what have you. Now when I tell you that the wartime ration was two slices of bacon and one egg per adult per week! So that doing fire-watching was a great idea (*laughs*).[4]

But in the post-war period, student overcrowding quickly became a problem and a constraint on expansion. The problems of overcrowded and poor teaching buildings were felt acutely by the College authorities. The construction of new buildings was very difficult, especially at the Pitt Street site of the College of Commerce. Building control was in the hands of a local authority that prioritised housing, and when even new churches could not be built in the mushrooming peripheral housing estates, the educational institutions of further and higher education had problems in getting permission for extensions to their premises. Noel Branton recalls how, soon after the end of the war, the pressure on space became great:

> At first, of course, they started to increase, it was too near the end of the war for the authorities to sanction the necessary expenditure for any real enlargements. So but then the college fortunately had quite a large piece of ground which was not being used. And [Principal Eric] Thompson got round that by erecting wooden huts there to make three extra classrooms which relieved the pressure to a certain extent. Wasn't a satisfactory solution, but it was the only one open because the department wouldn't sanction any more money then. It was too near the end of the war you see.

The numbers kept growing into the 1950s. The foundation of the Hotel School added to the problems of the College of Commerce – it started at Pitt Street, but, being unsuited to there, it was moved to a newly-purchased country house, Ross Hall (now a private hospital). Though this relieved pressure at least temporarily at the main building, student recollection is of a society in which scarce resources were not yet being channelled into the provision of an improved learning environment.

The material austerity of the 1950s and early 1960s was reinforced by a puritanism that was bounded by some rules that, by modern standards, might be regarded as slightly extraordinary. There was a college-wide ban on a number of things – political parties and campaigning at elections being one, and also swearing, as James Brown recalls:

> Yes, young women who had been hired and come to work with us and people who'd come up the HNC route as technicians, their language was what I used to hear in Singer's and the shipyards, whereas when I was at Strathclyde and the 'Tech' before that, they had a ban on swearing. Within the Student Union, the only place that swearing was allowed was the men's beer bar. Anywhere outside that you could be picked up by one of the union officials and charged with ungentlemanly conduct and fined for ungentlemanly conduct for swearing in front of women. So that's a social change in thirty-five years.

Swearing or not, college was where many students felt they 'grew up' into adulthood. Many interviewees recall arriving at College in the persona of childhood, still attuned to its attitudes and outlook. Doris reflected:

I was a child when I left school, some schools turned out young ladies. 'Hutchie' said they turned out 'Young Ladies' but they didn't, they turned out children, fairly well-educated children, but nevertheless children with *no knowledge* of what the world was like . . . I think it may be different now, but all my contemporaries at school, and I still see them regularly, feel the same way. . . You know, it was a very sheltered life, a very sheltered *schooling*, we didn't know how to cope with boys. We really didn't. I mean it was – you learned very quickly when I went to 'Tech', but my husband said I went out with some real rogues at 'Tech' (*laughs*) but he reckoned because I'd been at Hutchie it was pure naïvety that I didn't get into trouble, you know I was, I really didn't know how to cope with them. I treated them as friends. It was an odd situation, when I think back, it was *really odd*, when I think what my grandchildren are like now and what I was like, *oohh*, I mean there's *no relation at all*.[5]

Male students were faced very quickly with one aspect of growing up – National Service. Until its abolition in 1960, every man was expected to undertake two years of compulsory military service, and in the case of college students this could be done either before or after studies. A former male student recalls the deleterious effect upon student numbers:

In these days, if you didn't pass onto the next year you had to go to the army, so (*laughs*) that kind of did a certain amount of emptying [of the class] . . . It just meant if you failed you had to go to one of the services, National Service, but nobody took the course just to avoid it. A lot of engineers, time-served engineers that I know, they went to the merchant navy after they became journeymen. And that became engineering on the ships and that exempted them from National Service. Then in their late twenties they came ashore and having avoided National Service, that was avoiding. Me it was just that was the way I was going.[6]

Not all feared National Service. Noel Cochrane recalls how he just missed doing his Service:

At that point people were still going to the National Service. It so happened that my birthday was eighteenth December 1939 and the cut-off point for people going into the National Service was October '39.

So I knew that I wasn't going into the National Service and because there were lots of guys coming back *from* National Service, who had been on quite exotic postings, there had been a guy in Japan, they'd been in Germany, they had been in various places and the stories were all quite exciting. So the guys of eighteen were actually looking forward going to National Service, so I was disappointed.

With most students confronting National Service, the Tech was a man's college with a very masculine air. Women were very few in number in the 1950s. James Laurie recalls that ten out of twenty-five of the students in his pharmacology class were women (in the entry class of 1952), but that this was wholly unusual:

> Most of the undergraduates who were female were either in the School of Pharmacy or the Department of Food Science which was an adjunct to the School of Pharmacy. I would imagine there were very few women studying engineering or fewer chemistry or physics . . . We accepted it again because we had nothing to compare it with although I would imagine a generation earlier in my father's time, there were *a few* women in my father's class I remember him recalling that in conversation.

The few women who did go to the Royal College recall how the era of austerity impinged on them more than it did upon men. But it was not just material austerity, but a kind of moral austerity. Women were often limited to a sartorial conservatism, as two former students, Pat Fraser and Elizabeth McCudden, recalled of the dress code of the late 1950s:

> PF   You didn't wear trousers, trousers were out of the question, we'd on trousers, we were ahead of ourselves, but never as students. We went hostelling and we had trousers. I mean I borrowed my sister's, I didn't have any. And maybe you borrowed them? I can't remember. But you wouldn't wear trousers as a student. Everybody had dark skirts and I suppose a sweater really.
> EM   A blouse and a cardigan.
> PF   A blouse and a cardigan.
> EM   We dressed like our mothers!
> PF   That's right! That's true! This was just – well of course '55 to '58 we were. So the war was over ten years, and really the war didn't hit us. It was before the '60s and you know the days of individuality, hedonism you could say, feminism and all that kind of thing. We were terribly conservative.

Wealth also determined clothing, and few students could afford the latest fashions (which in any event were heavily rationed well into the 1950s). A few students owned cars, but some others were struggling to make ends meet. Being a student was not an option granting immediate wealth. Those who chose to go to work often earned more, and showed it in their dress. Elizabeth McCudden recalls:

> I think my father was intensely proud of me, there was no doubt about that. I don't know that my mother was all that. I think she'd rather that I'd gone out and got a job and dressed like a factory girl. She used to say they were far better dressed than I was. I mean I was a student, so, I mean I didn't have any money to dress like that because the factory girls were earning. But she may have been proud of me, I don't really know. My father was quite visibly proud of me. But he was always much more, although he was a working man he read a lot.

Money was short, facilities were poor, and rationing continued on many things (some, like furniture, until 1955). This gave a distinctive feel to student life which for many was to be transformed in a seemingly more affluent late 1960s.

HOME, STUDENTS' UNION AND SOCIAL LIFE

Living in Glasgow, most students found the Royal College to be really convenient for transport. The main bus lines ran close to the College (in some cases stopping at the door in George Street), whilst the Underground was not far away. But where the city-centre location has really won over the situation of other universities was for out-of-town students, often domiciled at home. With long hours at College in the 1950s, it was still possible to live on the Ayrshire coast and commute by train. This was one of the distinctive features of life in Glasgow, as James Laurie recalls:

> I lived in Largs and I travelled night and morning. The train only took an hour and seven minutes from Largs, and I really honestly cannot recall ever being late for a nine o'clock class because the train was late. And I travelled home again at night on the 5.21 and was home in Largs at half past six ... Our classes were from nine in the morning until one o'clock and then the afternoon was occupied everyday from Monday to Friday with a lab from two to five. I think we maybe had one half day when we used to go and do some revision in the library, but they were talking this morning about the hours put in by students attending classes and how

the hours are nothing like nine to one and two to five, but that was the acceptable [thing] – certainly in the sciences.

A small number of students even managed to get home for lunch in the midst of the gruelling timetable of the 1940s. One student recalls:

I mean the great advantage to me of the College was that our lectures in the College, there was always three in the morning – 9.30, 10.30, 11.30, finish at half-past twelve. And I had a season ticket on the railway from what was then St Enoch's Station (which is now that big shopping centre) to Corkerhill Hall which was the Mosspark Station and a monthly season ticket, it wasn't very expensive, I can't remember, just a few shillings. And I used to come home for my lunch because I couldn't *afford to* buy my lunch at the College canteen, you see. And mother would have soup and, not always a middle course, she used to make plum pudding and custard, you see, and that was it, so I would go back to College. And the great advantage was that, the afternoons in the College were general laboratory periods, so if you were a few minutes late, nobody would notice so that it was quite convenient that way. So these are the little embarrassments that I had. I mean I couldn't sort of socialise with my colleagues to the same extent as you *might do* if you were down out having a meal together, you know.[7]

A decade and a half later, it was made clear to James Brown that if he was to move on from undergraduate to doctoral studies, then some sacrifices might be called for. He was quizzed by his professor and prospective Ph.D. supervisor:

'Are you a Roman Catholic?' and I said 'No, why?'. He said 'Well you'll have no objections to birth control then?' I said 'No'. He said 'Because being married would be okay, you would probably cope, but to have a family and do a Ph.D. together would be very difficult'.

The costs of being a student were high. James Brown's starting salary with Singer's in Clydebank in the 1960s was £19 a week (taxed as a single man this came down to about £13.50 a week), and as a Ph.D. student on a Science Research Council grant it was £9 a week (topped up by tutoring in design two afternoons a week to give a total of £11 a week). The alternative Aluminium Federation scholarship was £11 a week, with another £2 for tutoring making £13: 'I was about as well off doing a Ph.D. as I was as a single man, having just finished my degree with Singer Sewing Machine Company.'

90

Poverty was real enough for some students, and affected their diet considerably. One student recalls a special instructional lecture on keep fit, organised in the Assembly Hall, for 1940s students:

> We used to occasionally to attend a lecture in the exam hall – you know, when some guru would come in and talk to us about something. And I can always remember one lecture, and I mean I even laugh at it now. It was this fellow and all the professors were in the front couple of benches, and we were all behind, you see, and the whole bloody place was full, and this fellow was talking about the importance of keeping physically fit, you see – one of these keep-fit men, and we should join a gym and all that. Now you were talking to people that hardly saw a square meal from one week to the next, *we were all like bloody rakes* (*laughs*), and Professor Todd who was the professor of pharmacy, *and he was a great guy*, you know, a real character, and he was very Glasgow, if you know what I mean, oh the Glasgow accent you could cut it with a knife. And this guy was going on about doing exercises, going to the gym, and Todd couldn't contain himself any longer and he stood up, he says 'Look my man, in this country it's *brains we need no' braun*' and they all clapped (*laughs*).[8]

Pat Fraser recalls that home life in the 1950s was dominated by university work:

> It was a very safe time I think to be a student. We didn't have the wealth of problems that students have today. We had no choice. And when you don't have a choice you don't have difficulties. It's there so you take it and as I say it was quite like an extension of school. Because we went home and we looked up, we didn't learn our lecture notes, but we looked them over, there was no question of going out every night in the week. You would not go out on a Saturday if the exams were looming. You would go to the charities' dances and things like that.

Nonetheless, then as now, College meant mixing with a new group of people, and maturing and developing as individuals. An important institution in this was the Students' Union which played a key role in organising leisure and recreational activities in the Colleges in the post-war years. Dancing was one of the most popular pursuits and the Students' Representative Council of the Royal College had a specially-designated Dance Committee in the 1950s to organise such events. More than a dozen dances were organised at both the Tech and the Scottish College each year, including the grander events – the Christmas and Easter Balls, St Valentine's Dance, Halloween Ball, and the Charities' Queen Dance.[9] These were highly-structured activities, with jazz and dance bands, dancing competitions with prizes (including 'miniatures' for the men, but not the women), and occasionally a 'wheel of fortune' to appeal to the gamblers. At some of the bigger dances, organised in the Exam Hall in the Royal College, short films were ordered and shown in adjacent rooms, where refreshments were also served (lemonade and biscuits), and, in some cases, a liquor bar was organised. In 1957–8, the supplies bought from the *Dunrobin* pub for this purpose for the Easter Ball (formal dress) comprised four bottles of whisky, three bottles of sherry and two bottles of gin (for over 300 in attendance at an event that went on all night to 7am). Not surprisingly, there were no reports of over-indulgence. The Students' Union appeared to cater for all tastes, whilst inevitably embracing the changing fashions in popular music. The Dance Committee agreed that dance bands and jazz bands would be engaged on an alternate basis for College dances, and, in 1955, that the dances would include three 'old-time' dances in the schedule. Evidently, some of the bands were supplied with beer to lubricate their creative efforts, whilst others had to make do with tea – significantly supplied 'at the interval by a *lady* member of the Dance Committee'.[10]

Apart from organising regular dances, the Students' Union was the epicentre of a limited range of clubs and societies in the 1950s, and played a key role in charity work. The latter included participation in the traditional Glasgow Charities' Week in January, where activities included the organisation of 'raiding parties' outside the city to places like Airdrie, Stirling, Falkirk and Motherwell. Inter-collegial confrontations were common, including flour fights and 'raids' which, the student's magazine noted, 'although officially frowned upon, are still very entertaining if kept within reasonable bounds'.[11] One of the highlights was the Charities' Queen competition, where between fifteen and twenty beauty queens from all the Glasgow colleges competed for this coveted title. Sports were also central activities of many of the 1950s students. The Athletics section of the Royal College Students' Union included football, rugby, mountaineering and, by the early 1960s, ski-ing, whilst the Scottish College societies in the 1950s included the College Choir, Debating Society, Musical Appreciation Society, Drama Society, and Chess Club as well as badminton and table tennis. At the College of Commerce, Eric Furness, later professor of economics at the University, set up a mountaineering club in 1952 – 'using our newly-acquired car to take students into the hills on occasional Sundays'.[12] In an era when women were only starting to participate in many male sports, Jeanette

Figure 3.3 Student dance, 1946–7
A packed dance floor for a Saturday-evening dance at the Scottish College of
Commerce. Dance and jazz bands were the most popular. Despite the groomed
appearances, there is an air of austerity about the women's clothing during post-
war rationing. *Strathclyde University Archives.*

Smith recalled an unusual conflict in the early 1950s between the male and
female students:

> We played hockey at an ash field out at Cambuslang, where it was always
> raining. It was the kind of surface where you stayed upright if possible.
> Once we threw together a girls team to play our boys, and the bloodshed
> was appalling. They were used to playing football on grass and we had
> run out of elastoplast by the end of the game.[13]

Many of the degree subjects had societies attached and organised programmes of evening lectures and meetings – such as the Metallurgy Society
at the Royal College and the French Club at the College of Commerce.
Other groups catered for more unusual interests, such as the Society for

Figure 3.4 Charities' Queen, College of Commerce, 1950–1
Duncan Macrae (a prominent Glasgow actor later on the Board of Governors
of the Citizens Theatre) poses with the student Charities Queen and the run-
ner-up at a College Ball. This beauty contest continued at Strathclyde until the
mid-1970s. *Strathclyde University Archives.*

Figure 3.5 Royal College football team, 1950–1
A rather eerie picture of the first eleven, complete with assorted kit. The captain in the front centre looks like a player not to be messed with. *Courtesy of John MacLaren.*

Research into the Supernatural. The Norwegian Students' Society at the Royal College and the International Students' Society at the Scottish College reflected the existence of small but significant numbers of overseas students at both places. Religion was also much in evidence, with the Student's Christian Movement and a Catholic Society in the Scottish College, and regular fifteen-minute morning services open to all denominations.[14] For many, an important part of student social life on campus was centred on such student societies. These were considered by interviewees as not as varied in the 1950s as they are today, and there was more segregation by gender and social class. Two women students recall of the climbing society: 'We went climbing and we made tea for them coming down the mountain.'

Certainly compared to the 1960s and 1970s, the portfolio of student societies, clubs and activities within the Colleges in the 1950s was severely limited. This was partly due to pressures of space. The Students' Union at the Tech was originally located within the Royal College building, then later in limited accommodation in John Street. Men's and women's social spaces were separated, with a separate 'Female Union' called the Muirhead common room, which catered for all the fifty women (out of about 2,000 students) at the Royal College in the 1950s. It was just a big plain room, with a huge fireplace, a table and armchairs, and for recreation a table-tennis table, a radiogram and a piano. For a long time, it also contained the only female toilets on campus. Jeanette Smith fondly remembered the Muirhead in the early 1950s as a private social space where she and a friend banged out popular tunes on the piano, and where they could gossip: 'there we had peace to discuss everybody's latest conquests unimpeded by the boys'.[15] Pat Fraser recalled that the Muirhead was, 'where we had about five records, one of which was *The Goons*':

> PF   But I mean our Union, the female Union, was all pharmacy students for the most part. It was great you know! Dances were wonderful! You had men for each hand. They used to bring the women from Dough School and places like that. Dough's School is what you call, is it Queens College now? Home Economic College.
>
> EM   And the girls always seemed to be plentiful, prettier, and we didn't like that! (*both laughing*)
>
> PF   That's right! They came from Notre Dame training college for teachers which was all female as well.
>
> EM   That was the opposition!
>
> PF   We were all females together!

One main restriction was that the Students' Union rooms were only open in College hours, and neither had a bar. Eventually, the problem was addressed with the opening of the new five-storey Students' Union Building on John Street in 1959. This provided Tech students with facilities that matched the best in the UK, including a massive dance/assembly hall on the top floor, a smoking lounge with a television, a games room (with billiards and table tennis), a darkroom for the Photography Club, several halls and reading rooms, and a massive refreshment area and cafeteria. It also had a new Muirhead Lounge, which was officially lauded as 'one of the most attractive rooms in the Union. It has been decorated in feminine pinks and whites'.[16] The new Union building brought significant changes in leisure provision and widened amenities available, with access six days a week, normally until 10.30pm, though later at functions. The creation of political clubs in the early 1960s, including the Labour Club of the Commerce College and the Scottish Nationalist Club in 1962, also rang in the changes in student life and culture. Nonetheless, continuity appears more evident

Figure 3.6 Student Representative Council Officials, 1952–3
The President, James Donelly, is in the centre front and the Women Student's
Union President, Nessie Leitch, on the far right. Note the Royal College crest
much in evidence. *The Mask*, February 1953. *Strathclyde University Archives.*

than change, especially in comparison to the revolutionary changes in youth
culture that were to follow in the later 1960s and 1970s. Even the Students'
Unions exhibited much latent conservatism. As late as 1961, for example,
the Student Representative Council at the Royal College still contained
rules that included the imposition of fines (and expulsion in severe cases)
where members were judged 'guilty of behaviour unbecoming of a lady or
gentleman'.[17] There were occasional reports of trouble, such as during the
1959 Glasgow Charities Week, but this was an isolated occurrence in the
post-war era, dealt with severely by the college authorities.[18] Student
behaviour was clearly constrained by prevailing rules and regulations, and

the 'respectable' social mores of a society still dominated to a great extent by the influence of middle-class values. Only rarely were dissident voices heard, as in March 1959 when a student complained in the Scottish College of Commerce's student newspaper, *The Pitt*, of the authoritarian attitude of the college authorities who had 'powers which are virtually dictatorial as regards College life'.[19]

The experience of going to college in the 1950s and early 1960s could also involve socialisation into what for many students was another world. One of our interviewees noted how in the process he absorbed some of the values of a different social class:

> It was a *very startling experience* for someone who had come from a sort of modest Glasgow home because, first of all, the whole atmosphere was of hard work effort, unrelenting pressure and the behaviour patterns were completely different. The language even was completely different and it was a salutary experience . . . it was *eye opening*, in that you know people in normal converse would speak the way they did. *But* I learned that, you know, it didn't happen in all cases and I made very many good friends there, friends that were with me for a long time.[20]

Kjell Sandberg, one of the many Norwegian students that came to study at Strathclyde in the 1950s and 1960s, noted the difficulties adjusting to the high tempo of studying at the Tech, and how he and his coterie of friends from his homeland had to work hard even through to the late evenings on their studies.[21] Friday and Saturday evenings though were spent in the Students' Union, 'or some other dance hall to have a drink or two and meet with Scottish girls'. This resulted in many permanent relationships developing: 'Many arrived single and open for anything coming along. This resulted in many romances, some ending there and then, but also many with happy ending in marriage and family'. Kjell himself married a midwife nurse (Anne) from the Rottenrow Maternity Hospital in September 1963. One of the big events in the Norwegian students' social calendar was the celebration organised for Norwegian National Day on 17 May. Kjell recalled:

> In 1963 this was arranged in Largs and we all departed Glasgow in buses in good mood with wives and girlfriends. The hotel had prepared a great dinner and dancing for us, the committee had brought a Norwegian drink 'Aquavit', to be served with the main meal, however the staff had misunderstood and served it for dessert in wine glasses! . . . At night the appointed guards to be responsible for an orderly retreat had a long job collecting all. Some had also mingled with the other guests at the hotel

that likewise seemed to enjoy the Norwegian celebration. Arriving in Glasgow at 4am in the morning it appeared that the guards had been too determined in their duty and also brought into the buses two hotel guests.[22]

Kjell commented that the large Norwegian contingent at the Tech were predominantly male and mostly mature students in their early and mid-twenties. They tended to stick together and maintained a separate identity, not least through the Norwegian Students' Society. Nonetheless, he noted: 'From the very first day we found the Glasgow people, drivers, paper men, shop attendants, digs ladies, college staff, lecturers and fellow students very friendly, open and making all of us very welcome'.

Despite the prevailing social conventions, women students could have great fun at College in the 1950s and early 1960s. One of the female pharmacy students was asked:

Q What did you find people like in social life at the Royal College?
A It was great, marvellous (*laughs*).
Q And what were your first impressions of the College?
A First impressions? Just that it was full of – fellas. I mean it was just, ahm, we were very definitely a minority. No, I enjoyed it thoroughly, it was quite different from school, quite different from school. We were treated very well, as girls. We got the front seat in all the lectures. We had – we got – down in the refectory we got preference. The boys all had to stand in this great enormous queue and the girls just sailed past and went in, but that was accepted, that was the way things were, but we were very well treated.
Q Did you feel, your fellow female students feel, that you were break-ing a mould by
A No. We weren't conscious of that at all, not at all, we just took everything for granted.[23]

With so few women students at the Tech, it may have seemed as if women had many things their own way. At the College of Commerce one 'poor minority male fresher' in session 1950–1 complained of the place being swamped by young women just out of school, resulting in the male students not being able to get lunch or even a game of table tennis. 'We were almost glad to turn into the last lecture', he recalled, but then shock-horror, 'No! It can't be! I don't believe it! But it was . . . a female lecturer'.[24] In reality, of course, women's opportunities in higher education in the colleges in the 1950s were slim. As Pat Fraser and Elizabeth McCudden recall, this was a period when women were structured out of higher education. The only women students they could recall were one who did architecture, one who did applied physics, and virtually all the rest were doing pharmacy. They were only seventeen or eighteen years old when they came to the Royal College, but the male students in their pharmacy class were twenty-one or twenty-two, many of them as a result of having completed National Service and apprenticeships. Few of the women students at the University matched that kind of maturity – except one, as they recalled:

PF   But she stands out! I mean all she was, was a bit more fashionable.
EM   Very pretty.
PF   She was very pretty, she was a bit more –. She had boyfriends, so she went places at night, like the pictures and stuff. She lived [out of town], but she'd to catch the train home and all that kind of thing. There was no question of living together or anything like that.
EM   No, but she ended up having to get married and that caused a real stooshie. I mean that's nothing today. But we all spoke about it with a low voice.
PF   And you only whispered it to your pal. You wouldn't have spoken about it to anyone else.

Though this woman didn't finish the course at Strathclyde in that year, her 'maturity' was much admired:

PF   We were so envious of her because she was a nice girl –.
EM   She was still popular.
PF   Oh very popular. We would have thought of her as very risqué.

But most women at the University were far less adventurous in moral affairs in the 1950s. As Pat puts it: 'We were very accepting. We were there to be prepared for the world of work. And you work hard and then you get on with it and that was it. It would never have entered our head to kick up and want to be with the boys, would it?' And Elizabeth McCudden responds, 'Not really. But we had boys in class. And we did go down to the Refectory a lot and that was where the talent was usually eyed up. The guys would eye you up, and then when it came to the dances it would be that they danced with you and make a bee line for you and that was how it all worked. Nothing was said.' Jeanette Smith recollected that no alcohol was sold on campus when she was there in 1951–5, and that the Refectory where many gathered to socialise was 'a grubby, smelly hole where we could get dubious

100

Figure 3.7 Charities' Week fight, 1957
An inter-College student 'battle' outside the West of Scotland Commercial College during Charities' Week in 1957. Three students were reported to have been charged for their part in this traditional conflict that was said to have involved in the region of 1,000 students. *Courtesy of* The Herald.

food and coffee . . . Social life was much more sedate then'.[25] For all the fun to be had, this was another world from that of the 1970s, especially for women. Indeed, the foundation of the University in 1964 stands precisely at what many historians note as the cultural chasm that separated the moral universe of the nineteenth and first half of the twentieth centuries from that of the later twentieth and twenty-first centuries.[26]

Despite its poor sex-ratio, the poverty of its social facilities, and prevailing social conventions, the Colleges were places not just for study but for social mixing, dating, having fun, and making merry. Elizabeth McCudden recalled the influence of Radio Luxembourg on some, but by no means all, students in the late 1950s: 'We would have animated conversations about what we heard on the radio during the night. But the rest of them were stuffy and boring.' James Brown recalls the world of jazz at the Royal

College in the early 1960s, when Chris Barber and his band played at the Union, but that this was world beyond his geographical reach:

> Well he was playing here in the Students' Union, but I couldn't go to the Friday night dances because I couldn't afford to run a car and the public transport stopped early. You couldn't get home after about 11.15, that was the last train, so you were home by 12 o'clock. You couldn't be any later than that and these dances didn't get under way until after 9 o'clock in the evening, so it wasn't worthwhile going unless you lived in Glasgow.

Glasgow, like most cities, stopped for most purposes at about 10pm – the underground, the buses and the pubs. This compounded the problem of popularity for the Union. A former student remembers the old Union in the bowels of the Royal College in the years after the war:

> Our Union is, as I say, was where you've got a swimming bath now I think. You go in the main door and you go down somewhat to the left, down a floor along on the left and part of it was the 'ref' and I think on the other side was a gymnasium and what we called our Students' Union where you could: well do what you do in Students' Union and it was, as I say, just a cement do-da which is obviously now a swimming pool. So it was a bit rough and ready, the facilities weren't as great even as Glasgow University. They had that quite good union there when I was there, I didn't go very much because I knew at times I had a tendency to be lazy so I thought 'getting involved with one of these things is the last thing I need'.[27]

In 1963, in the midst of the formation of the university and the frantic planning for educational change, James Brown recalls how cultural change knocked at the doors of the Tech Student Union:

> Rock and roll started when I was at school, and then the Beatles came into vogue I guess about '62–'63. At that time it was waltzes, foxtrots, quicksteps, and when they started playing Beatles music instead of jazz bands, dance bands, my wife and I stopped coming to dances in the union at that stage (*laughs*). That would be about 1963–4, some of the dances were still the old type, but we used to sit out the dances with Beatles numbers (*laughs*).

Much of the on-campus socialising occurred at the Refectory where, with females allowed to jump to the head of the queue, the food is remembered as it was to be almost everywhere for the next twenty years in British higher education – a choice of sausage rolls, beans and bridies. For variety, students could go to a café along the road for chips, bread and margarine, and tea. But as Elizabeth McCudden recalls: 'Fortunately I got well fed when I got home'.

The temper of the times in the 1950s was pitted against the unrestrained social mixing that is now taken to be commonplace in British university student life. It was not just the imbalanced sex ratio between male and female students that was to blame. More fundamentally, casual conversation was more restrained between students of the opposite sexes. Elizabeth McCudden recalls the case of the rather attractive Norwegian male students, many of them aeronautic or mechanical engineers.

> They stood in a crowd in the corridor and they always stayed together and you'd walk past them and they would give you the once over. If you were shy it was really quite tricky to negotiate. And of course you couldn't have shouted any retorts in Norwegian back at them . . . And they didn't mix. Some girls did end up marrying Norwegians, so some of them must have mixed. In general they didn't mix, they kept to themselves. And they didn't have any female Norwegians, because they were mostly doing engineering.

Elizabeth goes on to recall a date she had with another student:

> I remember going out with a fellow from the Tech who was much older than me. I think he was twenty-five or something, and he was doing his Captain ticket – you know the Merchant Navy. And he took me out. We went to the pictures. Before we went to the pictures, he said 'Would you like a drink?' So I'd never been in a pub before and he asked me what would I like to drink and I said an orange juice because I didn't drink . . . He was quite shocked that I didn't drink, that I was too afraid to drink because I wanted to be whiter than white, exactly. But we were then.

Pub drinking was definitely off-limits to the respectable female student. The *Dunrobin* pub across George Street from the Royal College, in Albion Street, was the nearest for the male students. The post-apprenticeship pharmacy students were already in the army for National Service, and they went on a Friday night after classes. The female students recall that 'We thought they were on the straight road to hell. I mean they probably had a pint of beer at the time but none of us, we were never in the pub, even in our lunchtime or anything, it would never have entered our head.'[28]

103

Whilst the female students' lives were proscribed by the prevailing macho and patriarchal environment of Glasgow and Scotland in the decade or so after the Second World War, immigrant students' lives were affected by the disturbing undercurrents of racism at this time. Bashir Maan, a student in the 1950s, explained how white Scottish folk typically refused to be served in shops by blacks and how 'the people in the streets were grown up, they were part of the Empire, so they looked at every coloured person as a "coolie", a servant, a subject'. He says:

> In the '50s and '60s, your neighbours used to be very racist. Your Scottish neighbours I mean. If we were cooking and your windows were open your doors would be banged – 'close the bloody window, we can't stand this terrible smell of your cooking', you know. Some people got some records from India and Pakistan and if they played records – 'Put it off, this bloody bad music you are playing' and things like that. But the funny thing is that the main objection of having a Pakistani or Asian neighbour at that time, to the Scottish people, was that smell of their cooking.

With the immigrant population growing, and – separately – with increasing numbers of overseas students (who made up 10 per cent of British full-time students by 1961–2), the issue of the wider society assimilating students from different cultures was going to grow.[29] But racism could co-exist with the basic humanity of the poor and the working class. Robert Orr explained about the generosity in times of adversity he found in the Lochee area of Dundee, known locally as 'Tipperary':

> A lady chief lab technician who was the head that I worked under as a lab technician, persuaded me to go round and collect money for the famine in India [in the late 1940s]. And I went around an area in Tipperary which probably no middle-class person would *go near there*. I went there and *every house* except one I got money from, and I was really ashamed because there was an old lady who [was] well obviously a pensioner, who'd obviously had a hard life because she would be a spinner and it's the worst job in the mill you can get because you've got to go up and down steps normally, so she said 'Come along laddie, they're probably a lot worse off than us'. Now the mere fact that women in her situation could *perceive that somebody in India was worse off than she was*, she was a better person than I was.

Students sustained a long tradition of philanthropy in Glasgow. The Student Charities' Day is recalled as perhaps the biggest student-centred

Figure 3.8 Rev. Dr Billy Graham at Royal College, 1955
A packed Assembly Hall listens attentively to the famous American evangelist during his Scottish Crusade (which also took in the Kelvin Hall, Hampden Park and Tynecastle). Note the blackboard intimating the room number for the 'After Meeting' for those seeking counselling. *Strathclyde University Archives.*

activity of the session during the 1950s and 1960s. Funds collected went to a wide variety of worthy causes, including the Erskine Hospital to help disabled ex-soldiers. Pat Fraser recalls:

So Charities' Day in those days didn't involve just putting money in a can. You got dressed up. It was a bit childish again, as something. They gave you lorries, various firms sponsored you, and came and supplied you with a lorry, and you dressed it all up and you got on that and you went to the outskirts or the centre and collected loads of money. And it was all done, you know, with the right intentions. A lot of it went to very charitable causes. This was in the days before charity became part and parcel, or giving anyway became part and parcel and that was the outstanding fun part really. But I just remember the Charities' Day, also they had a special one for the Hungarian Uprising in 1956 . . . And they had a special one because Glasgow's kind of well known for its altruism and its charity and all that kind of thing abroad as well. They did that.

The mid and late 1950s was also a time of considerable religious excitement in Glasgow. In 1955 there was a major six-week 'Crusade' by the Southern Baptist preacher, the Revd Dr Billy Graham, centred on nightly services to 10,000 people in Kelvin Hall and a huge Easter Sunday service at Hampden Park in 1955 attended by reputedly 120,000 people.[30] Billy Graham was invited to the Tech College, and preached to a packed Assembly Hall. Yet, such excitement was not always as purely spiritual in focus. What is described as 'a religious society' was joined by two women students for 'the social life': 'We did it to look the guys up and down'.

One of the great traditions of student life in the 1950s was the holiday job. Students worked in large numbers for the Post Office as delivery personnel, wearing merely a black and red arm-band to designate their office. Students with cars (or even better vans) were at a premium, and got paid extra for working as van drivers by the Post Office. During the summer months, jobs were sunnier and varied. Pat Fraser recalls:

> Everybody had wonderful jobs in the holiday. We had a friend of ours who was a gravedigger and he made enough money to come back and he had a marvellous tan, remember? And a lot of them did hotel jobs on trains, eh not trains in dining cars in the trains, you won't remember that but when you go to London by train it was a three courser it wasn't just standing yonder at the bar. People worked in hotels on holiday, so there was no shortage.

Other jobs were to be had in hospitals and on the buses. For some immigrant groups, however, financing their way through their studies by working was more difficult because of prejudice and discrimination. Bashir Maan was restricted to door-to-door peddling in the 1950s, which he did whilst studying at the Tech and then at the Scottish College between 1953 and 1956. He explained:

> And I came to the people who my brother had befriended and they looked after me and then I started. They were pedlars. All the Indian-Pakistanis at that particular time in Glasgow, the number was just about 300, they were all in the peddling business . . . Selling door to door, that

Figure 3.9 Indian student, Royal College, 1948
In the smoky grime of Glasgow's Central Railway Station after the Second
World War, J. N. Desai (fourth from the left) leaves for India after completing
his degree in Textile Chemistry. *Strathclyde University Archives.*

was the only job they could get because there were no, I mean Scotland
always had higher unemployment than England and therefore no jobs
for foreigners anywhere, any coloured person, no, not welcome. 'The jobs
are for our boys, not for you', this used to be the answer...I started
peddling too with them, because there was no other way, no other job
available. So after I settled myself in peddling, I then thought 'Right, I
should join the evening classes'.

For Bashir Maan, voluntary and charitable involvement in the community
provided much of his social life. After a couple of years he found that his
thriving business and increasing involvement in the growing Asian community in Glasgow encroached into his studies, leading him to drop out.
But there were no regrets on his part, as he explained:

Well, what happened was that during this time I became *very involved* in
the Pakistani community and Asian communities affairs because being,
not the only – but very few people were educated, they were mostly

illiterate, mostly illiterate, only one or two. But I had this kind of, should we say in my psyche to help people, so I was better educated than others and I was willing to help, therefore I became more and more involved which impinged on my activities that I had to do as my living and I had to go to the College and so therefore I suddenly realised that I can't do everything altogether. I couldn't leave helping the people because they were in desperate need at that time; *very, very* highly marginalised, suffering from discrimination, deprivation, everything, and I was doing well in business. So I thought 'Well, why the hell have I got to go back?', to get a degree here, higher education was to go back and to get a good job there, I'm doing all right here, I'm making good money in business and why don't I just abandon the studies, you know? So I abandoned the studies.

CONCLUSION

Entry into higher education in the 1940s and 1950s was for returning servicemen and women a making-up for lost time, whilst for younger students it added up to an emancipating experience. But this was a world still very much gliding along old grooves, one that was still restricted by prevailing attitudes, prejudices, discrimination and, for some, by financial constraints. One of our interviewees commented that she only got by because one of her closest friends helped her out on occasions.[31] Moreover, whether through lack of money, or through custom, it was rare for students to live apart from their parental home in this period. This drastically curtailed the independence and social freedom of Tech and Commerce College students, in marked contrast to what many more English students were beginning to experience at this time:

> Really our student life was an extension of school it really was. We wore uniform in a sense, in inverted commas. We couldn't wait to get a blazer with a badge which wasn't our school badge. I'm talking about at the, at Strathclyde. And we couldn't wait to get a scarf that hung away down there. Remember?[32]

The student community was not only much smaller in the 1950s, but their lives also seem to have been more intimately affected by prevailing social conventions. This remained a largely privileged elite within a diverse Glasgow of some one million people. The Colleges were small and intimate places, but student experience could vary greatly depending upon gender, class, race and other factors. The cultural gap was perhaps most obvious in the contrast between the behaviour of some male students (many well-trav-elled, mature ex-soldiers returning to college in their early twenties) and the behaviour of the young female school leavers of seventeen and eighteen years of age. Moral and cultural conservatism was everywhere in evidence, as was a strong work-and-study ethic, with social activities consequently severely prescribed. Amenities were relatively poor with few opportunities and less time for social mixing than was to become the norm from the 1960s onwards. Students' lives were perhaps more regimented by family, college and social convention. In such circumstances, fitting in, and accept-ing the way things were, was more evident than rebellion and challenge. The oral testimony suggests this was particularly the case for the female students of this generation. This, as with so many other things in British social and cultural life, was to change quite dramatically.

NOTES

1. For a review of the 1950s and early 1960s in British cultural history, see A. Marwick, *The Sixties: Cultural Revolution in Britain, France, Italy and the United States c. 1958–c. 1974* (Oxford, Oxford University Press, 1998), pp. 41–246.
2. Testimony of Anonymous Interviewee 6.
3. Ibid.
4. Testimony of Anonymous Interviewee 3.
5. Testimony of Anonymous Interviewee 4.
6. Testimony of Anonymous Interviewee 6.
7. Testimony of Anonymous Interviewee 3.
8. Ibid.
9. See the Scottish College of Commerce, *Students' Handbook*, 1955–6, p. 13 (Strathclyde University Archives [hereafter SUA] OJB/10/1).
10. SUA, ref. JA/6, RCSTG, Students' Union, Dance Committee minutes, 7 February 1958.
11. *CRUST*, 1965–6, p. 61 (SUA, JD 2/1/1).
12. Written testimony of emeritus professor Eric L. Furness.
13. Written testimony of Jeanette Smith, in unpublished personal communication to Neil Rafeek, 30 October 2002. Jeanette studied pharmacy at the Royal College, 1951–5.
14. *Scottish College of Commerce, Students' Handbook*, 1955–6.
15. Written testimony of Jeanette Smith.
16. SUA, RCSTG, *Students' Association, Students' Union*, May 1959, p. 31 (SUA, JA/19/2).
17. SUA, RCSTG, Students' Association, Constitution, Bye Laws and Standing Orders, October 1961, p. 14 (SUA, JA/17/2).
18. *The Pitt*, March 1959, p. 6 (SUA, OJB/13/1).
19. Ibid.
20. Testimony of John T. Webster.
21. Kjell Sandberg, 'Impressions from a Norwegian Student, 1960–3' (unpublished

personal communication to Neil Rafeek, July 2003). Kjell graduated in 1963 – one of nine Norwegian students in electrical engineering that year.

22. Ibid.
23. Testimony of Anonymous Interview 4.
24. *Pivot: Magazine of the Commercial College*, session 1950–1, p. 12 (SUA, OJB/12/2).
25. Written testimony of Jeanette Smith.
26. See especially L. Heron (ed.), *Truth, Dare or Promise: Girls Growing up in the Fifties* (London, Virago, 1985).
27. Testimony of Anonymous Interviewee 6.
28. Testimony of Pat Fraser and Elizabeth McCudden.
29. BPP 1963, Cmnd 2154, Robbins Report on Higher Education, p. 66.
30. C. G. Brown, *Religion and Society in Scotland since 1707* (Edinburgh, Edinburgh University Press, 1997), pp. 163–4.
31. Testimony of Pat Fraser and Elizabeth McCudden.
32. Ibid.

CHAPTER FOUR

Merger, Moving and Management, 1962–5

The creation of the University of Strathclyde in 1964 took a little time to accomplish. The Royal College had been campaigning since the late 1950s for its elevation to university status, but with some increasing frustration. By the early 1960s, other universities were coming into being in various parts of Britain, based on entirely new campuses with no previous higher-education base. But the University Grants Committee (UGC) seemed to be ignoring the superior case of an existing institution – with its mature structures, degree-level teaching, and strong heritage in science and engineering. But events were to move with some rapidity in 1962–4.

MANAGING THE CREATION OF A UNIVERSITY

During the 1950s, the UGC had proposed to government that existing universities in Britain should expand and new universities should be created. The Conservative government accepted this proposal, and established the Robbins Committee to report on the future of higher education. However in the meantime, the government authorised the finance for the expansion of buildings and staff at existing universities (even though some, like Reading, resisted growth),[1] and, more significantly, gave the go-ahead for seven new universities – Kent, Sussex, York, Essex, East Anglia, Lancaster and Warwick. These were already well under construction by the time that the 300-page Robbins Report (1963) was published, which made the case for many more new institutions to meet the rising tide of demand for higher education. Robbins argued that the number of university places be increased from 216,000 in 1962–3 to a projected 560,000 in 1980.[2]

To meet this policy, the Robbins Report called for the creation of an increased number of brand-new universities; in the event, only the University of Stirling was designated in this category in the immediate aftermath of the Report.[3] But the Robbins Committee was extremely keen that technological education should expand faster than arts and social sciences. A spate of reports since 1945 had reported to government on the problems of technical education at all levels, and the decline of technical schools in

111

England and Wales heightened the sense of threat to British economic recovery in a world dominated by America and the economic miracles of Japan and West Germany.[4] Consequently, a second proposal made by Robbins was to elevate what it categorised as three 'SISTER' colleges into the British equivalents of the Massachusetts Institute of Technology.[5] These were Imperial College of Science and Technology, London; Manchester College of Science; and the Glasgow Royal College. Robbins acknowledged in its main report of October 1963 that the elevation of these three was already underway.[6] The three SISTERS joined a second group of colleges known as CATS (Colleges of Advanced Technology) in each being granted university charters.[7] In this way, Strathclyde was part of a major movement by the science colleges to create a new band of universities based mainly in the larger industrial and commercial cities.

Roger Sandilands, a student at the time, explains the consequences:

Strathclyde had been promised its charter in about 1962 or 1963, it wasn't actually formally awarded until, roughly, April 1964 [actually August] during my first year. That's when we formally got the charter but the doors opened, everybody who started in that programme in 1963 were embarking on degree courses and the old Associateships, the ARCSTs, the Associateships of the Royal College were made retrospectively, degrees. So from 1964 all the awards were degrees of the University of Strathclyde. Shortly after a bunch of CATs were elevated to become new universities and Strathclyde has tended to be lumped in as a CATs that was given university status along with Aston and so on, and Surrey and so on, and Heriot-Watt, when that wasn't the case. There were also several new universities – Stirling, Sussex, Bath, York, Warwick – they started about two years later, but Strathclyde, Imperial College and Manchester were on their own.

In this way, the move to university status seemed fraught, but in actuality was accomplished by what today would be regarded as fairly swift government and UGC decision.

The exact shape that the new university was to take was a matter of great moment. With the Royal College in mature discussions already with the UGC, Professor Noel Branton recalls that in 1962 the idea came from the College of Commerce for a merger:

It was really, I suppose, where we'd reached a situation where if that merger hadn't taken place, [Principal] Eric Thompson was going to apply to the Department [of Education] for university recognition for the

Figure 4.1 Scottish College of Commerce students, 1963–4
Outside the main Pitt Street entrance, around the time of the merger with
Royal College. The group includes one of our interviewees, David Paterson, on
the far left. *Strathclyde University Archives.*

College as it stood, and of course then we would be confronted too with
an accommodation problem. You see, they'd enlarged the [Royal] College
because we had these temporary huts and so on, [they] built a large
library and you know . . . and we were still under pressure. So there was
talk at that time of extending the [Royal] College. They were talking
about pulling down some houses that were in Cathedral Street and

extending that way, whether that would have happened or not I don't know. When the [Glasgow] Police took the College [at Pitt Street] or were after it, we vacated it.

The Robbins Report recommended that the Scottish Central Institutions, including the College of Commerce, should either develop in close association with existing or planned institutions, or the largest (clearly suggesting the Commerce College) be granted its own degree-conferring powers.[8] The Royal College was already on a trajectory towards incorporation as a university, but the offer from the College of Commerce had some attractions – increasing female staff and students, and a quantum leap in non-science subjects. Professor Tom Carbery, then a more junior member of staff at the arts-based College of Commerce, suggests that whilst many of the teaching staff at the Royal College were apprehensive, the officers were extremely keen. He recalls the circumstances of merger with the science-based Royal College:

> Well certainly over that year of '63 to '64, there was the growing inclination that there were going to be more universities in Britain, and that Glasgow was fated to have one such. The initial reaction as I recall it, in the Scottish College, was that it would be the Royal College of Science and Technology that would be elevated and we would just plod on doing what we were doing. We were a Central Institution answerable to the Scottish Office. We were conscious that whatever criticisms there had been in the past ... the place was doing better and better work and getting better and better results and was going 'up'. By that time we had over 100 members of staff. So we were perfectly happy and contented to be left *doing what we were doing*. True, we weren't on university rates of pay, we were on Central Institutions rates of pay, but the difference wasn't all that great. So, there was no great anxiety from the staff point of view to be concerned in this university situation, and that was true of the people involved in the degree work, as I recall it, but it would certainly be even more true of the people who were doing *non-degree work* because they could see that if they went into a university situation, there might be all sorts of problems created *for them*.

So, there was clearly anxiety amongst teaching staff involved in non-degree work, and amongst those for whom research seemed a difficult career development to construct. As Tom Carbery points out, the non-degree work made up the greater portion of the College's work. But there was an even greater problem:

114

One of the ironies is that were there to have been a merger as there was, between the two colleges, it would have been better if it had happened in the late '50s *rather than* in '64, because until the late '50s, the Royal College of Science and Technology *was that* – it was a college of science and technology, it had no arts involvement *at all* . . . The criticism had been made that they were turning out engineers who, well they might be able to spell profit, P.R.O.F.I.T. but they certainly would never have thought of spelling it with a 'ph' and an 'et' because they had no feel for such matters.

However, the Royal College had an Industrial Administration Department from 1947, based at Chesters in Bearsden (this was the precursor of the Business School), and had already recruited in 1963–4 professors in four subjects – history, economics, psychology and politics. The College of Commerce moved quickly to promote the merger idea, and it seemed to meet the perceived problem of lack of breadth with the Technical College. The College of Commerce added significantly to the business, arts and social studies elements of the new university – what was perceived as the key humanities wing to nearly every new university of the 1960s. The two Colleges were not strangers to each other. The College of Commerce and the Technical College jointly set up a special department for day release in business, called the Glasgow School of Management Studies. Glasgow University had been thinking of the same thing, with the same name, and, as Professor Branton recalls, one of the professors at Gilmorehill made 'a very big attack on the Principal of the technical college'. But staff were reportedly generally enthusiastic for merger. Professor Branton recalls: 'I think it was generally accepted, and after all you were heading now, you knew, [for] this status.'

The selection of the name 'Strathclyde' for the new University was surrounded with some controversy. At the time, the name was associated with the ancient kingdom of Strathclyde in the so-called Dark Ages preceding the establishment of a united Scottish Kingdom. Later, in 1975, it was to become known in the Strathclyde Regional Council, which existed until 1996 as the major local authority for west central Scotland, and in the name of Strathclyde Police which persists today. But at the time, 'Strathclyde' was not a well-known name, either in Scotland or outwith it. In Roger Sandilands' recollection, there was more than a little resistance to it:

And many people, you know, at Strathclyde, at the Royal College, didn't want to change the name. They felt that the Royal College was so prestigious in its own right that they didn't want it to change the name to this peculiar word Strathclyde, 'what on earth is this Strathclyde?'. In those days it was an almost unheard-of name, it was something dredged up from the distant past, the old ancient kingdom of Strathclyde. And someone had a bright idea to call it Strathclyde and only subsequently has Strathclyde become a well-known name. The [local-authority] Region was established quite possibly because Strathclyde University took on that name, that name became prominent when previously it had not been, and then when regionalisation occurred [in 1975] it occurred to people to follow suit, dredge up the old ancient kingdom of Strathclyde's name.

One former professor of engineering recalls that 'the place was so well known as the Royal College and had its own degree, the Associateship, and it was actually *very well known* internationally, so many people, and I guess I had this sort of feeling too, felt that it was a missed opportunity when we called it the University of Strathclyde.'[9] With such widespread status, many regarded it as a shame and a missed opportunity to lose that part of the name. 'Because it was so well known for science and engineering many people felt it should have been called something modelled after Massachusetts Institute of Technology, you know MIT. Although the Glasgow Institute of Technology might not have had the right ring to it because the abbreviation would have been *GIT* (*laughs*).'[10] Though the name might be wrong, many thought the aspiration was right. Andrew McGettrick,[11] professor in computer and information sciences, recalls that

> People were using these sort of phrases that the likes of MIT, that Strathclyde should turn into a sort of MIT for Scotland, or for the UK or something of that kind. And I thought that was, I mean a technological university and you know – emphasis on maths, technology and so forth – I thought it was the right kind of aspiration to have.

Another possible issue was that of the location of the new University. There had long been an outside possibility that the Tech College would have relocated in the 1950s to East Kilbride, Scotland's first new town designated in 1947 to act as a population overspill for Glasgow and as a new regional economic centre. Located around fifteen miles to the south of the city, East Kilbride was created as a spacious new town with model living conditions (including initially, until 1952, a rigorous moral climate of prohibition – no public houses).[12] Professor John MacLaren recalls how the College governors had met the issue:

In the 1940s, when Sir James French of Barr & Stroud was Chairman of the Governors, there was a great debate at that time, whether the College . . . should move out to East Kilbride. Heriot-Watt in Chambers Street in Edinburgh had had to go out to Riccarton and had had their foot in both places for donkeys' years. There was serious discussion. Remember, mechanical engineering in the west of Scotland in the 'Tech' was the caucus and the National Engineering Laboratory was being set up out at East Kilbride. But they *decided* to stay in Glasgow. For what it's worth, they did the right thing for the wrong reasons. What were the reasons? The main reason was that we had three times the number of evening students than we had day students. They were coming from Ayr, Kilmarnock, Falkirk, Stirling, in the evening. As I say three times the number of day students . . . I engaged seventy part-time assistants to help the day staff to cope with them, and if they'd moved out to East Kilbride then, the ball was on the slates for these people. The argument might have been 'Ah, but Falkirk, Kilmarnock, Stow College are going to come up in the world, we will move out to a higher academic level out at East Kilbride'. But it didn't happen and they stayed in Glasgow. And another possible reason that I'm not entitled to speak on is that the relationship with the Glasgow Authorities was always very good . . . Now Glasgow was more technologically- and trade-bent; Glasgow University was *highly regarded*, but was more academic. I think Glasgow Council had a soft spot for 'the Tech'. The Royal College building was built in 1905 or so. Now, the University stretches all the way from George Square to Glasgow Cathedral. I think the Governors made the *right decision* for the wrong reasons.

Andrew McGettrick recalls the same issue of moving out of the city was raised in the 1960s, and it is clear to him as well that the right decision had been made. He recalls: 'Strathclyde made one decision and Heriot-Watt made the other – Heriot-Watt moving out to the outskirts of Edinburgh and Strathclyde staying put in here. And I think at the time most of us felt that Strathclyde had made the right decision in the sense that we managed as a university to expand faster than Heriot-Watt did.' In this battle, there is a view that Strathclyde understood well its constituency of students and how they needed to live at home, have first-rate transport links, and access to city-centre attractions.

For all the controversies and unsettling of existing traditions, the merger was nonetheless exciting. Karen Morrison, who at the age of seventeen years joined the Engineering Department in 1963 as a secretary, recalls the feelings:

I think there was a buzz, I think there was a buzz that we thought 'Gosh, we're going to be a university' etc . . . But I could remember, there was quite a buzz and I remember when we were granted the charter there was a service in the Cathedral and a lunch down for all staff down at the Kelvin Hall . . . There was a service to dedicate the new university and then to include everyone, *absolutely everyone in the university was invited*, and we had a very nice lunch in the Kelvin Hall and the time off to do that obviously, so, it was a big thing.

David Paterson, an economics student at the College of Commerce, found the student body a little apprehensive about merger and charter, with some worried about the status of their vocational training in a supposedly more academic environment. Yet, the majority feeling was one of excitement in the build-up:

I think there was a feeling that people at the College were going to graduate from the University rather than get a diploma from a college. And I think that was, I think that was the single most-important *factor* or the single most important message that people took out of the news that there was going to be a new university in Glasgow, and it would incorporate the Royal College and the Scottish College . . . I think, most people felt that their years of study were going to be rewarded with a proper degree from a British university rather than a college diploma.

David Paterson acknowledges that a united University was more quickly established than some had predicted. With it came a collective sense of identity: 'I think within a year, I graduated from Strathclyde and that was at really the end of the first year of Strathclyde's existence, and I think by that time everybody regarded themselves as a student of the University of Strathclyde.' The stark divide between the students of the two former colleges was fading:

I think it had all by and large disappeared by that time. I think the name of . . . Strathclyde was a wee bit – I think it was regarded as almost a cop-out. It seemed to be a funny, rather odd choice, but in retrospect I think a good choice . . . There was a single student body. The two student bodies were wound up. It was run, the new student body was set up more or less on the same lines as what both of us had had before because there weren't huge differences between the two colleges. And I think it took off very quickly and really quite successfully.

118

Figure 4.2 College of Commerce Administration Office, c. 1952–3
This typical mid-century office lacks computers, telephones, photocopier, post-it notes or even the personalised space which are all familiar today. *Strathclyde University Archives.*

The excitement of the merger and chartering of the university was still evident to Hamish Fraser, a new member of staff, when he joined the Department of Economic History two years later. He recalls the sentiment around the place:

> There was undoubtedly a sense coming into the place that it was going somewhere, I mean that was very powerful. You did get a sense of dynamism about the place. It was full of hopes and expectations it was going to go and I mean to be fair that continued, I think it continued through to the '90s almost despite hiccups and ups and downs. There was a *determination* to succeed.

The merger was more a process than an event. Staff and teaching moved from Pitt Street eastward across to the main campus in a flow of personnel, equipment and students. There were surprisingly few problems reported. 'They seemed to fit in quite nicely as accommodation became available,'

Figure 4.3 Sir Samuel Curran
Director of the Royal College of Science and Technology Glasgow from 1959,
architect of the merger and university charter, and Principal of the University
of Strathclyde 1964–80. *Strathclyde University Archives.*

Professor Noel Branton recalled. 'Of course, some of it had to wait for
buildings, you see, and that sort of thing.' Departments changed and
merged, names changed. Professor Branton became the first dean of the
new Business School, whilst the Department of Commerce became the

Department of Economics. The creation of Strathclyde degrees required some considerable planning – some for the creation of entirely-new degrees, but some for the elevation of existing degree-level classes into in-house degree courses and awards. As well as the College of Commerce's LSE-validated Economics degree, the Tech College had subjects like engineering, pharmacy and applied chemistry in which there were existing degree or degree-level courses that had been taught over many decades, but validated and awarded by Glasgow University. In engineering, students enrolled for the Glasgow degree continued until 1967–8, whilst new-intake students enrolled for the new Strathclyde degree. In mining, there was an existing degree that was only taught at the Tech whilst the degree was awarded by Glasgow University (without it having a mining department). The arrangements were complex, and varied from subject to subject. Disentangling the connections between Strathclyde and Glasgow universities took time, and

Figure 4.4 Dr Eric Thompson, Principal, Scottish College of Commerce, and later Vice-Principal, University of Strathclyde. *Strathclyde University Archives.*

121

was greatly assisted by the staff at Gilmorehill during the interim arrangements. But what was quite distinctive, if not unique, about the formation of Strathclyde University (as distinct from almost any other in the UK) was that the two existing Colleges had gathered decades of experience in teaching and examining degree courses. This expertise embedded in the two Colleges conferred a very real sense of there being a university already in being.

The creation of this University depended a great deal upon the vision and leadership of Sir Samuel Curran F.R.S. (1912–98). Curran had a distinguished career in atomic physics, including war work developing centimetric radar, using cavity magnetrons, at the Royal Aircraft Establishment, Farnborough, and at the Telecommunications Research Establishment at Swanage, and later Malvern. This gave radar new accuracy in finding U-boats in the Battle of the Atlantic. Curran also played a prominent part in the invention of the proximity fuse, which allowed increased effectiveness of ack-ack against enemy bombers and V1 flying bombs. He then worked as part of the Manhattan project in the USA on the development of the world's first atomic weapons, whilst his wife Joan (neé Strothers) worked on, amongst other developments, 'Operation Window' – the use of clouds of metal foil by British bombers to confuse enemy radar, including the 'creation' of a phantom invasion force of ships in the Strait of Dover on the night of 5–6 June 1944 as a diversionary tactic for the D-Day landings down the coast at Normandy. After the war, Sir Samuel had a spell at Glasgow University, but left to become Deputy Chief Scientist on Britain's first hydrogen bomb project in 1955–9. It was then that he returned to his native Clydeside.

Curran was appointed principal of the Glasgow Royal College of Science and Technology in 1959.[13] His campaigning work to raise the College to University status was critical, but so too was his work as the University Principal from its foundation in 1964 until his retirement in 1980.[14] His vision as a scientist was for a university of breadth and of quality. Only a man of proven research ability who had accomplished so much for Britain and the allies in wartime, could command the respect of academics across so many disciplines, and establish the University in the consciousness of the British academy. Professor Richard Rose of the University's Centre for the Study of Public Policy says of him:

I have enormous respect for Sam Curran, first of all because there was no side, no catch. When he hired me there was no nonsense. 'If you succeed we'll back you'. And I knew the other side of the coin said: 'And if you're no good you're another bloody mistake up from England' (*laughs*). And I have quoted those Curran rules since to various deans and vice-principals. 'If you succeed we'll back you'. Sam was a lad of parts who thought everybody *could* be as good as he was and he was in favour of everybody having a chance. But if you weren't up to it, whether you were an undergraduate or you were a professor; don't expect sympathy because he grew up in a world where you either did or you didn't, and he earned his eminence.

Rose is second to none in his admiration of Curran: 'I tell people that the man who hired me was an applied natural philosopher. What did he do? – Made atom bombs (*laughs*).' And those who participated in the merger of the Colleges and the chartering of the University in 1964 agree on the pivotal role of Curran. His determination to succeed in meetings on merger and charter, especially within the Royal College, ensured that a single vision was going to succeed. John Paul in Bioengineering reinforces this impression. He recalls that the merger needed enthusiasm, and it was the Principal who inculcated it from the start:

> Sam Curran was *a driver* and he wouldn't take 'No' for an answer. And he could be quite rude in Senate if he wasn't getting his own way. He bulldozed University status through the Senate, and he bulldozed it through the University Grants Committee and the Privy Council. He could be *very abrasive* if you spoke up against his wishes in Senate or in a committee meeting, but having said that, out of the meeting he was the friendliest person.

Gustav Jahoda,[15] emeritus professor of psychology, recalled: 'There was no nonsense about him, you know, no pretensions, unlike some other principals and vice-chancellors I can think of, who were pompous and so on. He was a very straight Glaswegian of *the old sort*.' Tom Carbery summarises:

> What I'm stating is that the general impression is that Britain decided that it needed new Universities and at the same time it had to improve itself on the technological front, and it needed new universities and a College of Science and Technology for immediate promotion. Sam Curran grasped that opportunity, grabbed the ball and ran with it.

There were tensions to be faced in the merger of the two Colleges. This was evident amongst both staff and students, and it was apparent to David Paterson as a student at the College of Commerce. To him there was a clear sense that his own College was 'looked down upon' and was 'perceived to be a lesser institution compared with the older universities, compared with . . . the Royal College of Science and Technology'. From the student angle, he reflects:

> I think it was certainly perceived as an inferior institution. And at the time of the establishment of Strathclyde, when we were trying to form one integrated student body out of the two colleges, it was very apparent to me that the people in the Royal College *really* did look down their nose at the Scottish College of Commerce and felt that they were really doing the Scottish College a big favour by taking them over and absorbing them into a proper academic institution.

The Commercial College, he recollects, had a name as the place where shorthand typists went to learn, giving it a feminine character at a time when higher education had a masculine image. Lacking the traditional faculties of the older universities, the College had a different place in the educational firmament:

> So it was regarded very much as a kind of technical adjunct, a necessary service to the business community in the west of Scotland I think. And I think that was partly true and a wee bit unfair as well because . . . there was a lot of, there were some very, very bright students who for one reason or another ended up at Pitt Street – very bright people that I can, you know remember today. And I think they added a bit of distinction to the place.

The new university meant new things in some unexpected ways. One was the enhanced power of the academics as a collegiate community, expressed through a Senate on which there were not only professors but also elected members of other staff grades. This created novel situations, with the centralised power of the officers of the Colleges giving way to the more divisible and challengeable power of officers who were now facing a more empowered university community. Tough bargaining ensued by staff and representatives of the Association of University Teachers concerning pay levels of merging staff, since they had formerly been on two different pay scales. The University was regarded by many staff as being highly supportive of AUT submissions to the University Grants Committee.[16] But at the end of the day, some staff were surplus to need as there was duplication of positions. This was a period of intense worry for some staff.[17] Many staff were accommodated in new courses, and some staff left but, in the main, staff secured positions in the new University.

Figure 4.5 The new learning environment
The main lecture theatre in the new McCance Building, seen in 1964 shortly after it opened. It was the one most used for large arts and social studies lectures. The view onto the open terrace some five floors above George Street was an unusual feature (that could be blacked-out when needed). *Courtesy of* The Herald.

BUILDINGS INTO TEACHING ZONES

The foundation of the University created a new name on the educational landscape – one that took a little time to sink in. One applicant for a job recalled:

I applied for a job in the University in November 1965 as an assistant secretary in the newly-formed television unit. I hadn't actually heard of the University before then, and in actual fact had great difficulty in finding or locating the University because nobody knew what it was. And of course I was seventeen and very naïve, and didn't realise that what we'd always called the 'Old Tech' or the Royal College had actually become a university... My interview was on the Monday so on Saturday when I was in town I came to George Square, walked along George Street hoping to find somebody who'd heard of the University and I couldn't find anyone who knew of its existence and eventually I just located the building from the street name.[18]

Even six years later, the University was not altogether a prepossessing prospect to the job applicant. Ann Mair,[19] first computing officer in the School (later Faculty) of Arts and Social Studies, recalls her first impressions of Strathclyde: 'Didn't know where it was. Came out of the train, took a taxi (*laughs*), from Queen Street Station to here, was sat down. I was stupefied, I mean I was lost at that period... It was spread in odd buildings.'

The new University got its name, its charter and even its staff fairly easily. But creating the actual place for learning and research was a hard physical task, and one that had to happen astonishingly quickly. Karen Morrison came as a secretary to the Engineering Department when the Royal College was still a very small physical place compared with today's mushrooming campus. She remembers it as:

A lot smaller. *Very much smaller.* There was only the Royal College building, half of what's now the Weir Building and the Student's Union. That was all that was there at the time, that was the Royal College... There were tenements *all around*, tenement buildings all around Cathedral Street, all the way up over the side streets, right over to what used to be Parliamentary Road which doesn't exist anymore. We had the buses and the trams, obviously the hospital was there, the maternity hospital was there, but it was all tenements as far as I could remember all the way along Bath Street until you came to the sort of shopping areas that have always been there.

Brian Furman remembers the decrepit nature of the campus on his arrival as a lecturer in 1969:

When I first came to Strathclyde University the Taylor Street end of the campus there was this *old gym*, the university's gym, sports facilities were there and that end of the campus was completely run down. There were no nice residences, there was no student village. On Rottenrow there was the Balmano student residence and it was a fairly run-down end of the

campus and then of course the university started a programme of building the halls of residence, the Birkbeck and then the other halls of
residence and then the whole student village was developed, of course the
Barony, right down to the Barony Church and the residencies on High
Street. So there was an *enormous* change in the campus . . .

Alan Riley[20] in Estates Management was one of those who re-modelled the
buildings to the needs of an advanced university:

> I just came here straight in '65 from David Dale College, a pre-
> apprenticeship course, served my time here as an apprentice electrician
> and I just stayed on. This is the first job which I ever had . . . *It was very*
> *good actually.* You had a variety of jobs, you worked in everything, every
> aspect of the job you worked on. I worked in the heavy cable, pulling big
> heavy cable end off, putting floodlights up, things like that. We done
> everything in they days, there was no contractors whatsoever came in.
> We'd go to the labs in the Royal College building, the Weir building, and
> the workforce was only eight or nine electricians, a foreman and an
> assistant master of works. That was the workforce and everything was
> just done in-house and it was very good.

The maintenance staff of the university has been a jewel to the institution.
Though the scale of the operations has changed, the various departments
(including the gardening staff) have reliably sustained the working and
aesthetic environment during extremely rapid change.

The campus at the time of the merger was very limited in size. Karen
Morrison recalls how the new university took shape in varying styles of
white concrete. The starkest was the Livingstone Tower. Seemingly, every
1960s new university needed a tower of some description, function and
height, and Strathclyde's was an office block similar, some have said, to
London's Centre Point. Karen reflects on its bright colour:

> Well, it was a building of its time really, wasn't it? I don't think we
> thought anything, we probably thought 'goad, that's a bit ugly, look at all
> that orange'. But apart from that you didn't really give it a great deal of
> thought . . . There were so many skyscraper things going up at the time
> you just thought 'Oh here's another one, yeah, okay'.

One of the new departments that moved into the Livingstone Tower was
Geography. Tony Martin[21] recalls that the building wasn't quite operated to
the standard of other universities of the time:

The problem was that Livingstone Tower hadn't been developed as a university building. It was a 'spec' [speculative] office building built by Sir Robert McAlpine and the university had taken it over. So one of the first committees I was on I suppose was the Livingstone Tower amenities committee and this was the mastermind of Nobby Clarke who was the head of English, I. A. Clarke, but everybody called him Nobby, who really tried to *improve* conditions in the tower . . . It was basically a pressure group to try and get Estates and Buildings to do something for the building and do it rather quickly, because most people at work were *coming in* and a lot of us had come in from purpose-built university buildings and many of us in fact had better conditions as research students . . . I remember as a research student at Liverpool I had a key to the building and I could get in any time of the day or night . . . They barely had a staff in the Livingstone Tower in those days, and it obviously was a problem of access. I remember coming in on a Saturday evening about five 'o clock, half past five, after you'd been a day in the field. And the only way you could get into Livingstone Tower as a member of staff was to ring a clockwork bell and hope the janitor heard you. And I can remember when [one staff member] appeared, he wrote a stroppy letter to the Principal saying 'We're a technological university, why do we have to have a clockwork bell on the thirteen-storey building?' (*laughs*).

The first Psychology Department laboratory was located in an old stationery store in Montrose Street that was full of machinery. Gustav Jahoda, psychologist and anthropologist, recalls an early embarrassment:

I remember one occasion when I invited a distinguished professor from overseas, and he gave his talk. First of all he was *astonished* at this kind of setting and went up these old stairs (and I should tell you, he came from San Francisco). Suddenly, in the middle of his talk, the whole place started rocking; *well we were used to that*, but he *blanched* and thought there was an *earthquake*. It was just the machinery. So the conditions were pretty rough.

New buildings were erected with the successes of new units and departments. Karen Morrison again:

I remember when they built the Wolfson Centre because Bobby Kenedi, who used to be professor of bioengineering, I can remember the day he got the grant from the MRC, I was in his office at the time he got the go, the Medical Research Council for going ahead to develop

128

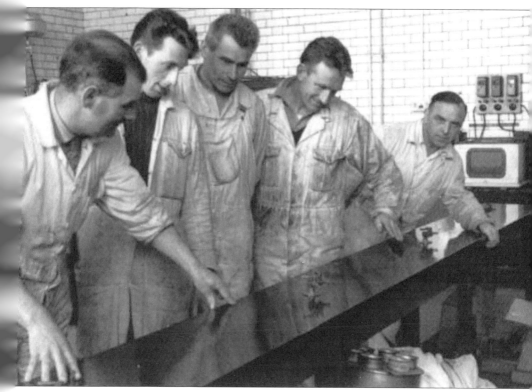

Figure 4.6 Royal College maintenance staff, 1961
A group of painters assessing a job in Royal College lecture room 401.
Strathclyde University Archives.

bioengineering at Strathclyde. And it took off from very small things and grew from there, and then of course Sir Isaac Wolfson gave him the money to build.

The tenements that surrounded the Royal College were knocked down to make way for new buildings, leading to one unexpected consequence. Karen Morrison again:

I remember when they knocked down the tenements they had an influx of mice . . . Oh yes, we had a *huge* influx of mice. They used to eat the paper in the cupboards and we used to come in and find this smell of – because they had urinated in the cupboards. We used to open the stationery cupboard '*Oh God*' you know, and then you'd find chewed corners of packets of paper . . . The droppings were all over the place. So the chaos went on for a very long time, the influx of mice . . . years, several years I would think because obviously there was so many build-ings . . . But we had these mice for a long time and that was upon the sixth floor, 'How the devil did they get up here?' you know . . . I can remember putting my phone on the floor in case it ran up the cable.

The buildings had their own structural problems. Dr Brian Furman in Pharmacy recalls the sometimes watery route to his own office in the Edwardian-vintage Royal College building:

Well we were, the Department was based in the Royal College and was spread out between the fourth level of the Royal College, or what's now called the fourth level on the Royal College, and the roof. So my office, my first office, was on the roof and I had to go across an *open space* to get to my office and, as you know, the climate in Glasgow isn't the most wonderful and there was a number of hazards associated with that. First of all the rain, you habitually got wet going between anywhere else and your office and secondly, in the winter it was, the roof became very icy, so there was another hazard. So it was, you know, *an interesting experience (laughs)* and my laboratory was also on the roof, several laboratories were on the roof as well, in those days.

One story has it that in the building of the Students' Union, piles for the foundations had to be driven down close to the tunnel roof of the High Street railway line that runs east–west under the whole length of the University campus. According to the story related to John Paul, as he admits possibly anecdotal, 'in mid-morning when railway traffic was zero, a track inspector came rushing up from Queen Street Station to say "You've dropped a pile into the High Street tunnel" *(laughs)*. And if a train had met it, there would have been a *disaster*.'

Despite some of the early additions, the campus was still small. This was a major difference from Glasgow University which already sprawled across Gilmorehill up in the west end of the city. Glasgow benefited from a strong Victorian core of a campus around which new-build structures were absorbed, with some remarkable success. Robin Alpine[22] reflected on the Glasgow and Strathclyde campuses when he made the journey from the one to the other in 1962: 'Well it was very much more concentrated in terms of build-ings, apart from Pitt Street. But down at this end there was very much sort of, there was just the Royal College, the building above, McCance and the Livingstone Tower and for a long time that was sort of it.' By contrast to Glasgow University's more piecemeal expansion, the University of Man-chester in the early and mid-1960s set about re-modelling and expanding

Figure 4.7 Transformer Laboratory, c. 1964
The new Royal College building high-voltage electrical transformer lab. *Courtesy of Ronnie Simpson and Department of Electronic and Electrical Engineering.*

what has been called its 'education precinct and student village' into a grand design that, inevitably perhaps, seemed never to be realised but remained what was described as 'an empire on which the concrete never set'.[23] Strathclyde had fewer buildings of older stature on which to rely as a core, though various mature structures (like the Maternity Hospital) split the campus and prevented a gelling of the site.

The merger was not merely combining two existing institutions into one university. There was also the addition of new departments, indeed an entire new academic wing in essence, to be accomplished. This was the addition of arts and social studies. Dr Robin Alpine, who was effectively head-hunted for Strathclyde from Aberdeen University by Professor Kenneth Alexander, commented upon the contrasting nature of Strathclyde with other Scottish universities of the time:

> So apart from the small number of people, it was very much more a sort of science engineering institution. So to that extent it did seem different from Glasgow and Aberdeen, it didn't have a broad sort of faculty, so there's that difference. Although that changed very soon because we come to the merger and that then changed things very much.

The addition of arts and social studies was seen by many at the time to foster the dimension required for the University to justify its status. The Department of Economic and Industrial History was formed in 1963, but the word 'Industrial' was quickly dropped. Hamish Fraser, later to be professor of modern history, joined as a young lecturer in 1966, and recalls how the first head of department, Professor Edgar Lythe, obtained a name-change:

> I think he felt that this [the word 'Industrial'] was not entirely *respectable*. I mean, bear in mind Strathclyde was formed as a university *before* the concept of a technological university had been thought. It did not describe itself as a technological university, it described itself as a university with a particular interest in science and applied science. I think somewhere like Bradford or Loughborough, I can't remember, these were the first to actually use the term technological university, but that was two or three years after Strathclyde came into being. And I think the idea of bringing in the arts and social sciences was to turn the place into, *rightly or wrongly*, what was regarded as a real university, and it was only really in the '70s that, again, there was this return to emphasising, or apparently emphasising from time to time, you know, that it was a technological university. The whole *aim* as I understood it anyway in the late '60s was to broaden it.

Indeed, many recall the hostility of at least one university principal in Scotland in the early 1960s who sought to ridicule the pretensions of 'applied' science as the basis of a university at all. Professor Tom Carbery had been a student at the College of Commerce from 1952 to 1956, and then joined the staff in 1961. He well recalls the attitudes of the time:

People in universities like Glasgow and Edinburgh would make scurrilous observations about 'plumbers' and people running around with micrometers in the Royal College. They were seen as non-cerebral, non-intellectual who got their hands dirty and worked with oil and things like that. They weren't doing *real*, academic work, of which universities were held in high regard over long centuries, because they weren't doing the classics, they weren't doing law, they weren't doing medicine, they weren't doing divinity, these were the *real* academic subjects. If you look around at who were the principals of universities throughout the UK, it was arts people, it was historians, it was classicists, it was English literature men, it was, maybe the odd chemist and the odd physicist, but it was *never* any engineers or anything *of that nature*. And so, despite the fact that *they were doing good work*, not least in chemistry and physics, *they too were subject* to severe and unwarranted criticism.

The rise of arts and social sciences seemed to be unstoppable in the British university expansion of the 1960s. The brand-new universities (with no precursor colleges) had to deliver rapid student expansion to balance the books, and the promised dominance of science students simply evaporated nationwide – partly because science students cost more to educate and were literally too expensive to matriculate in very large numbers, and partly because of the swing away from science subjects at school and university levels.[24]

In this atmosphere, Tony Martin, arriving as Assistant Lecturer in the Geography Department in 1966, recalled the situation of the new institution:

You used to get letters addressed to 'The University, Strathclyde, Scotland', because obviously most universities were named after the city in which they were in. But there was a lot of rivalry in those days between Strathclyde and Glasgow. And if you rang Glasgow, of course you had to go through the switchboard, and the receptionist up there would say '*the* University' and we were still looked upon very much as being 'the Tech'.

Barrie Walters in Modern Languages, and later Dean of the Faculty of Arts, has a similar memory:

I remember my doctor when I first came up here and one of the first consultations I had with him, he said 'What do you do?' and I told him I worked at Strathclyde and he said 'Oh you mean the Tech'. I said 'No, I mean Strathclyde University', he said that he was a graduate of Glasgow which 'is a real university', he said.

The problems of establishing university identity as a whole within a wider consciousness were replicated for the disciplines that were new to the institution. Individual departments had to forge reputations within their discipline nationally and internationally, and this was a task fraught with confrontation with all sorts of snobberies, prejudices and ignorance. Robin Alpine in Economics recalls being offered a lecturing post at Birmingham University and turning it down.

> Somebody at Birmingham, who was on the interview panel, a very well-known economist ... was obviously *amazed* that I would turn down going to Birmingham, which was a very good institution and some very, very good people, just in favour of coming here. You know it was, he thought this was quite odd. So in that sense there was that sense this was an upstart of a place you know 'Why are you going there?' ... And he had a very good reputation. And when this guy in Birmingham sort of heard the other person was coming from Glasgow he said 'Well, you know, obviously that changes things. It's obviously going to be a good department.' So I think there was perhaps some sort of snobbish sort of amongst people that didn't know there was the general feeling the 'Tech's' an inferior institution to Glasgow University.

Expectations and cultural clashes were to some extent inevitable. Robin Alpine again:

> Strathclyde in terms of the social sciences here had developed from scratch in 1963, so people coming in were aware that it was a university environment and what a university job involved. And it didn't just involve sort of teaching but you had a, you know, you didn't have the long holidays that students had, you know, you had research and things to do and so on it wasn't just a teaching job. Whereas the Scottish College was much more sort of [a] further institution. The people there had been there for quite a long time, and were used to a different sort of working environment: a lot of them did take the long holidays and they didn't have the same requirement for research.

The Pitt Street building of the former College of Commerce stayed in existence for several years after 1964, and merger in real terms was actually quite a slow process. Roger Sandilands, who was here as student and lecturer from 1963 onwards, recalls links to the Commerce College staff and students:

We didn't have a lot to do with them until 1972 when they moved physically to John Street as they called it in those days. There was Pitt Street which is now the headquarters of Strathclyde Police. I used to go up there quite a bit during my final year because the library there had all the journals and no one was using them and I used to go up there, get peace and quiet and whereas they might have been taken out from the Andersonian Library I could always guarantee I could get access when I needed them there and peace and quiet to read, get my head down. But generally we didn't have a lot to do with the Scottish College until '72 when they all came down physically, and in Economics we merged and we took on all their economists . . . But you know the thing is, think back to 1963, in England 5 per cent of eighteen-year-olds went to university, in Scotland it was about 10 per cent. So even if you were at Strathclyde which was the bottom of the pecking order in those days – in Scottish terms there was Edinburgh, Glasgow, Aberdeen and St Andrews and Queen's College Dundee which was I think, had just broken away from St Andrews and then there was Strathclyde and a couple of years later there was Heriot-Watt. So we were much less prestigious than these long-established institutions. And they tended to look down on us, but when you consider that only 10 per cent of Scottish students went to university, the quality of the students in those days was quite high, even at the margin, even the margin of the least-esteemed university, the staff and students were *good* by comparison to what they are today at the margin when you are taking on 30 to 40 per cent. So, yeah, it was stimulating.

Some young staff found that there was an old mentality to break down in the creation of the new university. Tony Martin in Geography recalls the art of persuasion needed to broaden library acquisitions: 'I can remember trying to get books. I remember asking for something in Danish that I'd been able to get in Liverpool as a research student, and I got this memo back . . . [that] said I couldn't have this because nobody could read it. And so I sent . . . a memo back in Danish and I got the book (*laughs*).' Professor Thomas Maver, at the forefront of new research method and concept in architecture from the late 1960s onwards, found that the effort to bring research money into the institution was being resisted by those of an older school who believed that, as he described the attitude, 'research was just draining down effort away from teaching'. The idea of a commercial culture to exploit research for direct financial gain was still largely anathema at that time, as it was in most of higher education, but more seriously 'there was a kind of reverse snobbery' that Glasgow University could do these kind of 'fancy things' but Strathclyde should continue along rather old grooves.

One thing that new staff brought shortly after the merger and charter was the democratisation of the new University's institutions – its committee structures and forms of government. In the School of Pharmacy, as in other parts of the institution, there was a tradition of more top-down management, but younger staff pushed for the creation of collegial systems of decision-making. Dr Brian Furman reports:

> I think there were four of us actually, who decided that we actually wanted the Department [of Pharmacology] to be run *differently*. We wanted to make changes and it was a credit to the head of department then that he, instead of saying 'Look I'm the boss, you'll do it my way' said 'Well if you want change, let's talk about it and let's do it' and as a result of the activity of four of us, so I was one of the, if you like, the troublemakers, four of us changed the whole way the department operated. So we established committee structure – finance committee, postgraduate committee, all these kind of thing, research committee – and the department began to establish the pattern which has *now* spread probably throughout the whole of the science faculty anyway...

The testimony from those who were new members of staff in the mid-1960s strongly bears out this case – that it was that generation entering during the radicalisation of university management across the United Kingdom who pressed for the introduction of what they regarded as democratic decision-making systems at every level from department to senate. A simple process like the taking of committee minutes and the formal recording of decisions of meetings was reportedly new in certain parts of the institution, and was seen as the introduction of a professionalism pursued by new academic members of staff.

The 1960s and early 1970s were a period of frenetic change from red-brick (or red-sandstone) college into plate-glass university. These are categories of university commonly used in the writing of the history of British higher education. But, this was not merely a metaphorical change; it was also a literal change that posed serious and direct problems. For example, in the early 1970s, Tony Martin was accustomed to lecturing to architecture students in the bowels of the old Royal College building, an Edwardian pile of red sandstone, white-tiled walls, stone staircases and heavy-duty ironwork. One day, without warning, his lecture venue was changed to the new Architecture building – a prize-winning construction of concrete, copper panels and glass. Only alerted by a note on a door, Martin went straight to the new building, delivered his lecture, and then raced out to warn a colleague who was due to follow him at the lectern. Being unfamiliar with the new building, he came close to serious injury:

At the end of the lecture I lit my pipe, came down and the next thing I knew I was lying on the pavement outside. And of course in those days the tiles in the inside of the building were the same as the tiles outside, and in fact I'd run through a plate-glass window. Not a mark on me, but I'd run through a plate glass window... The janitor picked me up and sat me in a chair... and then the professor of architecture, Frank Fielden, appeared. Now he looked a bit like Robin Day, with a big spotted bow-tie, and he came up to me and said 'How are you?' and of course my only thought 'Whoever designed this building needs their brains examined'. Somebody told me it was him that had done it, but anyway he took it in good sport, and I was whipped up to the Royal [Infirmary] to have my eyes looked at and a tetanus injection just in case... They then put a bit of wood and an aspidistra in front of the window and my colleagues in fact used to call it 'the Tony Martin Memorial Aspidistra' (*laughs*), but I think I was very lucky, very lucky then.

As red-brick and sandstone gave way to plate glass and concrete, Strathclyde transcended two traditions of the British university sector.

THE WORKING ENVIRONMENT

The university is a complex community and economy, and few realise the extent to which there is diversity in the beast. The maintenance, modernisation, expansion and repair of the built environment is the responsibility of Estates Management, and this major sector of the university has not just its own tasks, materials and staff, but its own educational regime. Alan Riley recalls how he started in the University just after the charter, and obtained what he regarded as a very good apprenticeship in the University:

When I was in here in '65 to '69 when I was serving my time, it was a five-year apprenticeship, but just prior to my time coming up, they cut it back to four years and because of the City and Guilds qualifications, I qualified for the four years, so I only done the four years but it was a totally different, it was different altogether as I say. We didn't have to answer to the managers we've got now, we'd two charge-hands, one foreman and one assistant master of works as he was called then and that was all we answered to. And the Assistant Master of Works and the foreman, they went round and done everything, they marked everything out that was to be done, and you just went up and followed their instructions. And it was totally different – totally different now.

Karen Morrison in Engineering recalls the simplest things being done more simply in the 1960s:

> Things were very much simpler, you could do things by phone call then. You could phone somewhere in the university like the stationery department which very lucky, very lucky then used to be located down in the Royal College where the lift used to be. And it was a Mrs Archibald who was there and you could phone up and say 'Have you got such and such in stock?' And she would say 'Yes', and you could go and get it if you were desperate for it – not like nowadays where you've got to order things in triplicate with a budget code, and we didn't have budget codes. The University worked on a running budget. Obviously there were running costs and research budgets for each department but they didn't ask us to pay for any screw screwed into the door or somebody coming to mend the lock or something . . . And the stationery was one thing. And you could phone up and say there was a door sticking and someone would come over and fix it, not like now where you've got to explain your life away and wait for about three weeks. So things were very much simpler, it was probably because we were very much smaller.

In other ways, the new University moved quickly to establish itself with a modern culture in the support professions and services. One was librarianship and library services. Malcolm Allan joined the Andersonian Library in January 1967. Coming up from England, he recalls the appeal of Strathclyde:

> I saw that as an opportunity as an expanding sector, and also an opportunity for people like me who had professional qualifications, but did *not have* a degree because at that time the newer universities were taking people from the public sector – the public-library sector, into the university, the academic librarianship, whereas the old universities insisted on a degree and not necessarily any qualification in librarianship (*laughs*) . . . The old established universities . . . trained people into their own methods, and unfortunately a lot of those were very *individual, to the place*, which was why there wasn't any national compatibility with library networks and things until much, much later. And it was the older university that was much more difficult to adapt.

One result, as he recalls, was the early advent of new technology in the Andersonian Library:

Figure 4.8 Andersonian Library, 1965
The rather more spacious University Library, located in the recently-constructed
McCance Building. *Strathclyde University Archives.*

The Royal Technical College library had got its first professional librarian in 1952 – that was Charles Wood, and who became the University
Librarian when it became a university later. But he brought the Royal
Technical College into the technology of the '50s and a little bit beyond,
in two ways. First of all it was the first library, and certainly the first
technical college library, to have telex, and that was you know the instant
knowledge of the day, even though it chattered away and made a lot of
noise doing it, but to have information mechanically transmitted in that
sort of way. And then when it became a university in '64, there was to
be a new structure of staff and so they needed a Deputy University
Librarian and . . . when they got someone it was Lawrence Ardern – Larry

Ardern as he was known. And he was a Manchester man who had been librarian of Manchester College of Technology and because he didn't have a degree they wouldn't accept him as university librarian at UMIST, and so he transferred up here as lecturer in the Scottish School of Commerce – Scottish School of Librarianship.

As a result of Ardern's appointment, another element of modern library technology arrived early at the Andersonian – microfilm and microforms technology:

> He had been in that since the 1930s, so he was very high up in the national scene of that, in microforms of all shapes and sizes ... We had one of the best photographic labs at that time – or photographic and micrographic labs in the 1960s and 1970s in the McCance, doing it in-house. We had microfilm camera, we had reader-printers of all breeds and sizes and also desk-top readers of various kinds ... So we could read and use microfilm, microfiche right down to microdot, ultradot and so on, in the early '70s which many a university couldn't, and we could print from a lot of these things.

This technology was of great value to students doing the new-fangled study regime – the dissertation. Bill Speirs recalls its importance to his dissertation: 'You could get the microfilm out and so on, and by the time I was in my honours year I would be getting up early enough to be in there at half eight in the morning and spend *a day* just working away.' Creating a university library for so many new disciplines and to new standards, capable of supporting not only booming numbers of students but also research, required vigorous evangelical action by the new librarians. Malcolm Allan was initially the Librarian of the Commerce College Library for five years. 'It was a single reading room there and I was the sole professional, I had two library assistants, permanent, but Scottish College was about 1,000 students and it was mainly the social sciences rump-end.' The subject of librarianship had moved out to the Livingstone Tower, but Pitt Street retained the commercial subjects – commerce had become economics, accountancy, secretarial studies and the new Strathclyde Law School, then composed of one professor and one lecturer. For Allan, 'it meant that I was Law Librarian and Business Librarian before there was such a thing as libraries for them'. The Law Library moved in 1972 into the new Stenhouse Building, and the library growth started to weigh heavily on the planning of expansion – and to weigh quite literally. Malcolm Allan recalls:

In the planning stage, or the last bit of the planning stage, and I got a phone call from Charles Wood, 'Malcolm how much does a cubic foot of law journals weigh? Is it about thirty pounds?' And this was because, if you were putting the Law Library, with concentrated stacks for every journal, on the top floor, where was the structure of the building and the girders, and where could they put the weight? And the answer to that was to take an approximate cubic foot of law journals from the library in Scottish College basement up to the kitchen on the top floor and ask them to weigh it for me on the kitchen scales! And it was eighty pounds, not thirty, and that was why the first Law Library had all its shelves wall-hung, the weight was taken on the shelves on the walls all round the room, apart from one corner, which allowed for concentrated book shelves over a girder, and the reading room part was then all in the middle and it wasn't long before that expanded and expanded further, in Stenhouse. But that was the beginning of the Law Library.

Filling the shelves was expensive. It took four years to find and buy a set of the Scottish Court of Session cases from 1820 to 1920 at about £1,200 from a sheriff court that was closing down, and grant funding was limited for the Andersonian which, technically, was an existing college, in contrast to entirely new universities like Stirling which attracted library start-up grants from government. So, staff had to cope with some of the peculiar difficulties of not being a brand-new university.

The merger created enormous changes for students – movement of classes, overcrowding in others, and considerable disruption to the facilities of study. Yet, it was an exciting time. One of the great changes was cultural. A formerly technological and science institution was suddenly playing host not merely to the commercial students from Pitt Street, but there were humanities and social-science students – a new breed, formerly only associated in the city with Glasgow University.

James Brown in engineering was one student who, at the time of the merger in 1964, felt the winds of cultural change in the student community:

There was a very noticeable *change* in the place when the numbers increased and the people who were in the Union changed quite a lot with the hotel school and the business studies joined . . . We found it amusing . . . We joked about it. One of my friends doing a Masters degree became a member of the bio-engineering staff and he used to bring us over to the staff club at lunchtime. And the standard joke then was these people in the colourful trouser suits with long hair were the lecturers in business studies (*laughs*) . . . I think we thought it was sort of second rate compared with engineering. It wasn't 'real', it was very commercial but it wasn't of anything like the academic and practical standard that was required.

The difference between the Royal College and Glasgow universities was still great in the 1960s, he feels: 'Strathclyde was very intensively technical whereas Gilmorehill had a lot of arts and languages and it was after the place became Strathclyde that it became particularly noticeable.'

Such attitudes were not missed on the part of students in Arts and Social Studies. Roger Sandilands recalls the adverse attitudes from Glasgow University, the Scottish Education Department (SED) in Edinburgh, and the students of the older Tech College departments:

> I think the Glasgow crowd looked down on Strathclyde. They insisted on calling it 'Ra Tech' rather than Strathclyde, and they felt very superior. And there was quite a fight with the [Scottish] Education Department because the Education Department wouldn't recognise Strathclyde graduates for teaching purposes, we weren't eligible to teach in senior secondary schools or something like that, initially. But Edgar Lythe fought that successfully and that was one of the prejudices against the upstart institution. Of course this was very much a technological phase, and there was a tendency amongst the engineers to refer to the 'Arts and Farts Faculty' (*laughs*) but that was okay, we took that in good part. I think they were quite happy actually to have an 'Arts and Farts Faculty' because there were many more women were brought into the university than had been there previously.

Stewart McIntosh,[25] an undergraduate at Strathclyde in the early 1970s, is one of many who recalls how students in the Arts Faculty called those in the science and engineering faculties 'the plumbers'. The disdain was good-natured, and in any event Arts students were well aware of the longer hours that science and engineering students spent in contact teaching. But there was real cultural division. As an Arts Faculty student, Stewart recalls:

> I'll tell you one thing that really shocked, not long after I was in the university. I was in the Student Union and there was this huge thumping noise above my head, a colossal thumping noise and I was told 'That's Freds'. I said 'What's Freds?' and they said '*Tom and Jerry* cartoons' and I said 'Why are they called Freds?' Well, apparently the guy who wrote the scripts is called Fred . . . but all the 'plumbers' used to go in and watch these everyday. It was considered a big thing for them, whereas none of

us would dream of going and watching *Tom and Jerry*, so our interests were quite often different, culturally, but sporting-wise then we all crossed over, you'd have all sorts and any particular team.

However, Diana Henderson recalls that arts students like herself *did* watch *Tom and Jerry*, but at the Pitt Street Union in the basement where 'once a week they showed "Freds", Fred Quimby Tom and Jerry cartoons, in the theatre. Amid a great deal of cheering we always sided with Tom who we reckoned was bullied.' A decade earlier, David Paterson at the College of Commerce was well aware of the sense of slight disdain evident from the Royal College towards the College of Commerce, but it didn't last long, certainly amongst the student body. Strathclyde became a communal identity, one that marked a transition from one stage of higher education to another, and one that also marked the emergence of a new meaning, breadth and intellectual challenge. He concludes: 'The university did grow up very quickly and integrated very quickly and established an identity very quickly, and I would think on the whole it was a very successful transition from the old two colleges into what has become one of Britain's leading universities.'

CONCLUSION

Between 1961–2 and December 1968, the number of full-time university staff in Britain more than doubled from 14,276 to 30,755. Whilst a proportion of this increase involved movement of some staff from the college and further-education sector, the vast majority were new staff, recruited in urgency from recent graduates, often without their Ph.D. completed or even, in quite a significant number of cases, with their Ph.D. not even started. Staff were in hot demand, and those of research potential and intellectual brilliance even more so. Many were head-hunted, even before the graduation from their first degree. Others were being recruited in what was then a highly unusual way – from industry and commerce. Strathclyde was in the market for staff as it was for students, and by 1968 had forty-five professors, 151 readers and senior lecturers, 359 lecturers, and fifty-seven assistant lecturers.[26] In double-quick time a university had been moulded into being. It was then that students had to be attracted and ushered through the doors.

NOTES

1. J. C. Holt, *The University of Reading: the First Fifty Years* (Reading, Reading University Press, 1977), pp. 176–7, 321.

143

2. BPP 1963, Cmnd 2154, Robbins Report on Higher Education, pp. 67–9, 277; G. Walford, *Restructuring Universities: Politics and Power in the Management of Change* (London, Croom Helm, 1987), pp. 5–6.
3. Ibid.
4. Ibid., pp. 6–7; M. Sanderson, *The Missing Stratum: Technical School Education in England 1900–1990s* (London, Athlone Press, 1994), pp. 154–5.
5. SISTERS – special institutions for scientific and technological education and research; Robbins Report, pp. 128–30.
6. Robbins noted and confirmed that the target student entry for the three institutions by 1967 should be: Glasgow 3,000 with 20 per cent postgraduate, Manchester (which became the University of Manchester Institute of Science and Technology) 3,000 with 25 per cent postgraduate, and London 3,500 with 45 per cent postgraduate; Robbins Report, paras 315–16, pp. 129, 281.
7. Walford, *Restructuring*, p. 6.
8. Robbins Report, pp. 132–3.
9. Testimony of Anonymous Interviewee 2.
10. Ibid.
11. Testimony of Professor Andrew D. McGettrick, interviewed 30 June 2003.
12. C. G. Brown, 'Urbanisation and living conditions', in R. Pope (ed.), *Atlas of British Social and Economic History* (London, Routledge, 1988), pp. 173–4. I. Maver, *Glasgow* (Edinburgh, Edinburgh University Press, 2000).
13. *The Times*, Obituaries, 19 March 1998.
14. See J. Butt, *John Anderson's Legacy: The University of Strathclyde and its Antecedents 1796–1996* (East Linton, Tuckwell, 1996), pp. 162–6.
15. Testimony of emeritus professor Gustav Jahoda, interviewed 21 May 2003.
16. Testimony of Anonymous Interviewee 5.
17. Written testimony of emeritus professor Eric L. Furness.
18. Testimony of Anonymous Interviewee 1, interviewed 26 November 2002.
19. Testimony of Ann M. Mair, interviewed 23 December 2002.
20. Testimony of Alan Riley, interviewed 28 November 2002.
21. Testimony of Tony Martin, interviewed 26 November 2002.
22. Testimony of Robin Alpine, interviewed 6 November 2002.
23. By Hugh Wilson, planner of Cumbernauld; B. Pullan with M. Abendstern, *A History of the University of Manchester 1951–73* (Manchester, Manchester University Press, 2000), pp. 103–20, at pp. 104, 107.
24. Sanderson, *Missing Stratum*, p. 155.
25. Testimony of Stewart McIntosh, interviewed 9 June 2003.
26. Data from A. H. Halsey (ed), *Trends in British Society since 1900* (London, Macmillan, 1972), pp. 208–9, 213.

CHAPTER FIVE

The New Students

The changes of the 1960s forged a new character to higher education in Glasgow. The creation of Strathclyde University was the foremost of the institutional changes, and fashioned not just a new university but a new style of institution. The academic subjects diversified enormously as science, engineering and architecture joined up with law, arts, social studies and business. This brought expanded numbers of students and new types of student. The 'Tech' and the College of Commerce merged and developed as an academy of breadth.

WIDENING ACCESS

The first year of the university brought new students from strange places. Roger Sandilands, a student in the Arts School (later Faculty) from 1963–4, recalls:

> In my year it was a very good balance between international, English and Scottish, but half of us were Scottish I would say, about a third of us were English or from England, and there were several from Hong Kong and Africa as well. So it was quite cosmopolitan in that sense and a real university atmosphere.

One change was the arrival of female students in significant numbers. Indeed, one of the major cultural transformations of the 1960s was the reconstruction of gender roles. The pressures for increased women's access to sexual lives, to economic opportunity and leisure-time activities was also extended, of course, to education, and there was enormous pressure building up amongst women for widening of opportunity. This was no mere opening of gates, but involved very profound change of attitude to the nature of work on the part of women as well as men.

One of the most masculine of subjects was engineering. It was an area of the academy where women were virtually unknown, whether as teachers or staff. Karen Morrison did not remember any women: 'No. No, I don't remember any [women] students in engineering, chemical engineering – not in the '60s when I came. Probably going towards the '70s, yes, we had some, but it was very few by comparison with today when we have a big percentage of students.' John Webster, now emeritus professor of engineering, recalls that: 'Way back in the early '60s it was recognised that there was a problem in that so much of the country's talents, particularly in maths and physics, which of course was the touchstone, were girls, and if they came into engineering the system was not *conducive* to them. I mean they were not – the philosophy was not suitable for training or employment of girls in engineering.' This meant that women were entering in to certain subjects more than others. As with pharmacology in the 1940s and 1950s, so in the 1960s and 1970s the languages and more generally the arts and social studies were areas where female students were an increasing proportion of the total. In economics, the department was nearly always what Robin Alpine recalls as '99 per cent male'. He describes this as 'an odd thing . . . not policy', just few women applicants for posts. And it was initially a bit like that in the student population studying economics too:

> The student side initially used to be much more predominately male. I don't know whether it was thought that economics was a sort of science-type subject you know, back in the '60s you know and it wasn't the sort of thing that girls did you know? And there were other things, which they were more likely to do like history and modern languages and so on. But gradually it's changed and now it's at least 50/50 and there's no obvious difference. But initially it used to be very predominantly male.

Strathclyde was rather slower to increase the proportion of women students than both the new-campus universities and one of the leading red-brick universities, Manchester, where by 1964 they made up one-sixth of science students, 43 per cent of theology students, almost exactly 50 per cent of arts students and 53 per cent of education students.[1] Yet, the change was dramatic. In 1957–8, women made up a mere 7.2 per cent of the students at the Royal Technical College. By session 1967–8, they made up 22.8 per cent of students at the University of Strathclyde.[2] One of these was Diana Henderson, educated at Hawick High School, and rejected both for the Army and for teacher-training at Moray House College in Edinburgh. Out of the blue, in autumn 1966, Strathclyde accepted her for arts and social studies, and she drove to the city for only the third time in her life, leading her towards a law degree and, like many, a distinguished career. It would take another thirty-two years until women exceeded men at Scottish universities, but the 1960s were the beginnings of the great project of gender equality in higher education. However, the numbers of women entering science and engineering never reached the numbers that Sir Samuel Curran, the first Principal, hoped for in 1969.[3]

Figure 5.1 Pin-up at Strathclyde, 1965
The rising number of women at the University was felt immediately in the mid-1960s. A dress revolution was starting, but the era of jeans and jumpers did not arrive until after 1970. *From* The Mask, *Strathclyde University Archives.*

At the time of the merger, Glasgow was a city divided by the geographical barriers of class. There were vast areas of essentially almost one-class living. Education was about overcoming sheer ignorance – an ignorance that the schools of the wealthiest and most expensive kind had singularly failed to rectify. Roger Sandilands recalled at the Royal College in mid-1963 a classmate from the middle-class suburbs of the city who knew little of working-class inner-city areas like the Gorbals:

> I remember a very good friend of mine in the class . . . lived in Bearsden and her family were very middle class, quite rich. I remember once she asking me whether it was true that in the past the people in the Gorbals, the children in the Gorbals, ran around with no shoes on and, well I didn't actually *see* that but I understood that was the case and she was quite shocked. When she came to university I think it, for her, was quite an eye-opener, even though she was from Glasgow. She went to Jordanhill School and I guess her father drove in, in his Rolls-Royce from Bearsden. So she was quite cosseted from the reality of working-class life in Glasgow and I was much less so than her I think.

Bill Speirs was brought up in a working-class family in Renfrew, his father for most of his life being a fitter-turner at Babcock and Wilcox. Though an uncle had been to university, his was still a community in which the university was a strange and far-off institution. From the social perspective of the working class, a university had the great capacity to destroy some of your own roots, to remove you from pals, to alienate you from the place from whence you came:

> Lots of my pals saw going to university as a *snobby* thing to do and I was edgy about doing it, but then it just looked interesting and my parents were dead keen on it. But by going to Strathclyde I was going to be able to do a degree I was interested in but still keep in touch with my pals.

It was the apparent capacity of Strathclyde to allow the working-class entrant to sustain the threads of his or her heritage, to maintain that link with the community of background, that was seen as distinctive and for many vital. To get on, Strathclyders did not necessarily want to get out. Yet, for Bill Speirs, there was still some culture shock in his first week:

> I didn't know anyone who'd gone and I was *extremely nervous about it*, and quite pleased, probably fair to say that most of my early memories of week one and so on were of more of the Student Union than of lectures

Figure 5.2 Students' Union, 1965
A group of male students relaxing around the jukebox in the first-floor lounge in the Union building on John St. *Strathclyde University Archives.*

or whatever and; but *very nervous*. But a couple of things that within, probably within a couple of months came home to me was that there were a considerable number of people there who spoke posh, who I realised weren't actually any brighter than I was and, it's not that I despised them or anything, it's just gradually I became a bit more confident.

Getting a measure of staff and fellow students brings a sense of ability. He continues:

I realised that some of our lecturers weren't absolute geniuses, I actually found that quite a positive thing. It is not that they were bad, and there were some that were, *really were geniuses*, but the fact that there were some people you could identify with, 'Hm, maybe I can do this'. Having said that, my first year I was, I just scraped through everything because I spent most of the first year going to discos, the sort of things that first-year students *shouldn't do* but funnily enough do quite a lot, but I just scraped through every class, but again quite a few of my pals didn't and they had to do re-sits, so that in itself was a confidence builder.

As emeritus professor John Paul recalled in an earlier chapter, Royal College classes in the 1950s were already becoming cosmopolitan and crowded. From the engineering student's point of view, James Brown recalled: 'At that time I think most of the students in the class who were Scottish lived at home and travelled everyday, but there were quite a few students who were from India, from Norway, we had a good number from there and there were one or two English students.' The College of Commerce was not a stranger to overseas students either, since there had been a surge in the number from India for a time in the 1950s.[4] Roger Sandilands in Economics in the Business School also recollected the international flavour:

> Yeah, I remember being friendly with a couple of guys from Nigeria, one was a Hausa and one was an Ibo, so I began to get some vague awareness of what that meant in terms of civil conflict in Nigeria, this is before Biafra, before the Biafra conflict. I was quite friendly with a guy from Hong Kong but really it wasn't that international. I was very friendly with a guy from India as well.

Development economics was attracting both grants and students to the University, and this made the classes in many subjects have a postcolonial feel to them. Religious traditions and requirements had also to be met. One male Muslim student from the Gulf was uncomfortable about being alone in a room with a female lecturer or support staff, and brought a chaperone.[5] Overseas students tended to come in waves. John Webster, successively student, lecturer and professor in the Tech and the University, remembered the Norwegian students in the 1950s, the advent in the 1960s of students from Malaysia, Singapore and Hong Kong, and then another wave of Malaysian students in the late 1970s and early 1980s.[6] Overseas students continued to come, especially from south-east Asia, to not just engineering but to business, law, the arts and the social sciences.[7]

Scotland in the 1950s had few resident non-white people. Afro-Caribbean and African families were never to become especially numerous, having remained into the twenty-first century comparatively rare north of the Border compared to central and southern England. But Glasgow is now the centre of Scotland's Asian population, which originated overwhelmingly in immigrants from what is now Pakistan, and is mainly Muslim in religious

Figure 5.3 Postgrads hard at work, 1964
James Brown and three fellow mechanical-engineering postgraduate students
relax in their cramped and cluttered study room. *Courtesy of James Brown.*

background. It remains the case that Scotland's Pakistani population was
slower to grow than in most English cities, but the community nonetheless
became, by the mid-1970s, a vital characteristic of the city and nation –
evident to most other Scots in the proliferation of high-quality Indian
restaurants which made the city regarded as one of Britain's premier curry
cities. But the Asian population of Scotland did not begin in the restaurant
business, but rather in peddling.

Bashir Maan, historian and leading figure in the Muslim community of
Glasgow, recalls his journey from Pakistan to Britain, Glasgow and eventually to the University of Strathclyde:

> My father was a small landholder and he was very keen on getting his
> children well educated. In our family there was one or two people only
> who were educated ... but the Jaats are the farmers' class, who never *felt
> the need* of educating their children because they had enough resources to
> make a good living *from the land*. But my father was of a different kind

151

of thinking and he thought that the children should be educated, though he wasn't educated himself. So after I had done my primary, the high school was quite far from our village and I couldn't travel as I was only about ten years old, we were four miles and my father couldn't afford a man to take me and bring me back, you know. So he sent me to my grandparents who were about 200 miles away on new land they had been given during the colonisation of barren lands in the Punjab. They had a high school next to their village, so I was sent there for the high school after primary to secondary school.

Bashir spent four years being educated in the Punjab and returned at thirteen or fourteen years of age to his village because by then he could bicycle to school. From there he went to college in the nearest town, Gujiranwala, where he studied up to B.A. level when, in 1947, he failed English and had two further years to clear that exam. But 1947 was the year of the Partition of India and Pakistan, and Bashir became involved in politics and the rehabilitation of refugees coming to Pakistan. Though degrees came to be awarded to some in return for charitable work amongst the refugees, Bashir declined: 'I was so kind of proud, "Oh I'm not going to get a charitable degree, I want to do it myself" but *I never found the time* to appear [for the examination] again.' He worked for the civil service in Lahore, and then heard of a scheme to train boys in the Royal Navy, encouraging his younger brother to go in 1950. His brother spent two years in Portsmouth and was then transferred to Rosyth in Fife, and with two other Pakistan lads they came to Glasgow to have a look at the city. There they met some Pakistanis in the street – members of the peddling community.

The Pakistani peddling community had been formed in 1918 when Asian and other overseas sailors were demobbed by the Royal Navy and the Merchant Navy at Glasgow docks. Bashir Maan researched their history for his book, *The New Scots*, and tells what happened:

So all the coloured persons, Asians, Arabs, everybody was paid off. These people then congregated in the city docklands and they had some sort of colony set up in the docklands when they were coming in and going out of the country. So they were there and they couldn't find any work. Some of them were doing just selling wee trinkets in the streets or casual labour or even *begging*. So eventually one of the Pakistanis went to a Jewish shop asking for a job, in the Gorbals, and he said to him, 'Listen boy, no job for you, no job for us. You see what we have done, our boys are pedlars, I'm now a warehouseman, I started as a pedlar and I made good and now I'm a warehouseman and I supply to my own people but the trouble is my own people are also now getting better and getting into other businesses and they are abandoning this trade and there is a vacuum there. *You* can start this.' He encouraged him, and he even gave him the material and said 'Here, these are the things which you go and sell, go out and sell.' This one man, his name was Nathu.

Within weeks Nathu was making a good business and others joined him in the work. Many Indian Muslims and Yemenis returned to their homelands in the early 1930s, and by 1926 there were only about thirty or forty people remaining in Glasgow. But the peddling business was good for those who remained, and the community rose to over 100 in the 1930s and to 300 or 400 by the time of the Second World War. By the time that Bashir Maan arrived – in 1953 – some families had spread out over Scotland, numbering 400 to 500 in all, with 200 or so scattered in Edinburgh, Dundee, Aberdeen and even into the Gaelic-speaking Hebridean Islands. He joined an evening class at the Royal Technical College to study textile chemistry as it was an up-and-coming industry in Pakistan. He did well in his first year, but started sensing failure in his second year because of a lack of technical and scientific knowledge. He then transferred in late 1954 to the West of Scotland College of Commerce to study accountancy, and during his two years there he became very involved in the Pakistani community and Asian affairs.

The national prosperity of the late 1950s led to a labour shortage, and employers started to recruit immigrants. In the north of England and the Midlands immigrants already in factory work were bring laid off as some traditional factories closed, especially in textiles. So, Pakistanis migrated from Yorkshire and the Midlands to Glasgow. This expanded the culture of the Asian community. Hitherto it had emanated from two village family groups, one of which came from the Punjab, but the new groups coming via the north of England planted family groups from new places – from Mirpur, from other parts of Punjab, from Sindh, and from the Frontier Province of Pakistan. With existing language skill in English, the Glasgow community of Pakistanis had changed by the early 1960s. About half of the waged members of this community were employed on the Corporation buses, but about half were in factory work. Bashir Maan describes the situation:

Some were in these factories making bread and chemicals, chemicals because they were very dangerous jobs, breads, again, because they had to get up at four o'clock to go to the bakeries and buses because they were unsocial hours from six in the morning to right at twelve at night, the shift system. These were the only jobs available to them, but also another change occurred in the '60s was that some people who had made money, they then started to go into small businesses, small businesses like, mostly it was grocers, corner shops because the Scottish people were selling them and these people, the Indians and Pakistanis, started buying those shops were being sold by Scottish people. Now the trouble they found was that no customers would come in during the day, so they had to keep their shops open till late at night to make a living. During the day if a person saw, at that particular time, a black face behind the counter, they would walk out . . . Some would come in and buy whatever they need but most of them would walk out and go to the next shop which would be owned by a Scottish person. So these fellows then realising that they are not making a living, they started opening shops late till eleven or twelve at night because after six Scottish shops used to be closed, by half past five/six o'clock. So after that, they were *forced to go into the shop* and buy and *from there* then the relationship developed. Once they got to know them they realised they're not that bad (*laughs*).

As a result, the retailing sector in the city was transformed by the advent of Pakistani-run general stores and supermarkets.

It was at that point in the mid-1960s that the children of the expanded Pakistani community, with good English, started going on from school to university. The university of choice in the city, says Bashir Maan, was Strathclyde:

A   When it became a university, then a lot of our children were coming, were joining the University of Strathclyde, yes. I think most of them now *are* in Strathclyde from the ethnic minorities. There are some in Glasgow [University], there are some in [Glasgow] Caledonian [University] also, quite a number of them, but I think still most of them in Strathclyde.
Q   Is there any reason why Strathclyde?
A   I don't know because I think it has a good reputation and the provision here for students here are, I think –. You see Glasgow is an old university. They have their old ways and old systems. Strathclyde in the beginning, it was *new*, everything modern, *all the new ways*. So they could, should we say *relate*, with the young people better than Glasgow. I think that was the reason, and now Caledonian's even newer (*laughs*).

Sometimes, the universities in the city have made entry difficult because of extremely harsh requirements for ability in grammar. But these have often

Figure 5.4 Evening class, 1966
This Department of Commerce lecture was part of the University's extensive evening courses. *Courtesy of* The Herald.

been overcome. Asian students had a preference for highly technical degree courses – engineering, medicine, accountancy, and more recently law. This movement into what are seen as tough courses, with the highest entry requirements, is typical, says Bashir:

> The parents made sure that their children go into education which would help them in getting a good job because they had tough competition. You had to be, and even *now* I tell my people, that you've got to be a little better than your white competitors before you get the job. If you are at level with him, or even *slightly better than him*, you won't get the job, he will get the job. You've got to be *far better than him* before you get the job. So therefore the parents made sure that they went in professions where

there was a demand for the new kind of people. Most of them went into medicine and the rest accountants and engineers and all that.

Amongst home students, Strathclyde quickly acquired a reputation for attracting a very high proportion of first-generation undergraduates – students from families without a heritage of higher education. Hamish Fraser recalls that this contrasted with Glasgow University which had what he calls 'a strong distinct middle-class ethos' and one familiar at most British universities from Aberdeen to Sussex (where Fraser had undertaken his two degrees). 'That was the university world,' he says. 'You did get a great sense at Strathclyde of them trying to do something different and it was attractive. It always did attract a *large* number of mature students.' This reputation was not acquired slowly, by bringing mature students into the university in small numbers. It happened with a bang. In 1963, with a new School of Arts and Social Studies, staff were put in place in four departments – History, Psychology, Economics and Politics. This gave rise to a late decision to admit students for the academic year 1963–4, but with no time for the normal selections system, it was agreed to take from eighty to 100 students for the new arts degree. But, as Fraser remembers this meant that 'they had to go and find these students'. By one account, it was Edgar Lythe of Economic History who informed contacts at the London School of Economics and said to them: 'Right, if you've got any rejects who are quite promising, tell them to come here'.[8] By another account, it was Kenneth Alexander of Economics who broached this route for would-be LSE students to come to Strathclyde that year. Robin Alpine came to the Economics Department and taught in session 1963–4, just prior to the merger and chartering of the University. He recalls having to do service teaching elsewhere in the College, including chemical engineers: 'That is what I got! Which was interesting!' But he also remembers that 'the other thing that made the first year very different at Strathclyde in 1963 was that we got a lot of LSE rejects.'[9] Roger Sandilands recalls the tremendous buzz in 1963–4 of being a student in that first year in the Arts Faculty:

There was about twenty or so people who were to have gone to the LSE. I mean they were *good students* and even if they weren't good students, their background wasn't all that wonderful. The fact that there was ninety odd of us in the class but the staff/student ratio was about five to one/one to five. So we had weekly tutorials, the lecturers all came to our parties, we got terrific individual attention, we were all pretty much doing the same thing so we were all going through the same sort of course and we knew each other *extremely well*. And I suppose nowadays

156

when students are taking all kinds of mixtures of classes from all over the place, but then there were only six departments and we had five subjects so we were all were pretty much doing the same thing. And meeting weekly in tutorials we got to know each other very well. There was a party almost every week, maybe twice a week and there was a lot offered to us. They put on their best lecturers, so that people like Edgar Lythe who was *fantastic*, he was a *just superb* lecturer. When he finished there was a standing ovation for his lectures – *really, really stimulating*. There was a guy called Eddie Gibb who lectured in economics in the first year, he was very exciting as well. Schaeffer in Psychology, he was very good. A guy called Dr Alistair Howie, he lectured on Monday, Wednesday and Friday at nine o'clock in statistics, that's compulsory, statistics for us all. And we had about three lectures a week in each class, five classes, about fifteen hours a week although actually psychology didn't get started until January.

The Norwegian connection has been a significant element in the Strath-clyde cultural heritage. They came to study many different subjects. Those in economics, Robin Alpine recalls, were more interested in applied than theoretical aspects of the subject, and opted for more quantitative parts of the discipline: 'they seemed to sense that this was important for business and so on and they were looking further ahead. So that in some certain classes they actually were more than half the class you know. And that sometimes led to some mutterings among local students (*laughs*).' Tony Martin, formerly of the Geography Department, remembered how the Norwegians made an impressive impact of patriotic fervour at the graduation in 1966 of HM King Olaf V when he received the honorary degree of Doctor of Law:

My first contact with international students was in architecture. There was quite a few students from Norway and Iceland, one or two from the Lebanon and Israel, and that gave a very important international aspect to that class. It came a bit later in arts and social studies but obviously the Norwegian link was very strong because the first graduation I went to was an honorary graduation for the late King Olaf of Norway and that was held in the Assembly Hall and the Robing Room was in the heat engines lab in the Royal College. And really obviously the Norwegian national anthem was played in those days and on that occasion and there must have been something like 200 to 300 Norwegian students who *sang it* and they just more or less lifted the roof off the assembly hall.

The Norwegian students were overwhelmingly male and, despite a reputation for keeping very much to themselves, they did bring a sporting culture to the University at the very time when winter pastimes were starting to spread like wildfire in western culture. Ski-ing was still a little-known sport in Britain in the 1950s, despite the creation in 1946 of the National Outdoor Recreation Centre in the Cairngorms, and sports like orienteering were only first introduced from Scandinavia in 1963. But the Norwegian students who came to Strathclyde, many to study engineering, brought in the 1950s and 1960s what Professor John Webster has described as 'a very healthy outdoor attitude', transforming aspects of the students' association sports programme with the introduction of orienteering and ski-ing.

Strathclyde sought very quickly to establish a reputation for considering non-standard-entry students – mature students with experience of life and a strong commitment to learning. Ironically, the initial impact of the University was to reduce the number of part-time students – from 2,852 in the Royal College in 1957–8 to a mere 945 in the University in 1967–8.[10] However, this seems to have been caused in part by the decline of non-degree courses, and in part by the rise of the return-to-study mature students. One of the fruits of this early policy was Noel Cochrane from Edinburgh who sought to enter universities all over Scotland using school-leaving examinations taken at college, but he suffered a disastrous diet of Highers exams in 1968. All the universities rejected him, except one, and he never looked back:

> Well going to university was a – I had never had an ambition to go to university. I could draw and I could see myself going to art college, but that was all. I could only see myself drawing but university just was beyond my ken, we didn't know anybody who had been to university apart from teachers you would have assumed. So it was entirely a new, new experience, didn't know what to, what to expect. I had very low self-esteem academically. You just hoped that you would get through the Higher English, the other Highers, that some way you were going to sustain that and improve. So it was very, very daunting. *But* actually arriving *at* Strathclyde and meeting up with a number of mature students who were coming from a similar background was very reassuring and . . . one of the strangest phenomena that I encountered was someone from the east, finding myself in tutorials, let's say history tutorials, and learning that the people in that tutorials were from Catholic backgrounds similar to my own and for the first time in my life I was experiencing a situation where the Catholics were a majority *(laughs)* in a group and that was, that was, you know quite, quite staggering and quite interesting. So that was one dimension to it.

Figure 5.5 The new Muirhead lounge, Students' Union, 1968
The 'Muirhead' provided a location for female students to gather, socialise, debate and organise extra-curricula activities (including cocktail parties). This room was the successor to the original Muirhead room in the Royal College building. *Strathclyde University Archives.*

As a married man and a father, Noel found university daunting not just because of the learning, or because he was from the east of Scotland, but – in yet another echo of the dominance of structures in Scotland – because he was Catholic and a trade unionist. He found Strathclyde important for the ways in which the individual could break through these myriad frameworks of exclusion:

> I found it, I found it very, very reassuring and, it was, there was camaraderie, which, which developed, *it didn't happen instantly* and probably it took by the end of the first year to establish that so perhaps it was, in retrospect, I was a fish out of water for a while and but by the time you had worked your way through tutorials and you know had some pub

sessions you had, you had formed relationships. And yeah it was good, especially knowing people that were, a lot of the guys would probably be coming from, you know political or you know sort of labour kind of union interests. My kind of energising source would have been through *church organisations* and that kind of thing, that would have been my kind of ideals and spur. I would have found that in common with some of the guys as well.

As a mature student, Noel found he probably worked inefficiently, certainly to begin with. He recalls:

I had no criteria to judge it by and I was, the whole thing was a complete kind of, I just *got by* and I worked *incredibly hard* and probably *incredibly inefficiently*. I just had to give everything I had *to it*, to the extent that you know my wife complained years afterwards I was burning the midnight oil and just over-compensating for a total lack of experience in any kind, notion of study skills, or study background, study discipline. So I was just throwing myself entirely to it . . . Yeah, well that was the way. It was just, it was just a case of, you know, sort of going absolutely for it because you just did *not have any experience of*, you were so *in awe* of the word 'university' and what the expectations were. It was a *totally*, for me it was a different world. I mean I didn't understand things like what is a 2:1, a 2:2, that was a mystical *shibboleth*, you know, it was language that you didn't understand, I mean you know even the notion of Honours was mystical language.

Noel ended up forming a close camaraderie with a group of History students known as 'the Coatbridge Mafia', one of whom (though not from Coatbridge) was the late Dr Graham Cummings, later a lecturer in the Department of History.

By the mid-1970s, Strathclyde was a haven for mature students. Ronnie Scott,[11] himself a mature student, recalls the significance of this in the context of war, being working class and families finally achieving that democracy of access for which the Labour tradition had stood for decades:

I think for a lot of them who were, a lot of them were from families who were trade union and Labour Party, you know. They identified themselves as industrial working class and this was, I suppose – going to university was, *for them*, was what their parents had fought for. You know it was a combination of something, it was a whole seeing through of the post-war, you know the health service and education and all these things.

160

They were the beneficiaries of work that their parents and grand parents had and predecessors *in* the Labour party had fought for and worked to make happen. So I think they felt themselves, they thought there was a tradition or there was movement they were part of . . .

This was as Ronnie Scott puts it 'something that was completely foreign to me'. His father had been a telephonist and office worker, his mother a seamstress, and their fathers had been respectively a career soldier and then a solicitor's clerk, and an electrical engineer. So, in comparison to many other students, his family heritage didn't have what he calls 'the same kind of politics or class background that they seemed to have that as a something they all had in common'. But this common Labour heritage was a powerful feature of the student population of the 1970s, perhaps one of the surprising features of the oral testimony collected in this project. It was a heritage that led from the personal to the political and then back again. Ronnie Scott describes it more:

So, there were all these kinds of dynasties and backgrounds and networks that a lot of people had in common, that I didn't. So that, this was all new to me. A lot of it was new to me and there was a lot of things that one did and one didn't do that seemed to them to be −. There was a political line on whether you, for example you bought Israeli produce or whether you bought − that for them, an awful lot of personal things were political or what *seemed* to me to be personal, for them were political. Things like, for example one that sticks in my mind is that, you *didn't* buy anything from a pawn shop because a poor person had suffered but had been − the pawnbroker had profited from the person's poverty, so that patronising pawn shops, for example, was not a thing that somebody on the left did. I've never been in a pawn shop in my life, so it was never something that I was going to do but that was probably because it wasn't respectable. But there, it was interesting meeting people who had. I suppose they carried around with them a whole, a whole body of thinking that, that came as a whole, whereas I think I was kind of gathering. I was trying to make my own system or my own meanings or my own ways of looking at the world, whereas a lot of other people seemed to have access to answers, through those kinds of systems.

The baggage did not just define the individual in the institution, then, but came to be a challenge to the individual exposed to it. The University was a place of its heritage, come 1960s new culture or not. The students brought Scotland to the University.

So, for all that there were new types of student bringing exotic new perspectives and widening the horizons of the learning culture at Strathclyde, the University continued to rely for membership of its student body upon its immediate base in the Glasgow conurbation. Tony Martin, formerly of the Geography Department and for long in charge of admissions to the Arts and Social Studies Faculty, recalled how the student population seemed to be defined by the limits of 'the Blue Trains' – the distinctive electric trains running on the Glasgow commuting lines. These electric trains were introduced on the Glasgow suburban lines from 1 October 1961 (after a failed introduction following two train explosions a year earlier), and were extended over the following thirteen years to virtually all central-west Scotland commuting lines into Glasgow, providing a fast, frequent and efficient service for commuters from as far away as Gourock in the west and North Lanarkshire in the east.[12] With Strathclyde in close proximity to all of the railway termini and central stations for these services, it was peculiarly well placed to benefit from the upsurge in students capable of using these services. The 'Blue Trains' reinforced how the constituencies of both Strathclyde and Glasgow universities seemed defined by the compelling geography of the 'live-at-home-student'.[13] These two universities had by far the highest levels of domiciled students at pre-1990 UK universities. The proportion of Glasgow-domiciled students at Glasgow University actually rose from 74 to 78 per cent over the period 1961–84, whilst the proportion of its students from Scotland rose from 92 to 95 per cent.[14]

Strathclyde staff came to recognise the distinctive west-of-Scotland ability to widen academic horizons yet remain oblivious to cultures beyond the backyard. Tony Martin remarks:

> I can remember one of our better students coming in knocking on my door on two or three Monday mornings running and said 'Were you *at the match* on Saturday?' or 'Did you see the match on Saturday?' and I didn't realise what 'the match' was and he seemed rather surprised when I said I'd been to see Clydebank play Stenhousemuir, and 'the match' to him was Celtic's match, it wasn't anything else, he came from the east end of Glasgow and it was Celtic's match.

Indeed, whilst the students in almost massed ranks supported Rangers or Celtic, university staff tended to disproportionately support the minnows of Scottish senior football (any one from Partick Thistle, Clyde, Queens Park, Morton, Stenhousemuir, the much-lamented Third Lanark, or Stirling Albion). This may be a distinctive feature of the Glasgow academic, not one found in Manchester, Liverpool or London. The sectarian-rippled chasm in

Scottish football culture, centred on the Old Firm, does compel some of the academic body to a deliberate support of the underdog, in part a proclamation of cultural neutrality. As a student in Liverpool, Tony Martin reports that he 'could watch Liverpool one week and then cross Stanley Park the next week to watch Everton play at home, but you couldn't do that in Glasgow'. Football, it should be added, was also an academic cement – both within the University and outwith it. Dr John Sanderson,[15] formerly of the Politics Department, recalls its significance:

> Well we had a team called the Keynesian Casuals consisting of people in the new faculty [of Arts]. Because a lot of us were fairly young and could still play. And we played, we played students obviously, low-level student teams and . . . the arts and social studies people at Glasgow . . . And we played two or three matches against the Scottish Police College [at Tulliallan] accelerated-promotion people . . . selected as the likely chief constables in future . . . I think they thought this was a good idea for them, they sort of built class *esprit de corps* and we had several very good matches against them . . . I remember *Dave Forsyth scored a sensational goal* from, with a strike from the touchline that went straight in the other corner, *incredible*, you know, if he'd done it at Ibrox they'd have been talking about it yet, you know.

Despite a good *esprit de corps*, there was still an initial problem at the time of the merger in getting the school leavers to know of the new subjects available for degree study at Strathclyde. Students knew widely the calibre of a subject like chemical engineering, but economics for instance had to graft to become known. Robin Alpine remembers what he felt was the struggle to gain widespread appreciation for the qualities of the new departments:

> You certainly got the impression this was the case with the schools. Fairly early on I became an assistant advisor of studies. What we had to do was interview the students coming in and go over their possible curriculum with them you know and so on and also with students in other years. And you got the impression that the schools they were coming from were a sort of biased selection of the Glasgow area. It possibly still is. Maybe not so much now but it certainly was then that the better schools wouldn't send their good students to Strathclyde, they would push them to Glasgow. Just because that's what they knew about you know. So I think there was some thing but I think it was more within the area of people who didn't really know in detail what was actually going on here. They just had perceptions they'd formed and they weren't going to change

them. Whereas people who were actually economist, in other places, recognised that there were actually some good people here and it was, you know, deserved its place.

The mix of students and expectations in the 1960s and early 1970s created novel demands. Some wealthier students brought with them people whom they treated as study servants. Some overseas students felt that their university fees should cover their typing, and expressed surprise at doing computing work in which they operated the keyboard. One recollection was of 'young lady students' who brought in their own secretaries. And then there were all the male students who expected to have women provide free help – especially with the typing aspects of computing. Staff observed that male students sought free help from girlfriends, even during examinable assessments. Ann Mair notes: 'I don't think anybody took it as more than normal that the girl would come in and do the typing, out of the normal . . . Oh yes. I mean their Mum or their girlfriend would always come and do the typing'. This is in contrast to the 1990s when keyboarding emerged as a suitably machismo undertaking for male students to learn the skills. But then, as Ann Mair concludes: 'That was normal. I mean (*laughs*) times have changed.'

The new students of 1960s Strathclyde were allegedly a tame lot, in some respects. Certainly, economics student David Paterson thinks that student culture, as it was to become known within a few years, did not exist in his time between 1962 and 1965 – despite the musical harbingers of change: 'It was the time, you know The Beatles and before that Bill Haley and the Comets, and the Platters, and rock 'n' roll and a kind of fairly innocent adolescence growing up. No drugs. Nothing that you recognise today as modern student culture, just didn't exist.' Robin Alpine recalls the difference between his days as a student at Glasgow around 1960, and the tenor of the classes five years later at Strathclyde. Glasgow students were, he says, 'different in terms of the way their hair, style and colour'. He asks whether it was because the institution was science and engineering-dominated. Even in sexual relations, he felt the change:

I remember a class I used to teach in the late 1960s, and there was one extremely attractive girl that took this class and she nearly always made a late entrance. In my day as a student if that had happened there would have been stamping of feet and all the rest of it. And she went up and took her place and it was actually lecture room 2 or 3 just along the corridor there, and you could hear a pin drop. I mean, there was just nothing, and I used to go say to my wife, 'You know, I can't believe how tame these students are!' You know I just thought, this would not have happened five years earlier, you know when I was a student at Glasgow, I mean.

He recalled a tradition of indecorum in the lecture theatres at Glasgow, one perhaps then ingrained in the culture of the older British male undergraduates:

> We got into trouble in one of the lectures because we were giving a female lecturer a hard time and we got this stern guy, one of the senior guys came and really, we were a second-year class and you really got a dressing down. You know there were paper aeroplanes, things you know, and we were told this was not acceptable behaviour. To go from that sort of environment where students could be sort of unruly and so on to this where they're actually docile, if that's the word.

If younger staff considered the arts students to be tame, other staff remember this as a good quality. Secretarial and support staff are often the ones who get the brunt of student problems, and problem students. Compared to today, the students of the 1960s behaved very differently. Karen Morrison recalls:

> It was much more formal. When I first came, certainly the early '60s, it was shirt and tie stuff and *you were in time for lectures*. Ah ha, which doesn't necessarily follow nowadays but then again that's society isn't it? And students didn't miss lectures then and they handed work in on time and if you asked them for something you got it, you didn't have to ask them twenty-two times like you do now... I think there was probably a little more deference as well because that was society at the time, we had rules and mores, and society had a particular structure where the boundaries don't exist so much now... In the '60s there was a huge bit [of change] because all of a sudden a teenager was a person and you didn't need to wear the same clothes as your mum and dad, you had different stuff to wear so you had an identity. So it probably started then but I think it's gathered momentum and grown much more in the '90s.

Better behaved they may have been, but the 1960s generation were also optimists. Looking back from our more pessimistic times, Barbara Graham articulates the common sense of the optimistic times among those who went to university in the 1960s:

165

HUNG UP

on
POSTERS
or
RECORDS?

Then Hades is your scene—
we have the pics and the
discs you want. Progressive
sound and vision, stacks and
racks!

hades
Poster &
Record
Shop
11 BATH ST
GLASGOW

MANDY SMITH—CHARITIES QUEEN
'72

Figure 5.6 The 'new' student, 1972
Tradition (Charities' Queen) and change come together in this image. The
confident demeanour and strikingly-different clothes of this 1970s student
demonstrate a radical transformation in student culture. *Strathclyde University
Archives.*

And my generation was really the first-generation that in any kind of mass way, we're probably talking somewhere between 5 and 10 per cent, but nearly everybody in my class at school was a first generation person at university. *That felt so good! This was really something!* And obviously it was going to lead onto something good! You know! Because, well in a way it was unprecedented. So if you did know anybody who had a degree they were a teacher or they were a doctor or they were a lawyer or they were an accountant or they were . . . they were something professional so it wouldn't have crossed your mind for a minute that it was going to be anything other than that you know. So I think it's something about students but I think it's also something about society.

CULTURE, HOME AND SOCIAL LIFE

Glasgow could provide a sense of being at the front-line of 1960s culture. For many who came to Strathclyde, it was a great time to be young and to be a student, and to be at large in Glasgow. It was a city of excitement and confrontation, though still known elsewhere as a city of drink, poverty, bigotry and violence. For such reasons, perhaps, the reputation of the place in that era has perhaps not travelled as much as that of the Edinburgh Festival and the irreverent humour of *Beyond the Fringe*. But for the discerning intellectual there was much going on in Glasgow.

Roger Sandilands came from southern England first as an Arts Faculty student in October 1963, just as The Beatles and swinging London were bursting out. He stayed to teach at the University. So many aspects of the culture and vibrancy of the city attracted him – including the Barras flea market in the east end: 'The Barras were great in those days; you could go down there and pick up records and fountain pens and books and clothes, whatever, for next to nothing. It was much more exciting, much more going on there, much more on sale there then than there is now, and I used to go down there quite a bit on a Sunday morning.' Even the social problems of the city attracted him, confronting the zealous social-science and economics student as if to say 'Fix me!' There was much in the city to excite the undergraduate. One thing he remembered was Duncan Macrae, a famous Scottish tragic-comic actor who was a member of the board of the newly-established Citizens Theatre in the Gorbals a mile or so to the south of the University campus (see Figure 3.4). It was a theatre that specialised in the experimental and the new of the drama world. Its rates were cheap to attract the student; even in 1975, its seats were only 50 pence on hard gallery benches. Roger Sandilands:

I remember one evening going along there to a production, this is about mid-'60s, when they were doing a spoof, a take-off of famous characters including the Queen. They had all these characters like Shakespeare and Churchill. And one of them was the Queen. They all had masks, the actors and actresses had masks on, and they were going to satirise and probably hold up to ridicule these various people and the Board of Governors refused to allow it to go ahead. Arrived at the theatre, we all sat waiting for the curtain to be raised and it was raised on the board members who explained that they weren't going to allow the show to go on because it was disrespectful to the Queen. And there was a *big, big* debate and people were urging the show must go on but it didn't go on. There was a big scandal but one of the people was this fellow Duncan Macrae, whose daughter Christine was a year or two below me, knew her fairly well and he came to here to talk at the University . . . he wasn't very happy about it, when he was defending the decision of the board at the Citizens Theatre, but these things were quite exciting, they were memorable occasions as an undergraduate.

There was a strong sense of the University as being drawn to the heart of cultural change and intellectual contest. Lecturers in various departments arranged for key public figures to come and speak, often to lectures in the relevant subjects – something that still goes on today when members of the Scottish Parliament, or novelists, writers and commentators, come to speak to and debate with Strathclyde students.

For some of the new students, their first home in the city was in one of the halls of residence – such as Diana Henderson who in her second term entered Beneffrey Hall, a large newly-renovated townhouse where 'We had a lot of fun there and I was able to meet other Strathclyde students studying different subjects'. Roger Sandilands stayed initially with relatives:

I stayed near St George's Cross. My first term actually I stayed with my cousin in High Blantyre, came in with her husband in the morning at eight o'clock or even earlier . . . We drove through the Gorbals in the morning, and in those days the Gorbals was the Gorbals, now it's been totally transformed, and we drove in and he dropped me off at Queen Street Station. I sat in the station reading the morning paper until, until I think eight or 8.30 when the Students' Union opened and then classes would be at nine o'clock, and, that was my first term . . . And in January 1964 I moved out of Blantyre to escape the restraints of living with relatives, and into a bed and breakfast place in Shamrock Street which is just off St George's Road, about 100 yards from the Cross, and I used to get the morning paper at 10.30 at night, the Aberdeen edition of the *Daily Express* sneaked out, and that was a great place, Mrs Thompson my landlady, she was a great lady, she had all kinds of itinerants. I was there sort of long term, over several months, but she had quite a lot of American sailors there, lots of them around in those days patronising the Beresford Hotel which is now next door to the Baird Hall, the Beresford Bar? That was a great pickup point for American sailors picking up Glasgow hairies.

In many ways, Scotland was still a place of the 1950s, not of the 1960s. As many have observed, Scotland's 1960s were really in the 1970s. The world of repressed moral freedoms, of highly-charged divisions between rough and respectable, of Trocchi's *Young Adam*, still resonated through the northern kingdom. This was rammed home to Sandilands in his second year:

The following year, when I was in my second, I moved to Elmbank Street which is just opposite Baird Hall, and there's a place still there, the King's Cafe, still there and Mrs Bremner from Aberdeen, she was my landlady the following year. I remember for two guineas a week, two pounds two shillings a week, I had bed and breakfast and she was wonderful. She always brought me tea and biscuits at night, and if I didn't get home before half-ten or whenever it was, she would leave me a glass of milk and cakes at night-time. And in the mornings she would come in about 7.30, fling open the wooden shutters, the light would stream in, and she insisted on my getting up for a cooked breakfast. I was very cosseted, and all this for two guineas a week and, that was *great*. So I stayed there in my second year and that was just being opposite the Beresford. I never went to the Beresford dances but I saw all the consequences. You asked me about the drunkenness of Glasgow, well, it's not much different today I don't think on a Saturday night but, that was the atmosphere, a lot of wildness, a lot of gang warfare too. I was never the victim of it and it never particularly worried me because it seemed to me to be mostly gangs fighting each other rather than randomly against other people.

Most students did not live so close to the city centre. Indeed, by far the vast majority of Strathclyde students continued to live at home with parents or guardians. Incredibly, as Ronnie Simpson recalls, one group of students made a wholly-unusual domestic acquisition:

I went into the Ph.D. programme and by that time we did have a flat out in Great Western Road, about four or five of us and it worked well to begin with, everybody took their share of cooking, cleaning and getting the messages and then that got into a bad state but we actually discovered an *au pair* girl who was fed up with the family that she was with and she came and stayed with us and looked after the house (*laughs*). So, we must be unique in that sense that we're the only group of students who had an *au pair* girl (*laughs*).

Some students found adjusting to university life was far from easy. For the new Scots – the immigrant Asians, predominantly Muslim, and their children who grew up mostly in the city – it was the society, not Strathclyde, that was the problem. Studying at successively the Tech and Commerce colleges in the 1950s, Bashir Mann relates the kind of context in which the early immigrant student had to concentrate whilst out of the classroom:

But the funny thing is that the main objection of having a Pakistani or Asian neighbour at that time, to the Scottish people, was that smell of their cooking we have to live with and now that smell has become so popular. You see, this is what I always say is, that it's the ignorance which breeds prejudice and which breeds racism. Once you get to know people then everything's fine. I mean I have come across very many instances when two families are at loggerheads, an Asian family and a Scottish family, and what I used to do was, when it was brought to my notice, and usually it was either the Scottish family who brought it to my notice, or Pakistani or Indian family, I went up and tried to see both sides and I then tried to ask the Pakistani or the Indian family 'Why don't you invite them one day for tea?'. And once they did that, they became very good friends. You see, it was *just not knowing each other*, being suspicious of each other, not understanding each others' habits and culture, which was the cause of the trouble.

In a very different way, Noel Cochrane found the learning regime a massive shock. When he travelled from Edinburgh to study in the early 1970s, the whole experience was earth-shattering for his family and children:

It was hell. It was hell and I mean, in so far that I had –. I was *totally committed to surviving* and getting . . . I was married in '65, Marie Louise was born in '68, that was the year before I went to Strathclyde. In '70 while I was at Strathclyde, the fifth of March Julie was born and then thirteenth of July '71 my other daughter was born. So that was three young children, my wife was dealing with, while I thought I was exclusively devoting my time to study . . . I just thought this is, if I'm going to do this I have to do this and go for it and I was *ruthless* . . . I was writing an essay and I found a hair lying on the paper (*laughs*), I said 'Oh *my God*, is this the worry? I am going to start losing all my hair?'

He acknowledges the selfish, male drive to his studies at Strathclyde, but equally acknowledges what it did for his career. He went into teaching, gained promotion early, and became head of a department. 'And that was reward for being that ruthless but that again that's to do with my personality. I just had to do the best I could and if it just meant giving everything that's what I did.' Strathclyde, like other British universities in the 1960s and early 1970s, developed agencies to assist students in the transition to university life. Barbara Graham came to Strathclyde in 1974 with a joint remit in careers advice and student advisory work. She recalled the type of issue that she faced:

In those days of course virtually all the home students had grants and perhaps their grants hadn't come through. Perhaps they had seriously fallen out with their parents, their parents would refuse to sign the appropriate application form, we would then be intervening with the awards agency saying we have somebody here in hardship, really exceptions need to be made. We were administering funds which the university itself had, that sort of thing. But you would also get . . . people who were dreadfully homesick, people whose lives were wrecked because their boyfriend had walked out on them, you know all these sorts of things.

She recalls the absence of professional training for her job in those days, and how counselling was learned out of the 'university of common sense'. Special-needs students were an important development of the work of the new universities, and Barbara helped to run a club for visually-impaired students from all over the Glasgow and west of Scotland area, a club called Outreach, assisting with readers and special facilities in the library. 'It was all grist to our mill at that time. So it was an incredibly varied job.'

With the university's student base living overwhelmingly at home in the 1950s, 1960s and 1970s, the culture of the institution was obviously much affected. Whilst many of those who stayed at home did so for financial reasons, being unable to contemplate the expense of study at a campus university or a city university somewhere else in Britain, even students from middle-class families with much better financial resources chose to stay at home. This was the west of Scotland heritage. Ronnie Scott recalls how one female student led a highly-structured life:

I was in everyday but didn't have a fixed routine and I remember talking to this woman . . . who was an accountancy student and her father dropped her on his way to work in the morning and picked her up. So her working week was nine to five Monday to Friday. It was her father's working week so, which I suppose is good preparation if you're going to be an accountant, the likelihood is that your working the kind of hours her father's working. That seemed, well – you've got a lifetime of working nine till five, why? You know you've just escaped school, here's three years where you could maybe relax a wee bit in terms of hours but –

So, the social life of the University was dominated by the minority who were not residing with their parents. Roger Sandilands recalls the key role in his life of the Cross-Country Club of the Athletics Union:

Every week we either had a race at home in Glasgow or the other week we would be in Aberdeen, Dundee, St Andrews, Edinburgh, Belfast, Dublin. We went around a lot and so every Saturday night we would be in a pub somewhere singing and drinking and going to the dances afterwards, there was always a dance on a Saturday night. We got to stay over in Aberdeen and places or else we would take a coach to Edinburgh, stay until one o'clock and take the address of the girls we'd picked up and come back on this bus and so on.

He remembered that 'we used to go all over Scotland running against Edinburgh and Aberdeen and St Andrews and so on and even went to Ireland a couple of times on tour every other year we had an Irish tour to Queen's Belfast and to Trinity College, Dublin and that was great fun and amongst the runners there were some real west-of-Scotland characters, you know, folk singers . . .' It was also international and socially-levelling:

I was very friendly with a guy from India as well. He wasn't in our faculty but I was friendly with him through networking but partly because my social circle was around the runners, about ten or twelve runners, and most of them were in other faculties and only one or two were from the Arts Faculty. There were lots of engineers and chemists and pharmacists and so my social life tended to gravitate around those people rather than around people in my class.

Strathclyde students like all students knew how to enjoy themselves. Roger Sandilands recalls that 'I was not much of a drinker myself,' but that 'I used to take care of people who were incapable of getting themselves home (*laughs*)'. Student dances at Strathclyde and Glasgow Unions were the basis of much student socialising. Glasgow Men's Union at the top of Gibson Street, he recalls, was a Fort Knox:

> It was very, very difficult to get in. They had *very, very strict* policing of entry. If you were a female you could get in no problem, but [still] had to show you were a bona fide undergraduate full-time student at Glasgow University to get in there on a Saturday night.

Relations between male and female students were not made promiscuous overnight in the 1960s. Sandilands again:

> Well it was much more strait-laced *than today*. It was much more cautious, I think that the pill was only just coming on stream. I think there was much more caution about sexual relationships because of the danger of pregnancy but there was a lot of sex that didn't quite go all the way (*laughs*), I think that might sum it up. On the other hand there were girls who were pregnant in our class and there were people who were living and sleeping together, so it wasn't absent. My feeling was that, at least among the students at Strathclyde, the undergraduates of the day, here, they were much more I suppose strait-laced is the word. I was unaware of – there was almost no drugs, almost, one was vaguely aware of some people using drugs but it was *very, very rare*. I never came across it directly myself at all, not till I went to Canada, but one was aware of it being a problem down south . . . certainly we were aware that in the south of England it was a den of iniquity by comparison to here. People drank hard here, much, much more drink than in the south of England, but I would say much more caution sexually and almost zero drug taking, so that made a difference.

David Paterson started as a College of Commerce student and graduated a Strathclyde University student. For him, the 'social life was great'. It was not quite what it was to become:

> I mean, we, by today's standards it would be regarded as very tame and innocent, there were no drugs. I have no recollection at any time and this is up to the mid-1960s, I think the idea, one had heard about drugs as something absolutely dreadful and awful, one, you could not at that time imagine the idea of recreational drugs or any of that nature. The only recreational drugs were the traditional ones of tobacco and alcohol and eh? women.

Many respondents recall the very great influence in Glasgow, as indeed in most Scottish towns and cities of the 1950s and 1960s, of the folk-song movement. Roger Sandilands draws an important character sketch:

> And the other big difference between Glasgow and the south of England is that once again there is this folk-singing culture, folk clubs, and people would go to a pub and they would be singing, sometimes they were kind of sectarian but that was minimal. If we did sing sectarian things it was done with a sense of humour rather than seriousness. I wasn't really aware too much of the sectarian problem, I was aware that it was there, out there in the city, but not amongst the undergraduates . . . We had a folk club in the university and there were folk clubs out in the town and you'd go to the pub and the chances are that someone would be singing *Wild Rover* and someone would be strumming a guitar or a banjo or a mouth organ and *that you didn't get down south*, it was much *colder*. The atmosphere I think and that, I liked it, it was warm and communal. There was also the rugby culture where the rugby crowd. I'm talking about the students still, the rugby students, they would also be in the bar and they would be singing their rugby songs which were crude and sexist and so on. The runners were, us at Strathclyde and also the other runners at the other universities were *different* (*laughs*). They weren't like the rugby crowd. We almost never sang crude rugby-type songs, very rarely, we didn't think it was necessary . . . because we had a great repertoire of other things beside. The students at Strathclyde and Glasgow were the more outgoing, folksy, people who would have been more likely to strike up a song. You know, when we were down the British Universities cross-country championships in Nottingham one year, they closed the bar because they didn't allow singing. I think it was because singing in the south of England would be rugby songs and we would be singing the *Wild Rover*, 'at the end of the day', or *Northern Lights of Old Aberdeen*, you know, all those or *The Road to Dundee*, these sorts of songs, *totally harmless*, but we enjoyed singing them. But at Nottingham they closed the bar because we were singing, the Glasgow boys and the Strathclyde boys and there was a big row because apparently once they closed the bar they couldn't reopen it without a majority vote of the SRC. Ah it was *ridiculous* and you thought they were *crazy* anyway and *joyless*. Whereas it was the sense of fun and joyfulness amongst, I thought, about the socialising we did. There was a lot of hard drinking but it was also joyfulness and a non-aggressiveness about it.

The student folk scene was still in being in the mid-1970s. Ronnie Scott remembers one student performer then: 'Dave Douglass was unaccompanied, he would, you know, finger in ear and sing traditional north-east of England songs. There were some political or Irish material in there as well, but the bulk of it was a folk song repertoire.' But the 1960s brought diversity to the student social scene. By the late 1960s, a more modern style of student party was evidently in swing. Noel Cochrane recalls his shock, as a mature married student from Edinburgh, on attending his first student party in Glasgow:

> Anne, my wife, went through with me to this party, I'd never been to a students' party in my life before, so I think I brought drink and I don't know if she brought food. But of course when you arrived there, there was no food, absolutely no one ate and they hid their drinks (*laughs*). So there was no drink on the table. My experience of parties was New Year, and you came and you put your bottle down and people you know. But people would go into the toilet, lift the cistern out, take out a half bottle (*laughs*). *I couldn't believe it.* And at one point in the evening I got *very, very hungry* and I went through to look for food and I opened this fridge door and there were wee parcels of food wi' names on. I think I opened a packet of plain bread or something. I was trying to make a sandwich and somebody came ranting and raving through this was their food, you know (*laughs*). So that was, you know a measure of the extent to which you know I was a married man, who had never known *that aspect* of student poverty, squalor, the whole thing was.

The Students' Union acquired a reputation, that it sustained in the 1990s, of attracting some of the leading-edge rock bands of each era. Bill Speirs recalls that before he propelled himself into student politics, he spent his first year in going to discos and only scraping past his exams. One of the attractions in 1970, he recalls, was a now-legendary rock group and lead singer: Ozzy Osbourne of Black Sabbath.

> One of the other memories that I have of Strathclyde, when you're talking about when I first went there. In *week one* the band who headlined the Saturday night gig were Black Sabbath and it was the week that *Paranoid* [LP album] got to number one. It was just chance the social secretary had booked them, you know, months in advance and as it happened, so it was, well the place was absolutely *jam-packed*. I was deaf for hours afterwards *but* it was the kind of thing you don't forget, Ozzy Osbourne leaping about and, there you are, you know, 'bark'.

175

The Social Secretary at the time was Dougie Donnelly, who since the 1980s has been Scotland's premier television football and sports journalist. After the success of Black Sabbath, a few weeks later he brought Pink Floyd to the Union – who even then were giants and icons of the pop world; as Bill says in awe, 'and they were there'. Bill recalls that an even greater coup was planned – but sadly failed:

> The [Rolling] Stones were supposed to play, but they pulled out when they discovered that you had to be a student to get in, unless we had a reciprocal agreement with other students' associations and they reckoned that, that wasn't right so they didn't take part. But I mean during the time that I was there you had access at cheap prices to hear people like Pink Floyd, I never saw Family there, but Rory Gallagher – I mean just this incredible range of bands. And then there was always discos and events taking place.

Into the 1980s and 1990s, the Students' Union at Strathclyde maintained this reputation for clever and adventurous bookings of top and breaking talent. This reputation has certainly played its part in edging the decision of some new students in their choice of which university to come to.

Student organisations and activities were incredibly varied. If rock music wasn't a student's bag, there was always the Officer Training Corps (conducted jointly out of Glasgow University) which, though less popular in the late 1960s (with only one new recruit in one session), provided some additional pay (of 17/6d per drill night), good food, and access to hot baths (to supplement the one-per week permitted by the landlady).[16] The *Student Telegraph*, the Strathclyde University student newspaper, was a focus for news of all sorts – including, in the early 1970s, a scoop interview with Quentin Hogg, Secretary of State for Education. Bill Speirs remembers it from the early 1970s: 'I mean *Telegraph* was a good paper. There was always a good buzz about the place and I think a self-confidence about it was the thing that would stick with me, it didn't have to prove itself to anybody. It was in there.' The paper represented a focus for not just student culture but for the honing of new skills. Ronnie Scott recalls:

> The *Telegraph* was originally in the St Paul's building, although it is now in the extension to the Student Union building, originally upstairs in St Paul's. And it was, it had recently moved over to being typeset inside the building, so it was being typeset on old IBM Golfball – *brand new* at the time – IBM golfball machine and was pasted up by us, designed and pasted up by us and then taken through, physically taken through to the

printer in Stirling I think. So we all, it was absolutely a great education for, well for me certainly going into newspapers. I'm sure it was great for other people in the professions they went into, and wonderful access to things in terms of being able to – particularly things like being able to see a lot of concerts or see reviewed books or albums or –. It was a good broadening experience and also a lot of skills, a lot of skills to be learned: . . . writing, type-setting, paste-up, you know general newspaper skills, editing, editing other people's work.

Together with *The Mask* magazine, student journalism at the *Telegraph* was an important feature of student life.

Though the stay-at-home student population made up more than two-thirds of the total, undergraduate life was daring, adventurous and upbeat. Drink and drugs were as available in the city as anywhere, though many interviewees took the opportunity, without prompting, to put the record straight – as with Bill Speirs again: 'One thing I can say that I share with Bill Clinton is that I never inhaled; and, I mean in terms of the drug culture, I mean it's the kind of thing people would say, but it's actually true in my case.' However, it is important to observe that, as with Bill, there was little moralising amongst our interviewees: 'I'm not making a great moral song and dance about it,' he said emphatically, and others tended to make the same point. The other thing conventionally deemed to be on the student's mind is sex. Bill Speirs explains, as delicately as he can, the meaning of Strathclyde self-confidence in the face of the absurdities of student life at Glasgow University some two miles to the west. At this neighbouring institution, there were, for most of the twentieth century two Students' Unions – one for male students and one for women students, the latter known as the Queen Margaret Union (or the QM for short):

I mean, the only time that Glasgow would come up was arranging to get to the QM Union, you know, because at that time it was men and women-only unions, so all the Glasgow University men were excluding themselves from the Glasgow University women, so we took great delight in going along to the QM Union. But it would never have crossed our mind to feel in any way inferior to Glasgow. It was only *later* when people would ask these questions that I went 'What?', 'Why?', you know, there was a real self-confident buzz about the place.

So even in this department of life, the Strathclyder – well, at least the male Strathclyder – could feel with confidence he was scoring one over Glasgow.

GRADUATION

Diana Henderson recalls: 'My graduation from Strathclyde was a great event in a hired hall [the City Hall] somewhere in the city. I even bought my hood and gown and I was so proud of it! It was wonderful how the staff of the law department all came and wished us well and joined in the celebration.' The new students of the 1960s and early 1970s were the architects of our modern world, whether in the sciences and engineering, or in the humanities and social sciences. And Strathclyde students were undoubtedly workers. As Barbara Graham puts it, 'I suppose the starting point here is that the students who come to Strathclyde, both then and now, have not really ever been people who can afford not to get a job when they finish . . . So people, and this is still borne out in surveys today which some market researchers have done, that there is a very high intent to get employment.' The way in which their training at Strathclyde led on to careers has, however, changed enormously. Karen Morrison, secretary in the Chemical Engineering and related departments since 1963, signals the way in which the destiny of a student used to be linked much more closely to the precise skills and discipline of his or her degree, but how the call of employers and the economy came to be for diversity and flexibility. Students in the 1960s and 1970s went into traditional areas for chemical engineers, she recalls, and worked in local industries, notably ICI at Ardeer and BP and Shell:

> Petro-chemicals, oil and gas, these kind of areas. I think from the '70s, maybe late '70s onwards, they started to diversify a little bit, went into areas like banking and stuff like that and finance . . . But there's quite a lot of diversity now in employment opportunity. I think that's because the society as a whole doesn't want a specific degree in a specific area. They're looking for the best in whatever, to come and apply their overall skills. And we can kind of sell chemical engineering on the basis that it's a broad degree, that you're not limited to just such an area of employment, that you can diversity all over the place. Others find chemicals and stuff and pharmaceuticals.

The 1960s and 1970s were the highpoint of what used to be called 'the milk round', in which employers came to seek the best graduates for their companies. Barbara Graham had a special role to play in co-ordinating with the employers, and catering for their needs. Employer liaison was so different then, primarily as she recalls: 'because *hundreds* of employers came to recruit on the University campus, not a thing that happens now because you have applications on the net and employers using recruitment agencies.' The advent of web-based application has completely undermined the tradition

Figure 5.7 Metallurgy student, 1968
Courtesy of The Herald.

of the employers' fair. In some ways it was a chaotic venture. Barbara recalls:
'We had *so many employers* coming, that we couldn't *find enough rooms* for
them (*laughing*). We never turned them away, we always found something.
And obviously we still have good links with employers but it was just
different then, you know.' On the other hand, there were benefits:

> It all seemed so much simpler in those days because you would . . . put
> out notices and you would book the biggest hall you could get and you
> would once or twice run sessions on applications and once or twice run
> sessions on interviews. And some how or another large numbers of
> people came (*laughs*) I don't know whether they didn't have so many dis-
> tractions, ehm? But we often say things seemed to be so much simpler.

The demands upon graduates are immeasurably greater now. For one thing,
as Barbara puts it, 'The employers didn't have such expectations as they
have now.' Students in the early 1970s made a lot more applications than
now, but then the time for applications for most students is less. The

179

process of job application has become more time-consuming through new types of tests and elongated processes. Students now, Barbara notes of the early twenty-first century, have part-time weekday jobs in a way that was very uncommon thirty years ago, and a student has very much less time in which to make a wide number of applications for first jobs.

CONCLUSION

The new students of the 1960s and early 1970s were coming with new hopes and new aspirations. Various social and technological changes were well underway, and the baby-boom generation of the post-war world was grasping the rising opportunities with both hands. They came, many of them, from families with little or no tradition of higher education and, whether as school-leavers or as the growing band of return-to-study mature students, they were seeking education in a break-out from family and community tradition. In many towns and villages of the Glasgow conurbation, in the adjacent counties of Lanarkshire, Renfrewshire and Dunbartonshire, there was barely any acknowledged tradition in the early 1960s of being a university student. So the young and the not-so-young, the unemployed and rising numbers of single parents and divorcees, were coming to the new University in central Glasgow, with its good rail links and unstuffy aura, to make revolution. The thing is, there were very many different revolutions in the making.

NOTES

1. B. Pullan with M. Abendstern, *A History of the University of Manchester 1951–73* (Manchester, Manchester University Press, 2000), p. 166.
2. *The Times*, 11 February 1969.
3. Ibid.
4. Testimony of Noel Branton.
5. Testimony of Ann Mair.
6. Testimony of John Webster.
7. Testimony of Dr Robin Alpine.
8. Testimony of Professor Hamish Fraser.
9. Testimony of Dr Robin Alpine.
10. *The Times*, 11 February 1969.
11. Testimony of Ronnie Scott, interviewed 24 April 2003.
12. The Blue Trains were class 303 and 311 two-unit, central-corridor EMU trains built in Linwood. The service included the introduction of electronically-read, multiple-journey tickets, that constituted better value than the season-ticket system for groups like many students who did not travel every day. (Information from www.scottish-railway.co.uk, accessed 1 January 2004.)

13. Train-commuting Glasgow University students had to take additional transport to the main campus, using underground or buses, thus extending the commuting time from (say) Greenock from fifty minutes to Strathclyde to as much as ninety minutes to Gilmorehill.
14. M. Moss, J. F. Munro and R. H. Trainor, *University, City and State: The University of Glasgow since 1870* (Edinburgh, Edinburgh University Press, 2000), p. 283.
15. Testimony of Dr John Sanderson, interviewed 2 September 2003.
16. Written testimony of Dr Diana Henderson.

CHAPTER SIX

The 1960s Revolution

The decade of the 1960s is now widely regarded as a great fissure in the history of the west. The Second World War propelled the Western world temporarily along old grooves for a decade and a half. But the trembling of a new type of social change was being felt in the late 1950s, and by 1963 a cultural revolution had exploded in Britain as it did in Western Europe, Australasia and North America. A new spirit was in the air. The new University of Strathclyde was not immune.

EXCITEMENT

For many who came to Strathclyde in the 1960s, this was a glorious time to be alive. They were already infused with a new optimism, and a new sense of mission, even before they set foot in the portals. Tom Devine recalls his Lanarkshire upbringing as a 'fantastic time'. He goes on: 'Motherwell was a great, at that time it was a tremendous place, firstly for demographic reasons. No doubt the post-1945 baby boom, obviously of which I was part, and of course the '50s was just the break point before the *absolutely golden age* of the 1960s. So I mean I've only got very, very good memories of my childhood.' The opening of the University and the wider availability of maintenance grants did not mean that access was made easy. There was still a high academic hurdle, and many students felt really proud to have managed to gain entry. The new blood attracted to the staff created a growth mentality, with new departments being created. One lecturer in a science department recalls: 'There were lots of new departments and a great deal of optimism about how things should go, but certainly, . . . the chief thing was expansion and really some quite bright things . . . I think there was a general sort of optimism and it was a matter of sort of working together and helping to get things co-ordinated.'[1]

New courses with state-of-the-art teaching ideas and novel methods of delivery were developed – not least, as we shall see, in the area of computing and related technology. It is worth recalling that in the 1960s there really were two extremes of university expansion – brand-new universities on new (usually green-field) sites, and older institutions dating from the late medieval period or Victorian era. The green-field institutions started with clean

Figure 6.1 Grants demonstration, 1975
Strathclyde students march through central Glasgow as part of the NUS Week of Action on grants. *Strathclyde Telegraph*, 6 March 1975. *Strathclyde University Archives.*

slates and attracted vigorous and fearless staff, and some were hell-bent on educational revolution. At the University of East Anglia outside Norwich, the Vice-Chancellor urged his first graduates at the 1966 Congregation to embark on 'subversive activities', and the students and staff went on from 1967 to commence anti-Vietnam war protests, including one directed at their own Chancellor, Princess Margaret.[2] The older institutions faced real struggle for innovation. At Manchester, the loss in 1965 and 1966 of so many middle-ranking academic staff – the high flyers of the next generation – removed what social historian Michael Rose described as the mediators, or the footballing mid-field. In his discipline, he stated that the consequence was the appointment of gap-filler staff rather than the path-breaking new-agenda lecturers who were becoming prevalent elsewhere.[3] At Glasgow University, its own in-house historians note that the 1960s was a decade of remorseless battle between reformers and conservatives. It was, they say, 'an institution resistant to change with an outmoded curriculum still controlled by the cumbersome mechanism of consultation between the other institutions under the terms of the 1889 Act.' They continue: 'The

183

Senate remained deeply divided between the younger progressive professors and those against further expansion and the degree-awarding powers of the Royal College of Science and Technology.'[4] In this way, university expansion was very far from an unchallengeable consensus in the higher-education sector in the 1960s. For all sorts of reasons, anything smacking of change was vulnerable to the very powerful forces of reaction.

Strathclyde was an institution located between, not at the extremes of, these educational paradigms. Though mature in age and experience, it was still new in its governing structures and the development of new subjects, disciplines and faculties (or schools, as they then were). Starting really in 1962, the Glasgow Colleges were competing with other new universities for new staff – especially in the arts and social sciences. Students felt the excitement, and were embroiled in it. Diana Henderson was enrolled in 1966 for the B.A. Arts degree, studying British legal systems and four other subjects, but at the end of Campbell Burns' law lecture towards the close of third term she was among a small number of students taken aside and told that a Law Department was being formed and that they were invited to be the first students to study for a full law degree. 'Well, there is nothing like being flattered is there!' she writes. 'To be treated as an individual, to be plucked out of the herd and to be asked by someone we respected was a big step for young person in the '60s and I was delighted to accept.' Not just subjects but the campus itself exuded a sense of excitement in the 1960s and early 1970s. Ann Mair recalls that the campus cafeterias were meeting places that attracted staff and students late into the evening. Many staff were snatched, like Ann Mair herself, from industry to university. The research culture of a university was infectious, and was the place to be in 1970. Indeed, this may have been another form of 'brain-drain' – from industry to university – that along with the drain of skilled professionals to the United States and Australia, so affected the British economy at the time.[5] More predictably, staff were being attracted from existing universities, which were then suffering very considerable problems. One institution that experienced a potentially catastrophic outflow of experienced staff was the University of Manchester – this evident in December 1959 in twice the usual number of applications for promotion, and even more evident in the crisis session of 1965–6 when 250 staff resigned, equivalent to 29 per cent of the University's full-time academic staff of 870.[6] The University of East Anglia acquired many of its staff from nearby Cambridge in the 1960s.[7] Glasgow University had the highest losses north of the border, a turnover of 12 per cent of its academic staff in the late 1960s, many to what its historians described as 'the more progressive Scottish universities'.[8] Strathclyde took many from its nearest rival, but staff came from all over Britain to a university where teaching seemed to be not just a peripheral but a central activity. Some came further, as with Donald Fraser[9] from New Zealand, who joined the English Studies Department in 1971 and participated with Hugo Gifford and others in the development of the Strathclyde Drama Group and the University Drama Centre. A full artistic, music, literary and theatre community became one feature of the emerging full-scale university.

TEACHING

The 1960s did not merely bring new groups of students with new aspirations. It also introduced new lecturers to Strathclyde. They came for new subjects, of course, as the range of degree courses widened. But there was also a new breed of lecturer, staff with a strong commitment to changing society through education. For them, the university was not just a social service – it was the base for the fundamental re-ordering of British society.

One such was Hamish Fraser. A graduate of Aberdeen University, and still awaiting his examination for his doctorate under the legendary Asa (later Lord) Briggs at the University of Sussex, Hamish arrived at Strathclyde in the autumn of 1967. He recalled:

> I think we would use the idea of the missionary as much as anything. We felt we had this particular role to appeal to new groups of students, and of course the whole institution had a long tradition of mature students and at that time a lot of these people, and it increased in the '70s, were people coming from the shipyards who had been active in trade unions. The trade unions were actually giving them money to go and get degrees so we had a lot of very bright, very able people who were self taught and it made for lively tutorials. Tutorials where you sweated that really you knew less than some of the students.

This power of the tutorial to make you sweat was the stimulus for Bill Speirs, later of the STUC. He recalls his classes in arts and social studies:

> The other thing I *really remember* was that the lectures were all right depending on the lecturer. *Tutorials were brilliant.* It was just great, you know, having somebody that knew what they were about as your tutor, encourage you in a discussion and having people who were –. Though you hadn't maybe seen them before but were doing the same course and getting engaged in debate. And also that particular set of classes that I engaged in meant that I was, one day you were, or even in the same day, you would be going to a tutorial talking about . . . administration and

organisation, and then a couple of hours later you'd be along talking about the works of Aristophanes in the English class, and then you'd be off getting a discussion about just how exactly does policy get derived by political parties. The breadth of it was *great* for keeping your mind engaged.

The auto-didact socialist and trades unionist enrolled at Strathclyde, and continued to enrol, for several decades. Into the 1980s and 1990s, the prolonged collapse of Scottish heavy industry, and the trade cycles in all forms of engineering and the North Sea Oil industry, threw many into the search for higher education. The new economic order of Thatcher's Britain did much to promote the entry of mature students to higher education – including trades union organisers and shop stewards who lost positions through blacklisting. And many other mature students came also, and in the tutorial-based subjects they engaged with the new, young, wet-behind-the-ears lecturers. The learned, the thwarted, the angry, and the ambitious made their way in large numbers to university, and Strathclyde, as the working man's university, attracted well above its share. Hamish Fraser recalls these students with awe and with pride:

> I'm convinced, I don't think I'm remembering wrongly, that they spoke a great deal more than we had as undergraduates, and certainly one or two of the mature students often tended to quote rather outdated books. I can remember somebody who ended up as a professor at Heriot-Watt, indeed he may still be there, citing Thorold Rogers [a nineteenth-century historian]. Now I had never looked at Thorold Rogers, but he, with great confidence, cited this as a source to support some argument he was putting forward.

Education became a two-way street for young staff, with many mature students up to twice their age – worldly-wise, well-versed in literature, history and Marxist theory – holding court in tutorials with ferocious debate. Professor Richard Rose came from the University of Manchester, where he himself was considered one of the 'bright young men of the Government Department',[10] and he remembers how the mature students of Strathclyde formed a contrast to the much younger students at English universities:

> Let me give you a factual impression. The students I taught at the University of Manchester were very good students, they typically had done very well, they were well taught, good students, top of the sixth form from Lancashire, Yorkshire, grammar schools. Manchester was the

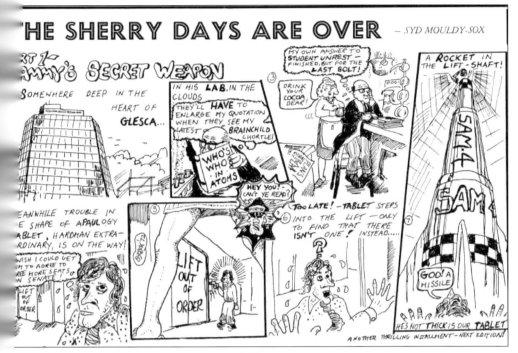

Figure 6.2 Student protest cartoon, 1972
The irreverence displayed here in crude but lurid graphics encapsulates the erosion of deference towards authority and the changed student culture of the 1970s. It depicts a confrontational relationship between the Principal and students, including over the campaign for increased student representation on Senate. *Strathclyde Telegraph*, 27 January 1972. *Strathclyde University Archives.*

capital of the north, it was a great university. It was their land in the slightly ambiguous sense of land, they felt at home there and they were very good and they had almost all had come straight from school. The students in Strathclyde, they belonged here, they didn't have a sense of inferiority about not being in St Andrew's or some important place like that with the English all around them. They felt very much at home, it was noticeable, there were more of them who were twenty-five and upwards.

One element of the teaching regime for arts and social studies lecturers was the provision of classes to engineers and scientists. This provision of complementary classes was seen to be an essential element in the broad education provided by a Scottish university degree, though many of the students concerned seem to have regarded it as a bit of a burden or a diversion.

Hamish Fraser recalled: 'I did it with a sense of mission, we also gave history to the engineers. We gave lectures to the engineers. I suspect it was maybe my third lecture was to 100, 150 engineers and that was an *utterly terrifying experience.*' In the late 1960s and early 1970s, there was a terrifying camaraderie amongst science and engineering students when they faced the young, bearded arts lecturer. This was fair game. One day, recalls Hamish Fraser:

> I came into McCance [Lecture Theatre] One, faced this large group and, I forget what I was lecturing on, and launched in, when all the lights went out. I had no idea how to work the lighting system and never been in the room before and checked it out and of course there were great cheers and hurrahs and in these days they flew paper aeroplanes and stamped their feet. I mean it's quiet [now], quiet compared to then. Eventually they got the lights on again and then I started again and lo and behold the lights went out again. They had clearly tampered with the system in some way and eventually one of them came, I was going for the porter to see if he could fix the lights, but eventually one of them came out and fixed the lights for me and the lights came on and I launched into the lecture.

History classes for engineers were, as Hamish Fraser put it, 'clearly a game – this was just an extra class, and this is how they reacted. After grief, one struggled through, confidence came.'

Grief, struggle, confidence. In those days there was not a great deal of staff training. Robin Alpine of Economics recalls his first days in 1963–4:

> I don't think there was very much emphasis in those days on training of university staff – I mean the way you talk. We didn't have any sort of training of what you have now in relation to lecturing. You know you were just thrown in and you got on with it (*laughs*). In at the deep end! The reason I stayed actually. My first job I had at Glasgow – actually I was a research assistant so I wasn't in a teaching department... And I hadn't thought of teaching at all.

But halfway through his first year at Glasgow University, he was asked to fill in for a more senior academic, and ended up with flattering comments from his students:

> What I found from feedback that I was getting was 'Look we understand it far better from you than we do from this guy'. And I thought well this

guy is right and also very good, but you know he was obviously at a level way above these other students. And I found I was getting on well with them, and I actually quite enjoyed putting things over. So that is where I sort of started, because I found it was actually quite an enjoyable sort of job to do.

In a sense, students took more interest in teaching quality in those days than did university management. And the staff of those early years caused tremendous excitement amongst the undergraduates. There were lecturers and professors who held their students enthralled in content and presentation. Roger Sandilands, a member of the first Arts School class of 1963–4, recalls Professor Edgar Lythe of the History Department. A specialist in Scottish economic and social history, Lythe acquired almost legendary status for his lectures, routinely getting standing ovations according to two interviewees. He commanded great respect, as Sandilands recalls:

Edgar Lythe? Oh he used to come in usually smoking a fag, he had no notes, he would just start talking, slowly, deliberately, very very clearly and just made the subject come alive. He was *superb.* I think he was probably the best lecturer as such I've ever heard. He was really, really riveting, he held our attention talking about economic history of course.

Diana Henderson remembers the applause and 'sitting in awe and admiration' at Lythe's lectures. Good lecturing was important to Noel Cochrane, a mature student in the late 1960s:

I just took notes (*noises to intimate scribbling quickly*). I was that sort of very conscientious about notes and I just accepted it as it was. I wasn't particularly critical of standards. You could tell, you could tell who was good or you could tell who's memorable because of their enthusiasm, Dougie Gifford was, you know, he jumped, you know he was *head and shoulders* in terms of other people because he had a, he just came at the thing with enthusiasm which bubbled over and I think that communicated to people and they got that.

Ronnie Scott, a student in the mid-1970s, also recalled Douglas Gifford: 'He's just a great speaker, somebody who really wants to make you rush out and read all the books that he's just mentioned.' Teachers at Strathclyde came with new ideas about the skills and the vision that needed to be imparted to students. Lecturers did here in the 1960s what other places were slower to do. Political science was a traditional book-based subject in most institutions on both sides of the Atlantic, but staff at Strathclyde had other notions. Speaking of statistical techniques, Richard Rose felt that students 'should know what the basic things were. The start was you should know how to collect data systematically. Well, you wouldn't think *that* hard in biology, you'd have frogs where in the Politics Department you have a survey.' And so at Strathclyde, political science students learned quantitative methods and conceptualisation of political-science problems:

> There was a course on how to collect data and they organised a survey, and we published a couple of them. I mean these were serious exercises, and I also got students out of the university into places like Castlemilk [a large so-called peripheral Glasgow housing scheme] where they wouldn't necessarily think of going unless some of them were born there.

The late 1960s and the very early 1970s witnessed the first major computer revolution for the University. It was in these years that computing became increasingly important for students, and the teaching content and the means of delivery of instruction were modernising very fast. This was an experimental time, when it was not always clear what would be the best method to deliver new skills. Indeed, change was so rapid that it was not entirely clear from one session to the next what precise skills were there *to be* learned. The revolution was initially amongst the postgraduate students. Ann Mair recalls that her appointment in 1970 in the Department of Politics, attached to Professor Richard Rose, was specifically to release lecturers from instructing students in computing skills. She recalls that 'they wanted someone as the buffer who would pick up the questions'. Those were the days of the new computer languages and punch cards:

> Now the students would be all postgraduate or staff. There were no undergraduates, well practically no undergraduates around at that time. The year after, a 'Computer Appreciation' undergraduate class was started with Keith Wilson Davis lecturing and me doing practical Fortran (a computer language) and SPSS (Statistical Package for Social Sciences) term about.

But in other ways, the 1960s had more in common with 1900 than 2000. For one thing, students wrote their work by hand. Karen Morrison recalls how student work 'would be hand-written; occasionally somebody would have a typewriter, but it would be hand-written, whereas now it's mostly by computer because most of them have got computers or laptops.'

In one particular respect the Scottish tradition of breadth in education was maintained. The Strathclyde Arts and Social Studies degree was deliberately given a unique five-subject first year, unparalleled in British, let alone Scottish, education. Bill Speirs, later to become general secretary of the Scottish Trades Union Congress, was attracted to it for this reason. Arriving in 1970, he studied English, economics, economic history, administration and politics, 'because I just liked the look of the degree . . . and the fact that you had such a *broad choice*.' Meanwhile, in the sciences and engineering similar pressures were occurring. One former professor of engineering recalls the change to the engineering student's curriculum:

It is very, very difficult. The width of knowledge is increasing all the time and you want to put more and more into the course, so gradually the amounts of physics and chemistry – not so much the case with mathematics, but the physics and chemistry has gradually disappeared in the sense that it's being done in the engineering departments but it's no longer called physics and chemistry. It's more appropriate to engineering and the chemists wouldn't recognise it as chemistry anymore, you know, so there's been more and more engineering crammed into the course I guess, and that started certainly in the mid-'60s . . .[11]

Yet, emeritus professor John Webster also recalls the pressure in midcentury to broaden the curriculum for engineering students. The creation of the Arts Faculty, he remembers, fitted precisely the trends in engineering education of the time:

There had been, a move, a detectable groundswell from the '50s, to the effect that the teaching of engineering was too restricted to technological subjects. They always had things like workshop organisation and management but they didn't have to look at the wider context, or engineering in the wider context of the nation. And this became known as 'the engineer in society' . . . a move to introduce courses in all engineering establishments which covered, extended to the engineer in society. Now, before 1964 when the Royal College was *still* the Royal College, there had been a number of members of staff in . . . – I think it was Organisation of Management, something like that – and they were actually located off-campus out at Chesters at Bearsden. And they had recruited a variety of people and one of them, who just died recently, was Professor . . . R K Shaw. So there was a nucleus of these people who were *in* the Royal College but in the sort of Management College section of it. And at that stage that Management College activity was supported largely by industry, it was not undergraduate students, people who come in from industry for a week's or a fortnight's course or something like that and in addition these members of staff would offer courses to undergraduates and we could involve an undergraduate element or a course in their discipline in the undergraduate courses. So of course when it came to 1964 they had right at hand a completely new liberal studies faculty. And there was no problem at all.

Meanwhile, staff in the Geography Department had the joys of the undergraduate *field-trip* to organise. Even with the relatively small numbers of the 1960s and early 1970s, this could be a chaotic and despairing job – and not just because of the problems that the students themselves posed. The 1960s was an era of intense government restriction over its citizens in ways that we would now think unimaginable. One was currency exchange control that limited the amount of money that a Briton could remove from the country (for a long time the figure stood at £50). Changing money and acquiring travellers' cheques had to be undertaken in advance of travel, and the sums recorded in the passport. Tony Martin, a specialist on Denmark, recalls the nightmare of trying to organise a field-trip during the sterling devaluation crisis of 1968 (when the fixed exchange rate was altered because of the country's poor trading position):

> I took a party to Denmark for a fortnight. And obviously all passports had to be collected in and we had to take them down to the bank to get the foreign-currency requirements written into the back of the passports. And obviously after we'd costed the field trip and got it all booked up, of course Harold Wilson decided to devalue the pound and that sort of put a spoke in our wheels because there were certain restrictions, even more restrictions.

One of the new features of many degree courses at Strathclyde was the dissertation, usually part of the Honours year. Few traditional universities had dissertations at that time, and even as late as the late 1990s it was absent from many subjects at the Scottish 'Ancients'. The dissertation brought a depth of focus to student study, honed research skills, and made students self-taught in a way that few conventional degree programmes did. Bill Speirs recalls his own undergraduate specialism: *Icelandic Foreign Policy 1945–70*. He says that it:

> Might sound terribly tedious, but Icelandic foreign policy was absolutely crucial at that time because they were sitting *right in the middle* of the strategic sea lanes between the Soviet Union and the United States and

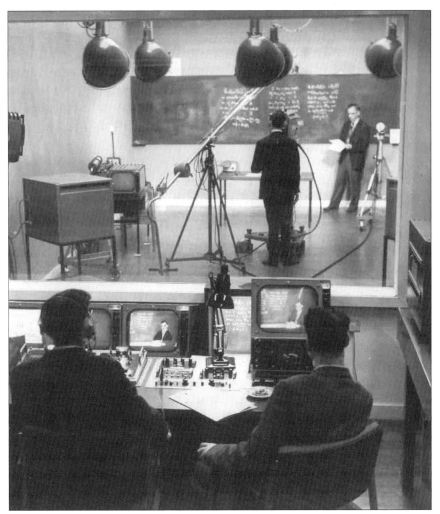

Figure 6.3 Strathclyde University Television Studio, 1964
The studio was used for the live transmission of lectures and, from 1965, for broadcasting the UK's first student-run television show (called Unit 65). *Courtesy of* The Herald.

there was all the battles that were always there about the US base at Keflavik, about the rights of Soviet shipping and submarines, where they could move, where they couldn't.

This work greatly empowered him:

But the thing was, at the end of it, I was able to say on both of those, 'I did that', 'I did that', you know, and it's not just 'This is what somebody said, this is what somebody else said' – 'This is original research I've done'. And the University was *great* in backing that up, just in making the facilities available and, maybe it was chance at the time I was there but the lecturers, the people who were involved, were *dead supportive*. So I mean, no, if you ask me negative thoughts about Strathclyde, maybe the food in the refectory wasn't that great but, no, it's all positive stuff. It's all positive.

Starting to come in too by 1970 were the first elements of the credit system, the semester system and the half-year class – what would now be called a module class. From the late 1960s Stirling University pioneered the semester system in the UK, but some subjects had such curriculum demands that they had to experiment with these systems. In geography in the early 1970s, as Tony Martin recalls:

We had *joint options* which I suppose . . . mirrored the breakdown later on in the University into semesters where a lot of departments in fact had to split a course into two. But in those early days in geography, historical and urban geography, economic and political geography were courses, so that the Geography Department in fact pioneered the idea of half options quite early on in the '70s to give students a better choice. And it was strange that later on when the semester system came in and the credit system came in, that all departments more or less had to go down to the half-option system.

Most of all, the 1960s offered small-class teaching. The first LLB class had nine students, including one future Member of the Scottish Parliament, and Diana Henderson describes it as 'like having private tuition really with tiny classes, individual attention and always open doors to go and talk over things that you did not understand.'

RESEARCH

Strathclyde developed a singular emphasis on applied work in much of its research. In sciences, engineering, law and social studies, there was a common goal of applicability to wider society whether at home or abroad. Lord Todd of Trumpington, the University's first Chancellor, set the tone. When asked about his first major success, the synthesis of Vitamin B1, he told a reporter in 1969: 'Did I tackle this just as a matter of chemical curiosity? Not on your life. I also had a picture in my mind of children dying of beriberi.'[12] Glasgow, as a city of social problems galore, was a magnet for

194

staff with research commitment in their own disciplines to social justice and equality. It was this applicability that attracted so many staff to the city.

The University opened its doors close to the time of the great internationalisation of academic life. Academics travelled further – not just for jobs, but also for research and for conference exchange. Various trends came together. First, international airflight became commonplace around 1970, and especially across the Atlantic. However, even in the early 1970s, American students characteristically made their way to British universities travelling 'steerage' on the QEII. Second, the growth of international organisations at governmental level called upon academics, in technical subjects especially, to become part of an international network of practical academics. And third, the collapse of European empires opened opportunities for staff to assist universities in the developing world. One former student who studied at both the Technical College and the University recalled:

> We always had an eye on the international scene. I mean the man who took over from Bobby Kenedi was a fellow called Jim Harvey, Professor Harvey, he was head of mechanics and materials until '81 from I think about '68. Jim had been educated in Stanford; he had studied here actually but had gone to Stanford. So he came with a view of the American scene you know and a number of our staff were also involved in Europe through the European Coal and Steel Community, so people were involved in that fairly early on. Once I got involved with my Ph.D. work, (I'm struggling to remember when I finished that, probably '71–2 I think, finished my Ph.D.) I was approached by the Atomic Energy people who were interested in the work and I very rapidly got involved with the Japanese, the Americans and the French which continued for quite a long time. So we had quite a kind of international flavour to that . . .[13]

Professor John MacLaren, of Mechanical Engineering, trained at the Tech College before becoming a member of staff, recalled the opening of new conference destinations – in his case, Franco's Spain that was still regarded in the 1960s as a nation with an undemocratic regime:

> In 1966 there was an international conference of the oldest technical institution in the world, which is very strange – it's the International Institute of Refrigeration. They held an international conference in Madrid, which was a very illustrious affair because the Spanish government was tickled pink that an international body of that standing, in conjunction with American . . . ASHRE . . . American Society of Heating and Refrigerating Engineers, joined with the International Institute of

195

Refrigeration to mount this conference in Madrid in the 1960s. It was a very posh affair. It really was great, because the government, the Spanish government, as I say was tickled pink with us going there . . .

International conferences were important venues for learning academic convention, and, in Professor MacLaren's case, for affecting research careers. He recalls:

The Spanish government really welcomed [us], and laid out the red carpet. Now the proceedings of that conference – I had my first worthwhile paper using computers to do this mathematical modelling of refrigerant compressors, but there were three of them, three papers. There was one from Delft University and one from Purdue University in . . . Indiana. The professor at Purdue University wasn't as raw and green as I was. He button-holed me and asked – the times were limited for these papers to be presented, [and he] talked me into presenting the three papers *together*. So I presented these first three papers on the computer analysis of refrigerant compressors and continued with that line of work from then on.

In some subjects, of course, international travel was the basis of research – as with Professor Gustav Jahoda in Psychology whose anthropological-based work took him all over Africa, to what became Ghana, Nigeria, Malawi, Zimbabwe and Zambia, and later to post-apartheid South Africa.

The city of Glasgow was itself a great focus for research in so many ways. As a city with a history and sociology of unparalleled industrial poverty, urban squalor, labour protest, urban pollution, social problems and work-induced medical problems, staff were attracted by the environs. Glasgow represented an important conjunction of research agenda and personal experience for staff arriving between 1960 and 1975. Roger Sandilands said: 'I felt for someone who's interested in doing economics it seemed a living laboratory of economics in action in terms at least of the kinds of *real problems* that economists should be interested in; unemployment, inequality, poverty, poor housing, social problems in general.' John Davies in Psychology found in the city and its conurbation the social materials for innovative study of addiction – whether to alcohol, drugs or tobacco. 'I began to see addiction in a totally different light as basically a social phenomenon rather than a medical phenomenon, and that was from working in places like . . . Blackhill and Easterhouse and parts of Castlemilk and so on.' In the new LLB class of the late 1960s, the students were invited by their lecturers to attend sheriff and high-court cases to hear some of the celebrated trials during those days of Glasgow gangland killings, providing what Diana Henderson describes as 'all a revelation'. When Professor Peter Robson joined the Law School in December 1969, he became involved in provision of 'store-front law' in the inner east end, at Dennistoun, and got some of his interested students involved too in what is now the East End Advice Centre. Robson started with a welfare component – variously called 'clinical law' and 'experiential law' – in his property course for students and then taught a welfare course on its own. As he describes it, law for the poor around 1970 was constricted by the professional fees and city-centre locations of legal offices:

> I can remember we would charge, we would charge a scale of fees depending on the cost of the property and if you bought a property for, say in those days, £5,000, which was *a lot of money* in the early '70s, I mean you'd have a very nice property for £5,000 in either Glasgow or Edinburgh, you'd be paying several hundred pounds in conveyancing fees, I mean a big wadge of money, and that was something which some people in the profession realised was not going to last and they proved to be prescient (*laughs*) because you can get your conveyancing done cheaper now than you could thirty years ago even though the house prices are now *stunning*.

Robson recalls that whilst some in the profession were reluctant, teachers such as himself 'saw some of the large number of people who were excluded from law, excluded from access to law, as a potential market'. Until the 1970s, the traditional location for lawyers was in the city centre; there was an expectation that clients went to the lawyer. Part of the revolution of which he was an element was the reversal of this:

> I can remember students doing research projects in the early days of welfare in the early '70s *mapping* where lawyers were and they were clearly not in the [housing] schemes. Lawyers have since moved out and even in the area like Dennistoun where I have been working, which is fairly close to the city centre, that used to have one law firm, and now within a half mile radius you now have seven or eight law firms in that area and the same thing has happened in some of the outlying schemes. And as I say some of them have also got some of the benefit of some of the developments from the early ideas, [mainly the] law centres. Again [they were] seen to be the alternative to profit-orientated legal practice in the '70s and these have continued, but hitherto, until most recently they haven't [been] centrally funded.

The city of the past as much as of the present provided new research openings. In History, Glasgow and its conurbation allowed scholars in industrial archaeology like John Butt and John Hume (latterly of Historic Scotland) to develop new techniques in recording and mapping the industrial heritage; it helped John T. Ward and Hamish Fraser to explore the heritage of labour rebellion and worker militancy; and more recently, with the advent of oral history, the industrial heritage has come to feature in new ways – in the experiential study of asbestos-related disease amongst shipyard workers and others.

Students were aware of the existing and emerging status of the research undertaken at the University in the 1960s. The excitement could be palpable. Bill Speirs, present in the early 1970s, recalls:

> I can honestly say that all the time I was at Strathclyde, I found it a really self-confident place. I just didn't find that people were getting hung up about, you know, where are we in distinction to Glasgow [University]. Now, having said that, I don't know, it may just have been the department I was in. The people in the Economics, Economic History departments and Politics in particular, they were at the cutting edge academically. I mean Richard Rose was the professor, disagreed with him politically but he was right up there – I mean, he'd been an adviser to presidents, he was always on the telly, you know, talking during election campaigns. Professor Bill Millar was always on the telly as well, John Foster was there and roundabout, they were publishing stuff all the time, they had books coming out . . .

The Department of Economics and others in the University became heavily involved in development economics. Roger Sandilands recalls that after spells in Vancouver, Latin America and Glasgow, he came in 1971 to a lectureship at Strathclyde:

> One of the first people I supervised for his Ph.D., which he got before I did – this was possible in those days – was Jim Love, the now Dean. He'd been in Ethiopia and he still was at that time and he was back and forward to Glasgow and I was his supervisor. He did a very good Ph.D. on commodity concentration, big issue in those days, particularly in African countries, and I actually did my Ph.D. after I was contracted by the UN to do a comparative study of housing finance systems in Latin America. So I did this work for the United Nations and I just worked it up into a Ph.D. In those days you could get a job without a Ph.D.

Occasionally, jobs were given without adequate frankness by referees. Gustav Jahoda in Psychology recalled that 'there was one research assistant who was a very able man, but unfortunately the two referees had not mentioned that he had psychiatric problems, and he came in one day armed with an air gun, put the target at the back of his door, and started shooting (*laughs*).' Such things, he adds, 'are all in a day's work no doubt'.

One of the great revolutions was that concerning computers. John Paul recalls the computing equipment available to him for his early research in the 1950s:

> I had done my computing on the university's *only* computer, a mainframe, which had a memory which allowed me a maximum of 200 variables. So I had to write a programme because I had a lot of data coming in and the same quantity x/n, had to be one thing one moment and another thing another moment (*laughs*). It was a very compact programme, but it took in data on punch tape and printed out data in sheets of numbers tables, so it had no graphics output.

Andrew McGettrick, professor in the Department of Computer and Information Sciences, came to the University in the 1960s after a Cambridge doctorate in Mathematics and taught on the new Computing degree. He recalls that the discipline then tended to be more about the computer than about computing:

> Well, the computers in those days – you had the computer and then you had, you know, databases and spreadsheets and compilers starting to appear and so on. And the course tended to revolve around the main, well the computer itself, and also the main software components that sat on that. And that effectively dictated what the curriculum was, with – there was some underpinning theory and some sort of mathematics in there as well, some logic. It's not changed a lot since (*laughs*). Lots of computing courses are similarly based on databases and compilers and hardware and so on, you know . . . there's an awful lot of the theory is similar now to what it was then. It's probably dressed up now, in more flowery, and more attractive language and so on, but, if you look around at what theory exists now and did exist in the '70s, well there's some, but there's a lot of it was around in the '70s.

Robin Alpine recalls working in the Social and Economic Research department at Glasgow University just prior to coming to the Tech in 1962, and he describes what passed for number-crunching in those days:

So I was doing computations, and we didn't really have computers much in those days, you ground calculations out on big huge big machines which couldn't do very much apart from multiply and divide you know but that's what you had to spend a lot of time doing and it took half a day to do something you could do now on a computer in a few seconds, you now, it's amazing the difference there.

The computing revolution meant using unconventional routes to becoming front-line in skills and knowledge. The use of computers in the social sciences was still very unusual in 1970, but Professor Richard Rose and others were keen on getting the best skills in an age when neither systems for training nor, more importantly, systems for examination of those skills in computing were yet fully in place. So, this University offered the rare opportunity to undertake political research with quantitative method. Professor Rose recalls:

Strathclyde was the first university in Europe to join the Inter-University Consortium for Political Research in Michigan which is the foundation of survey research in voting behaviour. So there was a budget line and my position with the Principal, Sam Curran, was that we were a quantitative department, we weren't as expensive as Chemistry but we did need some infrastructure and I knew that if I wouldn't get it from Strathclyde I wouldn't get it *anywhere* in Britain.

Ann Mair, first computing officer in the Department of Politics, recalls being employed without having finished her degree, selected ahead of postgraduate students and other supposedly 'qualified' candidates, for her practical knowledge, her work experience at IBM and crucially her ability in writing computer languages. These were heady days at the frontier of social-science methods:

We were state of the art, we really were. We had ICL computers in the university here and we had use of an IBM computer in Edinburgh which, a van went through at night with the cards for the program and came back in the morning. This was a great innovation and you had programs within SPSS and IBM Job Control Language. And one of the reasons I was employed was that I'd been working for IBM and I knew how to write Job Control Language. Professor made a clear decision to employ me despite having no degree.

The work was surprisingly physical:

The bulk of my work was for Professor Rose, and you would have a job sheet which was ignored rather than used; you would have a lot of pink memos. The stationery was *bright pink* and Professor Rose would type his own memos *furiously* with numbering points and you worked your way through doing point one, then point two, then point three, and some of the work was done simply on punch cards, it could be counter-sorted and we would use the little Olivetti Programma 101 computer, with its method of doing the Chi Square, if we needed to do the statistical underpinning having done the crosstab with the cards.

Professor McGettrick recalls the same physical element, of being something like a juggler:

In the early '70s, I mean a lot of it was to do with running programmes and punched cards, and the punched cards falling down and spilling all over the place, and submitting them, and finding you'd missed out a semi-colon, and taking three days to find that out.

The computers themselves were also much more physically-sensitive artefacts than they are today. John Webster, emeritus professor in design, manufacture and engineering management, describes how in the 1960s his department's huge single computer depended on the nursing abilities of its technician.

It was second-hand from Colville and it was housed in what had been a lecture room in the second floor of the Royal College and it was a notoriously-haphazard process to get it to work because it was a massive, it occupied all of this room. And it required very careful temperature control because otherwise it didn't work . . . Dr MacLean was one of the early mechanical engineers to take a detailed interest in computing. And MacLean would go up there on a Monday morning after a weekend to try and get something out of this computer and he would come back down after a while shaking his head and his explanation was 'The computer's got the cold this morning' (*laughs*) and this was simply the fact it was such a chancy beast, it had to be maintained very carefully at a level temperature. It had to have air locks on the door to make sure. Now, that was the first computer and it occupied all of this big classroom.

Despite their temperamental qualities, the computers of the 1960s and early 1970s placed a power in the hands of the very young researcher – the power of the technological frontier. 'I was getting the computers I wanted,' Ann Mair remembers. 'It was like being given a Ferrari or something. You

201

know, somebody would have a Jaguar or a Ferrari and other people would have a Mini, well I had the Jaguar.'

The pace of introducing computers varied according to discipline. John Paul feels that the Mechanical Engineering Department may not have been as quick as it could have been:

> Moving into the Weir building we started to get into more modern technology at the computer age. And I think maybe the department was *a little slow* in getting into the computer age because we had such a good base in calculators and, *hand calculators*, and again it was money, because a computer for each department was a big investment and it was long before the age of the desktop, and even when the desktops came out, they were a real investment. You would be able to get them for £1,000 now and they're much better and quicker, yes.

In architecture and building science, computers started to revolutionise the field at the same time as the University acquired the staff to rapidly expand the discipline. Tom Markus brought together the research funding and ideas, and Thomas Maver[14] arrived in 1967 to start the development of computer-based techniques for predicting the performance of buildings before they were erected. He recalls:

> I'd been working with computers in my previous job, very early days of computers with punch cards and rolls of punch paper tape. It was really *incredibly* primitive, and no computer graphics or anything like that. But I'd got interested in modelling the *performance* of buildings using computers while it was still on the drawing board. And in fact when the three-year project – this group was called the Building Performance Research Unit – when three-year funding for that project finished I set up the group that I've directed ever since which is called ABACUS, which stands for Architecture and Building Aids Computer Unit Strathclyde.

The revolution that the computers were bringing was not merely speeding up processes but creating ones that had never been envisaged before. The University was at the forefront of this expansion of conceptual limits. Maver again:

> I mean buildings are hugely different in that they are very large capital items and you don't repeat them. They are specific to the client and to the site and so on. So really what the idea was that you were really trying to prototype it electronically. You were prototyping a *model* of it rather than the object itself and that was quite a paradigm shift.

It was not just computers but wide swathes of technology and knowledge that changed from the 1960s onwards. In modern languages, the early use of language laboratories was extremely useful in testing students, but has since been superseded by the more useful video labs.[15] One student at the Tech in the early 1950s noted how his subject, pharmacology, had been essentially unchanged in knowledge or technology for the whole of the first fifty or sixty years of the century, then changed very dramatically:

A   So other than the antibiotics, pharmacy and medicine hadn't changed a great deal in the first half of the twentieth century... We now know but we didn't know then. Basically, the pharmacy course that I did in the 1950s was the same that my father had done in the 1920s, whereas when my son followed me into pharmacy in 1982, came here in 1982, there were three generations of us did pharmacy here. When my son came here in 1982 things had changed quite dramatically.

Q   Did you recognise much of what he was being taught?

A   Not really. We were working hands on. We were preparing our own infusions and extracts; emulsions, ointments, tinctures, we were working with the products that medicine had been using for 200 or more years.

Q   You were still pestle and mortar?

A   Mortar and pestle and doctors' prescriptions were written in Latin and we used an apothecary system of weights and measures where we talked about grains and scruples and drams and ounces... and gradually that system of weights and measures was superseded by the metric system.[16]

The change in pharmacy is emphasised by Brian Furman, lecturer in the School of Pharmacy since 1969. Over the last three decades, the subject has sustained its science-based element, but with increasing focus on the professionalisation of its practitioners – dealing with patients, legal aspects, and everything connected with medicines. As Dr Furman puts it:

The pharmacist is the custodian of the nation's medicines and therefore *has* to know *every aspect* of medicine but also, about the medicines, but also has to be able to deal with people and give appropriate advice on the correct use of medicines. And the emphasis on that has increased over the years since the 1960s when I did the course to now, when the course is now a highly professional course but still with a scientific element...

Indeed many of the interviewees give a strong sense that when their learning

203

started in the 1940s, 1950s and even in the early 1960s, little had changed in their field of study in fundamental terms for generations, and they felt they were 'plugging in' to a long-established subject, family tradition and city economy. Though this may not apply across the board, it is the interviewees arriving at the University in the 1960s and early 1970s who give the sense of very radical change to learning systems, the knowledge base and the technologies of their chosen disciplines. 'Even up until 1971,' James Laurie (a pharmacology student) remarks, things 'hadn't changed *all that much* although changes had taken place during the '60s and '70s.' But new disciplines brought the unknown to the campus. Professor Gustav Jahoda recalls the confusion of existing staff over psychology, psychotherapy and psychiatry, and the problems that some research techniques might bring to the institution:

> It was a psychiatrist who introduced Somato-typing, who tried to relate the *body* type and *body* shape to the type of mental illness which people are liable to. One of my newer colleagues had the idea that it would be nice to do some Somato-typing and for that you need to undress and take photographs in profile, front and back. He thought he would get some volunteers from among the students. So fortunately I got wind of that and I *slapped it down* because, as you can imagine they had preconceptions about psychologists. If they had been told he was photographing the students naked, that would have *just been the end*.

For secretarial staff, the changes of the 1960s seemed so distant now, but at the time they augured new methods of operation (and also to some extent new methods of teaching). Karen Morrison recalls:

> When I first started we had manual typewriters and we had the Roneo for stencils and we had a Banda machine which was an absolute pain, if you were a bit of a junkie on fluids and stuff you could have got high on the stuff. You had to put on the Banda machine which worked as a bit of a hit-and-a-miss sometimes, and then the electric typewriters came in and then of course IBM developed the golf ball which was terrific because you could change the heads. In engineering we do a lot of typing of symbols and formulae of course, so to be able to actually change a head and put the proper formula in was a revelation. So yes, those changes were enormous really.

Such changes were welcomed almost universally for the greater ease and speed of operation, as well as flexibility of procedures. Karen recalls:

going from a really thumping typewriter that you really had to bash like billy-o to something that had a very light touch that you could change the font to suit yourself. I mean that was night and day. And I can remember getting my electric typewriter and it came with almost bugles and fanfares. It came from IBM and it was what they called proportional spacing which obviously, depending on the size of the letter, it gave whatever the space was appropriate. And it came *packed, oh beautifully packed*, you'd have thought it was TNT or something and we weren't allowed to unpack, an operative from IBM had to come along and unpack it and commission it. Where nowadays you 'wheech' your computer out of a cardboard box and throw the packaging away and set it up yourself.

In the libraries of the University in the mid-1960s, new technologies were developed with great speed – notably microfilm and micro-forms – but space remained the biggest problem. Malcolm Allan recalls:

The Andersonian [Library] itself had this sort of central hall – the central well – which is rather like down below in the McCance now – a banking hall, it looks like – but that was the reading room area, but it meant it had no expansion because it had the car park below and it had faculty offices and the roof garden above and so to expand the library in the McCance was virtually *impossible*, but they managed it in several ways . . . And then they built on the Collins Gallery next door with the suite above it which was, at that time, it was a short-loan reading room to take that out of the library – . . . it was the early '70s – and they put a bridge across from McCance into that.

One of the areas where the universities pioneered new technology in the mid-1960s was the Television Unit. Strathclyde was one of the first to have the facility. Mathematics first-year lectures were recorded, but with no editing facilities, meaning that it had to be done in one take. One member of staff recalls this as creating 'a lot of tension'. There was:

Pressure on the staff to get it right and also to the academics who were presenting the lecture and you literally, it was still chalk and board. Even though we were doing it on television they were still using chalk and board and *if you dropped the chalk* we used to have to crawl about the floor, pick it up and hand it to them out of shot because otherwise you were going to have to start at the beginning again.[17]

The lectures for maths were broadcast at different times of day for many years as a way to alleviate pressure on student timetables. Eventually, after some five years or so, it became a film unit, operating for both Strathclyde and Glasgow Universities. The unit had directors, cameramen and floor managers as well as administrative support, and staff with the unit often got the chance to swap from one function to another. Some of the assignments were ground-breaking – such as filming an all-day open-heart operation, where the film crew were told that if they did faint, they were not to fall on the patient. At the Maternity Hospital, the film crew captured all sorts of operations on camera – 'natural childbirths and caesarean and breech births and, oh you name it, we did it.' From sewers to the Glasgow Underground, the Unit filmed the lot: 'if it moved, we filmed it'. From there, many staff moved on to television companies, the unit having provided one of the few sources of training for many who went to Scottish, Border or other TV companies.

The new university world of the 1960s and early 1970s was hard won by individuals fighting for new technologies, thinking out of the box about new applications, and creating what in effect became today's specialist disciplines. With the largest engineering school in a British university, even before the chartering of the University, staff and students were coming from long distances (including in some volume from Scandinavia) to join this prestigious sector of the University. With the National Engineering Laboratory at East Kilbride, the institution had a resource and staff quality that were the envy of the British sector.[18] This created a new liveliness and challenging atmosphere. Debate was endemic in the University. 'There was certainly a lot of debate and discussion about the way things should go,' reports Thomas Maver from Architecture:

> And what with the degrees of academic freedom and so on. And one of the agents of change I *suppose* was the amount of dosh that was available. I mean the resources were really, looking back on it, quite lavish in comparison to what we're doing today and there was far better staff/student ratio and new monies – you could bid for them and if you were to propose something sensible *they came*. It's much, much tougher now.

Lest anyone imagine that the new was in all ways an unalloyed good thing during the white heat of the 1960s technological revolution, Tony Martin from the Geography Department recalls some of the downside:

> Photocopying facilities weren't as good because it was *wet photocopying* in those days, produced a terrible smell. Your maps were produced on a

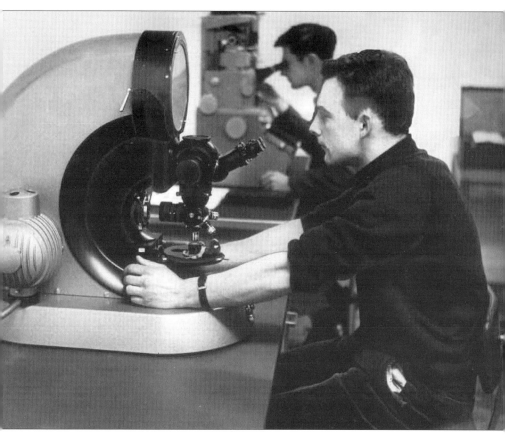

Figure 6.4 The technological university, 1968
Two students in the photomicrography laboratory of the Metallurgy Department. *Courtesy of* The Herald.

dye-line machine which give these terrible ammonia smells. You used tracing paper as a negative basically and you could churn them off on ordinary paper. Even, obviously geography was lucky, we had our own photographer to make slides for teaching purposes. But the other thing that stood out was we had calculators, and these things were about eighteen inches by about two feet and all they could do was the four major things in arithmetic. And they used to vibrate, and you'd feel the whole room vibrating when the students were using them . . .

Forty years later, a tiny £6.99 pocket calculator from Woolworth's will perform multiple-variable linear-regression analysis. But perhaps nothing signals the simplicity of technological advance over four decades than the advance from the blue typescript of the Banda copying system to the photocopying system.

STUDENT (AND STAFF) RADICALISM

The late 1960s and early 1970s witnessed students challenge university and state government across Europe and North America. New radicals like Daniel Cohn-Bendit came together with older ones like Jean-Paul Sartre to proclaim students not as in class struggle, but as a new permanent state of being.[19] Student revolt came to be on the minds of very many people – from those who saw it as political uprising to those who medicalised it as a condition.[20] There was genuine fear of overthrow of governments, as very nearly happened to the French President Charles de Gaulle in Paris in May 1968. Students at Hornsea Art College, the LSE and Essex University seemed to be leading the revolt in Britain. The rebellious student seemed to be everywhere in the Western world.

Meanwhile at the University of Strathclyde, things seemed a little quieter. Under the old Royal Technical College rules, students had felt banned from formal party-political activity in the buildings, and there was little that could be party-politics in the official student elections at either College. But Labour Party activist David Paterson recalls at the College of Commerce:

> I think student politics became politicised maybe after I was around. At that time it was, one did not stand on a Labour Party label or a Conservative Party label, I don't remember anyone doing that. Commercial College at that time was a pretty small electorate and it didn't really split on party lines. I think it was just a case of personalities and the number of people you knew and what you stood for in terms of how the university, the College Union would be run, you know, would we have the dances on a Friday or a Saturday night? You know that kind of pretty apolitical kind of issue. So there really wasn't much political division I recollect. I may be wrong, maybe I didn't see it but I didn't get the impression. I mean I never stood on the Labour Party ticket or a Socialist ticket or anything like that.

Yet, he recalls that the interest in and awareness of politics was genuinely greater then than it seems today. There was, he recalls, a great deal of political debate, especially once the University was founded in 1964:

> We had, all the political parties had political clubs in the University and they could attract big audiences to debates and so forth. I was active for

example in the Glasgow Fabian Society, and David Donald and I resurrected that, made it into a really major political forum in Glasgow with members of parliament and cabinet ministers and so forth coming up here regularly. And I think today politics probably for a lot of young people is a terrific turn-off . . .

The way in which political consciousness and discourse entered the student body before 1968 seems to have been rather different to what it was to become after that time. David Paterson again:

Although I said there wasn't any politics in student elections, and that's true, I think there was an awareness of the political issues of the day and you have to bear in mind that this is the time when the Cold War was, you know, and there were supporters of the alternative economics based on the Soviet model. And there were those of us who were much less certain about the Western capitalist system and so there was a clear divide, an ideological divide, and people could debate and maybe that's what's gone today, I don't know.

In some ways, the way in which politics operated until the later 1960s was – or perhaps had to be – subversive. Take music. One student recalls how amongst the Tech students:

There were some real west-of-Scotland characters, you know, folk singers, they would bring their guitars and I would pick up all of the Fenian songs that, well, *I didn't realise the significance of at the time* (*laughs*), but they were sung unless we were in company where we were told to hush because it was too provocative and, yes, there were lots of characters amongst the students and amongst the people in the city itself.[21]

British student radicalism was highly localised. One thinks of the LSE, Essex, and Warwick perhaps, and we may recall the Edinburgh University of Jonathan Wills and Gordon Brown in the 1970s. But everything was not as it seemed. John Gennard,[22] professor of human resource management, was a research assistant at the LSE from August 1967, and he points out that after the brief closure 'it became a place in which very little happened actually'. He says that the 'LSE reverted to what it always was':

I mean people always think the LSE was, if you like, a den of left-wing radical thinking, *it certainly wasn't* . . . The biggest student society in the

LSE was the Conservative Society, the Conservative political party society. So the LSE was a very exciting place to be, as a young lad it was great, I got great help from very eminent people but it was not, it was not the radical political hotbed (*laughs*) that people thought it was.

On the other side of the coin, some universities were so traditional that, as John Davies of Psychology remarks of his arts and divinity-based *alma mater*, the University of Durham, 'it was *dead easy* to be radical, you know'. He goes on: 'If you wore a donkey jacket and bovver boots you were a Marxist, and you were surrounded with people with blazers and boaters and punting up and down and boat clubs and things, and it was *very easy in the '60s*, you know, it was *dead easy* to be a revolutionary at Durham.' At the older Scottish universities, the system of student-elected rectors created a ready focus for protest over the role and rules of university governance. Yet, St Andrews University was regarded by most student radicals as tame in the late 1960s and early 1970s, dominated instead by the new 'far right' that was to come to influence under the Thatcher governments of 1979–90. When in 1973 the Labour student group at St Andrews organised a march on the administration block to demand to see secretly-held 'political' files on students, only one student turned up (and he was shown his rather innocuous file).[23] The new universities, by contrast, especially those that were arts and social-science dominated, acquired reputations for more apparently violent protest (for instance, the protests against the Queen at Stirling, and against Princess Margaret at UEA).[24]

By contrast, the science and engineering bias of Strathclyde has largely helped, in hindsight, to mask any reputation for student rebellion. Engineering students were generally considered less interested in political affairs in the 1960s, and seemed far less prone to student activism.[25] Moreover, by 1975 Strathclyde and Heriot-Watt universities were praised for having student associations that 'served as examples for the public sector in Scotland' (where representative councils held students rather at arm's length), and better too than English universities (where separate student unions operated with little clout within university governance).[26]

Yet, Strathclyde was not all quiet. Asked about student activism at Strathclyde in 1968, Robin Alpine in Economics replied:

There was a little yes. I don't think it was very obvious here. There was, I think – students did occupy a room or two for a while and so I think there was a, but it wasn't a large-scale thing. You know it was very much – you knew there were some mutterings and so on. And sociology became very important. You know, in '68 that kind of opened people's

Figure 6.5 The Students' Union, 1973
Many of the amenities provided by the Union are illustrated here in this drawing in the student magazine *Crust*. Note the blatantly sexist representation of female students. *Strathclyde University Archives.*

eyes. I remember I was an assistant advisor of studies, and sociology became so important that it was such a small department, they had to put a ceiling on the number of people they could take. And unless people had sociology down as one of their main subjects of their admissions form, you know application form, they weren't allowed to choose sociology. So I do remember that. It made a difference from that point of view. Certain subjects became the fashion to study, yes. So earlier than '68, numbers taking sociology were very small but it just suddenly went through the roof. I think they had a ceiling of about 100 students. That was about as much as they could cope with as a department, you know.

In a sense, sociology was *the* academic subject that defined the 1960s revolution in British higher education, the subject that gave both power and caricature to student revolt and teacher innovation. Ronnie Scott recalled what attracted him as a student to the subject at Strathclyde:

I found it a fascinating way, kind of pull, or a way of looking at things. I also find it and something I have reflected on quite a lot over the years, I also found it very de-stabilising, in that it – maybe this is the opposite of... other people having these kinds of *world views* of systems they carried around with them, that they had access to, that sociology, *for me*, kind of pulled the carpet from under me in a number of ways and it suggested that, eh? that there were a number of ways you could look at anything and all of them equally valid... And I found that personally quite unsettling that there was, I suppose, that at that point in your life you're trying to work out what your views are and things and trying to say 'Right I think I've got that pinned down, okay, that's what I think about that. Now what am I going to do about this bit?' And then sociology had the habit of kind of lifting the lid on these things you thought were, you thought you had or you thought you knew you had the answer, or you thought you knew what you were doing. So, personally an unsettling subject... because it, it suggests that there's more than one point of view and more than one valid point of view.

During the era of revolt in British university life in the late 1960s and early 1970s, the University Principal, Samuel Curran, possibly mindful of the student troubles at some universities with technological reputations,[27] reportedly observed on the apparent passivity of the Strathclyde students. Professor Richard Rose recalls:

On 1968 Sam Curran said to me 'Things seem pretty quiet here'. 'You'd have to hand it to the person who works up the engineers', he said with all the precision of a physicist. To my knowledge there were never any sit-ins in the McCance Building, but there were students who were willing to jump up and down. We had one student... who was arrested in class. Special Branch came in and lifted him.

Stewart McIntosh came as a mature student from a steel works in Rutherglen to study the B.A. Arts degree, graduating in English. Strathclyde provided the radical atmosphere in the early 1970s for his maturing political career:

I got then involved in student politics and in *Telegraph*, the student newspaper and in the SRC and I just enjoyed all that. I liked the idea, it was like a small version of how the nation's run, a lot of little sub-committees and there must be a big boring bit in me that likes the idea of sub-committees. I hate committees now, but it was a way of practising for adulthood in a way and I was very successful at it and became

Figure 6.6 Glasgow Charities' Week, 1968
What were you doing in 1968, Daddy? The flour-throwing battle between Strathclyde and Glasgow University students in John Street in February of 1968 resulted in six Strathclyde students being arrested and charged with disorderly behaviour after twenty-eight policemen were called to the scene. *Strathclyde Telegraph*, 13 February 1968. *Strathclyde University Archives.*

President of the Student Union, Students Association, which gave me a year off to run that. And I then went back, that was at the end of my third year, so I went back to do my Honours a year late as it were, and then I was very involved in the National Union of Students and I was [Scottish] Chairman of that for two full years afterwards.

The early 1970s witnessed construction of the core agenda for both student and political radicalism in Britain for the following three decades. Stewart McIntosh again:

All the time grants, grants was the really big thing, and a series of campaigns for equal rights for women, for gays, for people of ethnic minorities. We were very strongly anti-fascist, anti-Nazi, pro-good race relations, and very pro-equal rights for women. So those were big side issues, big grants were at the heart of it and that's what drove the whole thing.

Bill Speirs, also a student in the early 1970s and later STUC General Secretary, remembers how radical activity was fostered by students from Labour backgrounds:

It was all based around the Students' Association and what happened within in it and it tended to be – well, it related to, structurally it related to the elections for the Council, for the Student Representative Council and for the office-bearing posts as well as it being –. I mean, I went there in 1970. It also related [to] just all the campaigns and events that were taking place – the Vietnam War, the, it was Ted Heath's government and grants were, it was the time of 'Maggie Thatcher, Milk Snatcher' and 'Higher Grants, Lower Rents, No More Cuts at Our Expense' and so there was the campaigning stuff as well as, you know *broad campaigning* stuff, as well as the internal student politics. But when I went there the president was Dougie Henderson, now past Defence Minister, who I came across later on when [we] were both on the Scottish Executive of the Labour Party or the Executive of the Scottish Labour Party. He was succeeded by Stewart McIntosh who was my predecessor as Assistant Secretary at the STUC, stays down the road, now a journalist. So, I mean who was the president, vice-president, that sort of a thing had an impact on politics and they were all politically identified, I mean it tended to be people who were politically identified standing against those who were saying, you know, we are just going to look after the interests of 'the students' and it tended, at that time, to be the politically identified ones who got elected, but then there was just all campaigns.

Figure 6.7 Stewart McIntosh, Strathclyde Union President, 1973–4
Stewart was heavily involved in the grants campaign. He encouraged fellow
students to look beyond the University to support other trades-union campaigns (such as the miners), and to develop links with, and help, the more
deprived community that existed beyond the ivory tower. *Strathclyde University
Archives.*

The Students' Union was used in support of some of the big industrial disputes of the day. McIntosh recalls during the miners' strike of the early 1970s that:

> We would raise money for the miners and put up, literally, organise camp beds in the Students' Union for miners who were travelling from one part of the country to the other for their demonstrations, and we'd put them up, feed them, that kind of thing, offer hospitality. There was a very strong network of all these *kind of things* and it wasn't even thought of as anything special, it was automatic. If somebody asked and you had the resources, you just said 'Yes'.

So, if Edinburgh University had Gordon Brown, Strathclyde had a series of individuals who were to become important in Labour movement politics and trade-union activity. This continued into the mid-1970s. Ronnie Scott, a student in the Arts Faculty at Strathclyde, became heavily involved in student journalism and politics:

> I was in [the Student Representative] Council from my first year, which is not, I don't think is that common, because I had those kind of networks, because people were saying within a week or so saying 'Well you need to get yourself in council' or 'We want you to be in council, so here's how you do it' or 'We'll make you some posters; here's who you go and speak to; here's how you do it'.

The Broad Left, an anti-Trotskyist group, was composed mainly of the Labour Party and the Communist Party. There were major and very divisive political issues splitting the fabric of the student body-politic, notably the Palestinian-Israeli issue that was dividing the left in more complex ways than today. Yet, whilst student politics for some activists 'was a pillar of their lives, it was integral to their lives', for Ronnie Scott it was somewhat less: 'it wasn't quite a recreation activity, more than that, it was I suppose a moral and ethical element to it as well. But it was nothing like as ingrained in me, as it was in them'.

Strathclyde was regarded by some as the premier radical student institution of its day, certainly in Glasgow. Bill Speirs makes the obvious comparison:

> Things were happening and Strathclyde was there at the cutting edge of the National Union of Students and Glasgow [University] wasn't in NUS. Right throughout the period I was at Strathclyde, in terms of

Figure 6.8 Students' Union entrance, 1975
Students' Union diaries are shown on entry to the Union. The modern student
dress has been born. Our interviewee Ronnie Scott is raising his diary aloft.
Courtesy of Ronnie Scott.

where universities and institutions stood in relation to each other,
increasingly it was 'Where did they stand?' and 'What was their political
balance?' within the National Union of Students, and Glasgow was just
marginalised. Glasgow actually *was* marginal. They just didn't feature at

all. You know, if there was an Anti-Apartheid march through Glasgow it had been done through NUS and there would be Paisley 'Tech' would be there and Cardonald College and Strathclyde or whatever, Glasgow didn't have a banner (*laughs*), so in that sense, they just didn't really feature much at all.

The overthrow of the elected left-wing government of the Marxist President Salvador Allende in Chile in 1973, American withdrawal from Vietnam, the Watergate scandal, the Upper Clyde Shipbuilders dispute and work-in, and the miners' strikes of 1972 and 1974 – there were issues galore to confront the left-wing students of the time. Some lecturers played significant roles in various capacities in relation to these campaigning issues. But for the majority of students, the issues were, as Speirs puts it, 'small "p" political issues – grants, housing, you know, rents, first flats and the grants'.

So, Strathclyde was perhaps not the quiet backwater of radicalism that might be assumed. Certainly, the Union building was off-putting to some students – in part because it seemed dirty and untidy, in part because it did not serve good food, but in part because 'there were lots of very hairy and very left-wing students hanging about' who made some members feel uncomfortable.[28] Many noted Marxists of the 1960s and early 1970s passed through its portals – some to academic eminence elsewhere, including staff (like John Foster, who moved from the Politics Department to what is now Paisley University) and students (like Willie Thompson who became a professor of history at, successively, Glasgow Caledonian and Northumbria universities). In all sorts of ways, the atmosphere of the 1950s Tech and College of Commerce passed into a different era as new blood arrived. Yet, Strathclyde never experienced the large-scale, long-term sit-ins and protests of other universities that broke taboos, traditions of the curriculum, methods of government, and some vice-chancellors too (with some retiring early, it is said, after failing to curb student-led change).[29] Strathclyde University clearly represented a different collision of forces, in which the real target of protest was less internal to the institution than in the powers that ranged against the city's workers and industries, and their worsening position, and the rise of social problems that staff and students hoped to arrest. Certainly, the oral testimony in the present project conveys a powerful sense that the radical mission at Strathclyde was less to reform the University than to reform society. But maybe there was another factor. Professor Roy Campbell, doyen of Scottish history and lecturer at successively Glasgow, UEA and Stirling universities, told Norwich magistrates in 1970 that 'so many of the protesters come from middle-class homes where they have been pampered'.[30] Perhaps Strathclyders were just that bit less pampered.

Figure 6.9 Women students' float, Charities' Day 1965
Strathclyde University Archives.

THE UNIVERSITY COMMUNITY

A learning and researching institution has to be something more than the sum of its parts. A university needs to create an atmosphere that facilitates accessibility, social mobility, and a sense of achievement. Drilled and disciplined learning may be one part of the process, and it may have been a rather more significant element of university education in Britain in the middle of the twentieth century than now. But there was something else, something that administrative, security and support staff especially, contributed to the environment for both academic staff and students. Karen Morrison, secretary in Engineering, recalled:

We've always had contact with the students. This is very random I know, but we've always had contact with the students right from the word 'go', probably closer now but it's always been there. Even when the sixth floor was totally staff-orientated, the students would come to an inquiry window and ask, and it was only good interaction with departments. You didn't say 'I only work for so and so'. There was good interaction, you would muck [in]. We used to have a tea lady there, who came round there who came round with her trolley and gave us tea in the morning and the afternoon – halcyon (*laughs*).

The tea trolley was an icon of British life. Revered in films and television plays, in the middle of the twentieth century there was a rite of passage associated with the anticipation of the arrival, and then the service, of both beverage and biscuits from this mobile mini-canteen. It was something greater than its parts. In itself, the tea and biscuit may not have constituted that much in dietary terms, but the arrival of the tea trolley was a punctuation of the day, an occasion for democratic chatter, and unpretentious sport in an otherwise hierarchical day. It marked what others have noted about Strathclyde – its undermining of pretension and pomposity. Barbara Graham came to Strathclyde as a careers advisor in 1974 after working at two of the ancient universities of Scotland. Strathclyde struck her 'as being *so laid back* by comparison with the formality' she had encountered elsewhere. 'As I look back on it now,' she went on, 'I think it wasn't that people were laid back, they certainly weren't unprofessional, but they were very approachable and relatively informal by comparison of what I had experienced elsewhere.'

The University community has always had a major impact in the city. The cleaning staff alone constitute a significant employment opportunity, traditionally filled by women. Usually starting very early in the morning, cleaning offices, corridors and teaching rooms before most students and staff are even at their breakfast tables, the cleaners create the first bustle of the university day. They were drawn from a big geographical area, but a strong tradition developed for them to come from the east end of the city. Nan Stevenson,[31] one of the University's first cleaners, recalled:

From all over Glasgow, *all over Glasgow*, aye, yes. The majority of them years ago always used to always come from Easterhouse, we had a big, big crowd of cleaners that used to always come from Easterhouse, and actually they worked in the years they either left for ill health or they're all mostly away now but they were from all over Glasgow.

The university revolution brought more women onto campus, especially as younger research and academic support staff. This caused a certain degree of division in the female workforce. Most of the female employees in white-collar work were secretarial staff, and many of them had entered the university several decades before. This divided many of them from the new, bright, highly-educated and adventurous staff of the research teams. Ann Mair recalls how departmental secretaries in the Arts School '*had a lot of power*', and they let younger women staff know it: 'Because they, *well they said themselves*. Some of them, a lot older than I was remember, I was twenty-one, I was young, these women were twenty-thirty years older than me which meant that instead of being born in '50 which I was, they would have been born in the '20s and '30s and then into jobs.' Karen Morrison recalls the same power of the departmental secretary in Engineering in the 1960s:

> The head of department then . . . was Adam Thompson, he had a dedicated secretary if you like, and she was very much on a pedestal and she was – there was a kind of hierarchy. I suppose there's still a little bit of a hierarchy, but not in the same terms and things, I think, were probably a lot more *rigid* perhaps then?

But this was something you just accepted:

> I mean you're a child of your time, and any education and training you have relates to the society you are in at the time I think, so if we were taught secretarial stuff we were taught – 'You address letters so, you set them out so, the punctuation is so, and you close so,' – and various office procedures. And I suppose there was a kind of us-and-them where you felt that the academic staff were perhaps a little bit above you. Although you weren't daunted by it you kind of accepted their position.

As many historians have pointed out, many of the women born in the inter-war period had attained significant school-leaving qualifications. But sustained problems kept them out of higher education: insufficient family support, the Second World War, and the pressure to give up war-time positions to men on their return. This meant a generation of women for whom, as it has been widely said, 'liberation was deferred', and many of them remained in secretarial positions.[32] Ann Mair provides direct evidence of this:

> The secretaries at that point were often women who would have done very well at university but weren't given the chance. Remember they were

never allowed to stay on at school, but they would work their way up through the grades to become professor's secretary, *and it was a proper grade system*. And the professors left a lot of power in their hands.

The university was dominated by male lecturing staff, and a generation of women who had 'deferred' their liberation (often to their daughters) still tried every avenue to exert some influence over the gender issue. The University Women's Club was one such institution. Ann Mair joined it, along with a lecturer from the Economics Department. She recalls:

That was set up in the early days of the university by professors' wives who were worried about the *very, very few* women lecturers who were around. And the professors' wives were educated women themselves, some of them worked in, you know, very good jobs but again, they would get married and they wouldn't stay necessarily in their jobs and that, and that had day trips out and places to go and visit.

The Club suffered, she felt, from the mistaken motives and outlook of the wives: '*I enjoyed it*, but it was increasingly being ignored and derided by the lecturing females who said it was a wives' club.' At the same time a Women's Group was set up in the 1970s, with a more explicitly-feminist outlook, and in time it formed the intellectual nucleus of what became Women's Studies teaching.

Many of the staff of the new university were young. Yet, some of the traditions of the old Tech were quite congenial to them, and are fondly remembered, as with Robin Alpine and his wife:

Apart from going to the Uni to play badminton and my wife did as well, you know there was a badminton club at Strathclyde in the early days, you actually had to roll down a mat in the assembly hall and roll it away again at the end. But so we met some people. And the other thing was, I think it was the case then certainly, because there were only a small number of departments initially. You didn't really think you were just people in one department; there was much more intermixing amongst departments . . . People went for lunch in those days . . . You didn't just have it at your desk or in a departmental room . . . In fact it was the foot of the Royal College initially – there was a big dining room, a lot of tables and people had a sort of set lunch . . . You went to where there was a spare seat and you chatted with other people. They were sort of tables for four, and so you were talking with people who were [from] any other department at all in the University ... You got to know someone by face

Figure 6.10 Women's liberation?
A student breaks the mould in 1968, participating in the traditionally male-only beer-drinking contest in Charities' Week held in what was known as the 'men's beer bar' in the Students' Union. *Strathclyde University Archives.*

even if you didn't know his name, you knew the faces of a lot more people round the university. Even without being high up and being on important committees, even as a junior you met far more people just because of the environment of that time. And that was good. I think it helped you to feel you were part of an institution.

The scale of the institution assisted this sense of belonging. Most departments were compact, even in well-established disciplines. Dr Brian Furman recalls of Pharmacy:

The department was great, it was a small department, by modern standards, and it was a very friendly department, the atmosphere in the department *was good*. We had a head of department, Bill Bowman, who was a very sociable sort of guy, he didn't have any of the trappings of the traditional university head of, professorial head of department in those days. Everybody was on first name terms, it was a very good department, the atmosphere was very good.

Many interviewees recall the significance of food and food outlets to the good humour of the place. All remember the very fine canteens for staff and student in the bowels of the Royal College Building in the mid-1960s, and regret its passing. Even the new buildings had their culinary moments. Barbara Graham of the Careers Advisory Service recalls: 'The staff club of the entire university was one floor above us, we were at that time on the first floor of Livingstone Tower and there was a canteen and a staff club on level two, and people went there for scones and coffee in their morning tea break. It was delightful.' Good food in congenial surroundings seems to have lifted the spirits tremendously.

The campus became a hotbed of trials and experiments in the 1960s and early 1970s. One was the campus television show, as recalled by a staff member of the unit: 'The Students' Union or the Students' Association had a very popular Friday lunchtime show where the students actually operated all the equipment and they used to invite . . . people like Ken Dodd and speakers and things like that and it was very popular and that used to get relayed live to the Students' Union.'[33]

Politics infused more of academic and non-academic life in the University's early years than perhaps was to be the case by the end of the century. The institution was no single-party campus. In the History Department, for instance, there were left-wing and right-wing lecturers. John Ward, professor of Modern History, was a well-known Tory figure in trades-union circles. Left-winger Hamish Fraser recalls:

Labour and industrial relations were still extremely popular and there was a lot going on, trade unions were at the centre of almost anything, so it was exciting ... The unions themselves were very conscious of their history. I mean a lot of histories [were] coming out, and we had a regular stream of visitors. John Ward had good contacts with certain trade unions, particularly the General and Municipal Workers Union which tended to be kind of right-wing in its politics anyway. We had Scottish officials who would come and give talks to the students, and we certainly tried to take on doing things on the history of trade unionism and we also did comparative labour history as well. We did try to take it right up to the present, so clearly it's *seen* as being relevant to the developments that were going on at that time and John Ward was very active in the body called the Conservative Trade Unions Association, so it wasn't just seen as Labour. One was aware that there were other elements within trade unionism.

The early 1970s witnessed the consolidation of major social change in Britain, especially in relation to anti-essentialism: the equality of all persons irrespective of race, gender, religion, sexuality (and later dis/ability). It was a period when traditional radicalism was re-radicalised, when the socialist or communist was challenged by the feminist, anti-apartheid and gay-rights movements. Bill Speirs was one who faced a paradigmatic shift in his own radicalism, recalling how for himself and for many other Lowland Scots the first essentialism to be faced was that of religion. Sectarian attitudes, songs and hurt veined through the everyday life of children as well as adults in his home town of Renfrew, as in most of west-central Scotland. But he recalled how they were strangely dissipated, seemingly without thinking, at University:

So we got to Strathclyde, I was not aware of there being any sectarian differences. I don't know quite why it should have been like that but people who were pals, there's a pal X, Catholic, never crossed my mind particularly why he was a Catholic or not and *I don't quite know why*, it was just never much of an issue there. What sticks in my mind more of my early years there, was when I was getting more involved in the Labour Club and the Socialist Society and so on, was that we were being asked to take up this issue of homosexual rights as it was then termed, Gay rights hadn't come into it, homosexual rights. And at first myself, you know, and a number of others were 'What?', 'We're supposed to argue for poofs?', 'What's this, what's this all about?', and that was much different, but Catholic/Protestant? No. I couldn't possibly give an explanation as to 'why?'. For me it might have been different from other people but it just didn't, it didn't sink in.

If religious bigotry was dissipated greatly by higher-education expansion of the 1960s, and racism was exposed to reconsideration in our society in large measure through the anti-apartheid movement of the early 1970s, gay rights were perhaps the hardest for many people to absorb. Bill Speirs recalls that the question was 'What's it got to do with politics?' It was the hardest of all the essentialisms intellectually as well as in terms of personal sexual identities, for many people to accept. 'But,' he goes on, 'because it came up and because it was *so sharp*, it meant that the people who were advocating that we should be taking up the issue of gay rights or equality for homosexuals, as it then was, had to explain "why", had to put a case for it. And we listened to the case and thought "Aye, right enough".'

The University community did not exist as an island in the middle of central Glasgow. There is a strong lay tradition stretching back centuries in Scotland of reverence for 'the College', but at the same time there has always been friction between town and gown. In the 1950s, especially for female students, there were difficulties to negotiate in Glasgow society. Elizabeth McCudden and Pat Fraser recall:

PF   The ruffians were more rough and I think people with an education are more snooty. You know both cases. It was more of a class thing.

EM Even though I came from a working-class background my mother wouldn't have been happy me going to Barrowland, it was very – . . . it would have been frowned upon going to a place like that.

PF   There was quite a lot of gang warfare, not warfare but gangs and knives even then in Glasgow and I think it was more from that point of view.

EM Keeping out of trouble . . . But you know when I went to dancing at the Locarno I never owned up to being a student . . . I always said I worked in the buses or I did something like that.

In the 1960s, students became more numerous and more visible, the new television news broadcast their antics and sit-ins, and across Britain friction grew between town and gown. Alan Riley of Estates Management recalls the reaction of local people in the streets around the campus:

Any students, they didnae like students. They didnae. I used to drink in a pub down the town called *The Ingram*, and *The Ingram* was purely a working-class man's pub, you get a few females in it but when the

Figure 6.11 Strathclyde University Labour Club, 1967
SULC declared itself 'democratic socialist' in outlook and was one of the most
active of Strathclyde's student political organisations. *Strathclyde University Archives.*

students came in they always wanted to make a racket. The guys would-
nae tolerate them, you know – sparks, plumbers and others didnae like
students.[34]

Strathclyde was pitched into a high profile in 'the Town' by its sheer
location, by being in the very heart of the city, less than a stone's throw away

from the City Chambers and George Square, the city's principal public space. That visibility grew as the campus grew, expanding out from a single building (the Royal College) to consume entire blocks of the centre (and by 2000 an entire quadrant of the city stretching almost half a mile in length). So, as Barbara Graham has said of the University when she arrived at it in 1974:

> It was still relatively new in the sense of people calling it a university. So it would have been at a time if somebody jumped in a taxi and said 'Take me to the University', they would have wound up at Glasgow. But Strathclyde is always very *visible* in the city centre and through events like the Town and Gown Seminars, through the fact that we have connections into business and industry, chambers of commerce etc. I think that where it matters the University, all the time I have been here, has had good respect within the city generally – you know, the business sector and the civic sector.

CONCLUSION

Some Strathclyde staff pursued revolutionary tendencies in sartorial ways in the 1960s. John Davies of the Psychology Department recalls: 'For the interview you'd put your suit on, and then you'd turn up to start the job and you'd look like a refugee from *The Apache* [TV series] or something.' But after getting the post of research assistant, 'I turned up wearing . . . an affectation – sort of corduroy cap and pink jeans and flowery blouses and all sorts of things.'

For many the 1960s seemed less a time of revolution in the city of Glasgow, and at Strathclyde University, than it has since appeared to many commentators elsewhere in Britain, Europe and North America. Yet, ideas were changing very rapidly – ideas about who was eligible for higher education, how learning was to be delivered, what exactly it was that constituted 'learning', and how students (and staff, for that matter) were to explore the 'new' of the world. Richard Rose recalls perambulating the world in the midst of mighty changes in 1968 and 1969. He says: 'Student troubles were a sideshow for me. I was actually in Paris the Saturday before the events of May started on a Monday, and then went on to Vienna where it didn't start until after I left. I was gassed in Chicago, and the following year I booked my hotel a month before the Bogside rising.' This is a tour from student revolt against the French state, through wider student rebellion in Europe, to the Democratic Convention Riots in Chicago, and thence to the start of 'the Troubles' in Northern Ireland in 1969. Political science involved being there as well as reading about it, and these events brought to Strathclyde, as elsewhere, a sense of the immediacy of a world changing in ways that were not entirely clear to its observers then – nor in some ways even now.

NOTES

1. Testimony of Anonymous Interviewee 5.
2. M. Sanderson, *The History of the University of East Anglia Norwich* (London, Hambledon and London, 2002), pp. 187–222 at pp. 187, 189.
3. B. Pullan with M. Abendstern, *A History of the University of Manchester 1951–73* (Manchester, Manchester University Press, 2000), p. 99.
4. M. Moss, J. F. Munro and R. H. Trainor, *University, City and State: The University of Glasgow since 1870* (Edinburgh, Edinburgh University Press, 2000), pp. 278–9.
5. This idea is not really developed in any of the literature, but may be a factor worth further research.
6. Pullan, *University of Manchester*, pp. 98–9.
7. Sanderson, *University of East Anglia*.
8. Moss et al., *University of Glasgow*, p. 288.
9. Testimony of Dr Donald Fraser, interviewed 3 and 6 June 2003.
10. Pullan, *University of Manchester*, p. 155.
11. Testimony of Anonymous Interviewee 2.
12. Quoted in *The Times*, 11 February 1969.
13. Testimony of Anonymous Interviewee 2.
14. Testimony of emeritus professor Thomas W. Maver, interviewed 16 October 2002.
15. Testimony of Barrie Walters.
16. Testimony of James Laurie.
17. Testimony of Anonymous Interviewee 1.
18. *The Times*, 11 February 1969.
19. Daniel Cohn-Bendit interviewed by Jean-Paul Sartre on 20 May 1968, in H. Bourges, *The Student Revolt: The Activists Speak* (London, Pantheon, 1968), pp. 97–107.
20. Contrast B. and L. Ehenreich, *Long March, Short Spring: The Student Uprising at Home and Abroad* (New York, Monthly Review Press, 1969), with A. D. G. Gunn, *The Privileged Adolescent: An Outline of the Physical and Mental Problems of the Student Society* (Aylsbury, Medical & Technical Publishing, 1970).
21. Testimony of Roger Sandilands.
22. Testimony of Professor John Gennard, interviewed 15 July 2003.
23. Callum Brown's recollection of student activity whilst a student there 1971–5.
24. However, Michael Sanderson notes that the issue at UEA was not so much why there was revolutionary activity by students, but rather why there was not more; Sanderson, *University of East Anglia*, p. 220.
25. This was the conclusion of surveys contrasting engineering and social studies students conducted at the University of Manchester in 1963; Pullan, *University of Manchester*, p. 157.

26. D. Jacks, *Student Politics and Higher Education* (London, Lawrence and Wishart, 1975), p. 76.

27. Pullan, *University of Manchester*, p. 159.

28. Written testimony of Diana Henderson.

29. See Pullan, *University of Manchester*, pp. 172–203.

30. R. H. Campbell, 'Address to the magistrates of Norwich on student discipline and welfare', October 1970, quoted in Sanderson, *University of East Anglia*, p. 217.

31. Testimony of Nan Stevenson, interviewed 28 November 2002.

32. P. Summerfield: *Reconstructing Women's Wartime Lives* (Manchester, Manchester University Press, 1999).

33. Testimony of Anonymous Interviewee 1.

34. Testimony of Alan Riley, interviewed 28 November 2002.

CHAPTER SEVEN

The Legacy

The legacy of the University of Strathclyde has been evident in the lives of our interviewees. The vibrancy of their memories of their years spent in learning, teaching or working at the Royal College, the College of Commerce, or at the University in the decade after its formation, is homage to the centrality of the university experience in contemporary Scotland. The experiences represented in this volume are by no means exhaustive in range, but they are certainly representative. They show how being at a university shaped our world in the late twentieth century.

GRADUATES AND CULTURE

In October 1963, the Robbins Report signalled not just the expansion of British higher education, but its democratisation. Students with entry qualifications for one institution should qualify for another, it said. Universities should become less elitist not just by being more numerous, it said, but by being more equal: 'the greater the uniformity of university, faculty and departmental entrance requirements, the wider the range of choice for schools and candidates'.[1] What was being envisaged was clearly a society more profuse with educational opportunity, graduate employment and knowledge-based economic advance. Universities seemed set for a glowing future.

Yet, the 1960s appears in many recent university histories as a period of crisis. At Manchester, Glasgow, Reading and Edinburgh universities, institutions of some pedigree and tradition, there is in the work of their historians a powerful sense of the clash of different generations of academics, and between institutions and students. There is a sense that the troubles of the decade – the political liberation of the young (including the lowering of the age of voting to eighteen years in 1968) and the rise of youth culture with all its ramifications – fomented a gigantic clash of the generations that, in the absence of any alternative, took place at the campus of the British university.[2] This is even more apparent in the history of the newer institutions such as the University of East Anglia, where there were demands for student participation in decision-making – demands that almost inevitably had to be rejected to greater or lesser extents.[3]

By comparison, those staff and students who attended the University of Strathclyde in the 1950s, 1960s and early 1970s do not confirm the dominance of this theme in their memories of their workplace and *alma mater*. One factor to account for this may be the extent to which the University was perceived by so many of those interviewed not as the problem requiring rectification, so much as the solution to the problems of society. Those who taught and studied in applied and social-science subjects like economics, law, sociology, history and politics came to use their learning as a means of better understanding, and then transforming, the society in which they lived. In engineering and architecture, there is in the testimony a sense of using skills to solve the problems of poverty and overcrowded tenement housing, and the engineering problems of both industry and society at large. And in the sciences – as with Lord Todd – we discern the drive to solve the medical and related problems of a world to which a post-imperial nation had much to be grateful for and for which it had in the 1960s still much to do.

Another factor may be that the students who came to the University of Strathclyde were more dedicated to the practical than the hypothetical, to the real rather than the abstract. Even a simple thing like studying language as a spoken and not just a reading language was not totally accepted in the academy in the 1960s. One interviewee recalls at a previous college having an external examiner who would only listen and not participate in oral language examinations, and who, in some embarrassment, met a few of the students abroad and suspiciously avoided conversing in the language in which he was the examiner.[4] The sense of mission, as Hamish Fraser of History told us, was palpable, and the mission to teach led onto a mission to change the system outside the academy, less than that within it. Radical students seem to recall less of a battle against the University than against the state that paid grants too small for home students and raised fees for overseas students, against banks that did business with apartheid South Africa, and against an American military-industrial complex that bombed the people of Vietnam.

A third factor is the sense of the University as a new home for the generations who were coming from traditions in Scotland of marginality in educational and social opportunity. Though the proportion of the working classes in British higher education was remarkably (and perhaps disappointingly) to change little over the remaining forty years of the twentieth century, the evidence of our testimony shows that the University had a special place in the hearts of those from less privileged backgrounds. This applied to those from the Lanarkshire working class and lower middle classes, from Catholics, women, mature students and industrial workers, from trades unionists and those from anywhere in Scotland who sought a university experience in which tradition and flummery counted for less than the urgency of a wider social mission and skills with which to change things. As Ronnie Simpson reported, coming from a Fife mining community, 'I think you come from a background where there is no major libraries, no major educational buildings, and to come in *to a place like this*, you know, *it's just a new experience*'.

For these kinds of reasons, the experience of education recounted to us by staff and students bears a somewhat different stamp to the histories written by the professional historian from the University minute-book. The Strathclyde student was no stranger to the issues being felt by the student at Edinburgh, Manchester, UEA – or even, dare we say it, at Glasgow. But Strathclyde provided a grounded experience for students more likely to be from the less well-connected sections of the society of the west of Scotland. With so few going to British universities in the 1950s, there were still many of the middle classes, many women, many ethnic groups (including the Irish and the Asian) and many from overseas who found in Strathclyde a comfortable and conducive academic venue.

If there was distinctiveness to the Strathclyde student culture in the third quarter of the twentieth century, this seems even more true if it is looked at in the context of youth experience and the cultural revolution of the 1963–75 period. The type of experience our respondents speak about at College and University is at variance from the experience testified to by those interviewed for projects focused on cultural revolution.[5] Firstly, the interviewees do not place the testimony of cultural revolt at the forefront of their recollections. They do not call upon awareness of sexual liberation, drug culture and so on as the primary focus of their experience of the period. Second, the content of their testimony suggests, when it touches on these matters at all, rather that the experiences were somewhere to the side of their own; these were experiences 'elsewhere' (wherever that may be), of the immediately-following generation, or they were going on around them, but that they were not of immediate and central significance to the interviewees' experience at Strathclyde. The testimony here rejoices in the richness, the diversity, the humour and fun, the pain and the sheer hard work of student experience in the mid-twentieth century. There remains a sense that the period moulded the graduate world, and that the Strathclyde experience became less regimented, less puritanical, less narrow and more gravel-like than that of student experience before.

In this sense, there is a significant change between the testimonies centred on student and staff experience in the 1940s and 1950s and those centred on the mid-1960s onwards. It was a coincidence that the first student intake in October 1963 to new degrees happened in the same month as The

Beatles' *She Loves You* was topping the charts, and that the charter raising the University occurred in August 1964. But the start of the swinging sixties in these years, and the moral, religious and demographic revolutions that emanated from that, have changed the face of Glasgow, Scotland and indeed the western world. The University nurtured that revolution – even if in its birth there was no overthrow of educational precursors, and no outlandish student rebellion and occupation of the Royal College Building or of the new administration in the McCance Building. The revolution was a much more intimate one.

THE STUDENT EXPERIENCE

It is when one moves from the generic agenda of the social and cultural historian that the oral testimony can be 'read' to bear out the notion of distinctive features of a Strathclyde experience, and a distinctive Strathclyde legacy.

One characteristic of many of the graduates of the time was the extent to which work abroad featured after graduation. Britain in 1950 still had an empire, and then there was the development work in the developing nations of the world that followed in the 1960s and 1970s. The degree of travel seemed much greater then than now. One of the causes of this was the linkages between Strathclyde and the manufacturing companies in engineering and shipbuilding especially those with international links and contracts. Glasgow was an imperial city, perhaps the exemplar of the European city founded on production for export to far-flung empire. This still survived into the 1940s and 1950s, and made for international careers for many. One of our interviewees followed a route that was familiar to many Tech students of the time:

Q Did you get a job as soon as you left?
A When I graduated? Yes I went to Singer [Clydebank], I worked for six months each summer in John Brown's [also Clydebank] as a student apprentice, we had to do that in these days, not in John Brown's particularly but you had to go either to John Brown's, Rolls Royce [Hillington] or some of these places to get practical experience. Then when I graduated the usual groups of people came around interviewing us all and I got an offer of a job in Singers and it was ten pounds a week which I thought was a lot of money in these days, I took the job in Singer.
Q And how long were you there for?
A Twenty-seven years, not in Clydebank because about a year and half

Figure 7.1 Staff and students, Geography Department, 1971
Collage of students and staff produced by one of the Geography students. Dr
Tony Martin is depicted on the extreme left, reading *The Topper*, and Professor
Mervyn Howe is in the TV. Short skirts, flared trousers and long hair on some
of the men indicate the prevailing fashion. *Courtesy of Tony Martin.*

after I joined them I was transferred to the Italian factory for graduate training and I stayed there for nearly three years. And then in
1960 I went to the United States for six months to their head office.
And then I went for a year to Turkey to Turkey's factory to get *it*
started up. We used to help starting it up. And then I went out to
Pakistan and India where I was in charge of building up a factory and
making Singer sewing machines in Pakistan.[6]

As the number of Scots going to empire lessened in the 1950s and 1960s, the empire coming to Scotland increased. Strathclyde became an important university of choice for the immigrant Asian student, arriving in the city in the 1950s and, in subsequent decades, for those born in the city. As we have seen in the testimony of Bashir Maan, the Tech College provided a venue in which the postcolonial mission to overcome the imperial legacies – the racial prejudice, discrimination and injustice of empire – could be played out slowly and calmly in higher learning and the imparting of skills.

Fewer Scots-born students now head for long careers in overseas climes, but the number of overseas students coming to the university is sustained. Certain departments have a long tradition of overseas students. Brian Furman in Pharmacy has supervised twenty-five Ph.D. students since 1969, and the majority has come from overseas – in 2003–4 he has three Nigerians and three Chinese, plus others from Iraq, Iran, and a Palestinian from Egypt. The same thing was noted in arts and social studies. Tony Martin, admissions tutor and lecturer in geography, recalls the internationalisation of the student body:

> I mean to say when I first came most of the students, in fact we used to say they were on the end of the Blue Train, you know, the suburban railway which were called the Blue Trains in those days. But obviously *progressively* Strathclyde tried to move out until it got an international reputation and I think towards the end of my period here at Strathclyde we had students from, what, about 120 different countries, but when we first came, when I first came in fact, they were very much the west of Scotland.

Postcolonial development work was fostered in 1969 by the British universities' initiative to universities in developing nations. Dr Eric Furness, later professor in economics, was first chairman of Strathclyde's Overseas Development Unit, leading in 1970s to a link-up with the University of Ghana, and from there to the formation of the David Livingstone Institute of Development Studies, and, by diverse routes, to the placement of several lecturers in overseas universities.[7]

One strong feature of nearly all Strathclyde graduates has been the intention to work. The social background of most of the students of Strathclyde has ensured a culture of work-related studies, of knowing that the aim was to get a degree as a passport to the best position possible. But the opportunities for work have gone through major cycles since the 1960s in ways which were less marked perhaps for the smaller numbers of graduates of the nineteenth or early twentieth centuries. Barbara Graham from Careers Advice recalls:

If we're certainly talking of the '70s and to some extent on into the '80s, it would be an expectation that if you went to university and got a degree you would be doing a job which in some way was known as a graduate job. If I go back to the '60s when I graduated myself, never would it have occurred to any of us that we would not get a job or that we would not get a job that would be different from the kind of job we'd got if we'd left school. And certainly I think that was the way that students thought in the '70s as well. So they would be primarily applying for graduate training schemes with industrial, commercial recruiters, or perhaps more so in the case of arts students there's always been a high proportion of those going to do further study leading to occupations such as teaching, social services, librarianship things of that sort.

A further feature of the Strathclyde student legacy has been the intimate connection between the institution (and its predecessor colleges) and the family. Families from the late nineteenth or early twentieth century found occupations using skills they had learned through the Colleges, often in the same subject. We have seen already the significance of the family connections established in engineering through Allan Glen's School. But the economy of the west of Scotland was not solely industrial. The Royal College had a strong reputation in pharmacy, for instance, and created generations of family connection. James Laurie recalls two examples:

I have very fond memories of coming to 'the Tech' in 1952 because my name is Laurie and you seemed to register in alphabetical order and the chap I registered and stood beside in the queue to register was a chap called John Leslie and we still are in close contact with one another, and John Leslie ran a pharmacy in Cambuslang for many years and my father before me ran a pharmacy in Largs and succeeded to him. In fact there are now four generations in my family have come from Strathclyde, three to do pharmacy and I have a granddaughter just started in the Hotel School doing hospitality management just this year...John Leslie's father was a pharmacist before him and John succeeded his father and ran the business.

This legacy has remained vibrant. Strathclyde has sustained the tradition of family connection in engineering and science, and extended it into other and newer subjects. In arts and social sciences, as well as one generation following another, staff have noted the parent and child (often mother and daughter) coming to university together, or even on occasion the mother *after* the daughter. In law, Professor Robson conducted research in the late

1970s into his school's intake and found the family connection still strong: 'Our product has gone out there and has produced its own children. We are getting, you know, we are getting – second-generation people have come to Strathclyde which is a bit strange. You know, we had the sons of our former students, the sons and *daughters* of our former students through our doors.'

Another legacy is more complex to describe. The University attracted mature students in significant numbers from the 1960s, earlier than most universities in Britain. Return to study became a particular specialism of the institution, and it created a special relationship between the return-to-study student, career and family. Noel Cochrane recalls his success in his teaching career after graduation, and the determination – almost the selfishness of spirit – that got him through:

> I was like (*sounds to intimate speed*) and you know, sitting at the desk just *grafting hard, hard, hard, hard*. It was just very, you know as a special recruitment, you know [I] was very earnest, *everything depended upon this* you know in terms of. I had three children when I was at university. It was a tremendous responsibility to meet this challenge which I had *no*, you know, no kind of real expectation [or] preparation for, other than –. So I was – I was quite overwhelmed by it.

This is to what he attributes his success:

> I think that was personality. I think, I think that Strathclyde was just the opportunity to express that aspect of yourself you know challenge you to do that, it gave you a goal and once you had the goal you know you were, we were going to succeed. Previously, I had never been in, you know, the education system had never challenged me previously. *Jobs* had never challenged you like that previously, but here was a challenge that you took on. It was very . . . and failure to do it would have been a big loss of face. So I think that was the first time that I had encountered that and in the process of encountering, you know, discovered dimensions of yourself you just didnae know.

The mature student's commitment to study is legendary the world over. But in central Scotland, Strathclyde had a constituency that was more heavily populated by mature students from working-class backgrounds, sometimes unemployed because of the decline in heavy industries, and though this is very difficult to calculate, it does seem to many that the widowed, separated, divorced and single parent were unusually numerous in Strathclyde admissions. This made one mid-1970s student, Ronnie Scott, reflect:

How brave they were, in terms of – I mean speaking to some of them, what their personal circumstances had been, what they'd given up, what sacrifices they were having to make to be at university and how they, they weren't able to take part in, in any other student activities just because they had a child at home or they had other work to attend to or whatever so . . . that was one thing that struck me . . .

Mature students found a real enjoyment in the Strathclyde experience. In some ways, certainly in arts and social studies, mature students made the B.A. Arts degree their own. Stewart McIntosh recalls his days as a student of English in the early 1970s:

By third year I realised I really wanted to do English, so that kind of English suited very well. And a great time, it was without doubt the best years of my life . . . Oh yes, I had a tremendous time, I loved it. I had a reasonable grant, because in those days county councils like Lanarkshire and others were offering grants to working-class kids to go to university. And, oh there was a special grant, it was called the [Special Recruitment Grant]. It was a desire to bring people into school teaching, mature people. There was a great shortage of teachers at the time, and so you were guaranteed maximum grant including living-away-from-home allowance. So I had a flat three-quarters-of-a-mile from my parents' house (*laughs*). You wouldn't get that nowadays, would you? So that was all fully-funded, and it was great. And in the end you didn't have to sign up to be a teacher, no one actually *bothered to check*, no one came back to me and said.

This commitment of the mature student had vital aesthetic ramifications. Noel Cochrane did English studies, which became a parallel skill to his previous interest and training in art:

I can understand how probably I had the ability *in* English, but I didn't know it. Art was *demonstrable*, you could draw, but being articulate or even understanding how you're expressing yourself, had no currency, I had no measurable, you know kind of way of identifying this, but I probably you know –. So English was probably the most appropriate thing for me to do, you know in retrospect. And that's hindsight, you know, kind of life experience that tells you that you know.

From the late 1960s the University enticed creative and artistic minds, attracted perhaps by the space provided by study. Those destined to be novelists, writers, journalists, elements of Scotland's artistic and literary renaissance of the late twentieth century, came to Strathclyde for study. Strathclyde staff learned more quickly than elsewhere, perhaps, that for mature students the institution needed to provide a venue for exploration of commitment as well as of intellect. The committed mature student will find her- or himself in that space, and use it to the best of their abilities. In that space, the University is not the giver of commitment, but the provider of space.

The reputation of Strathclyde was formed with remarkable speed. This started with its own students, rather than with the Scottish Education Department or Glasgow University. Recalling that the SED initially withheld recognition of Strathclyde qualifications for teacher-training, Roger Sandilands remembers during his first year as a student in 1963–4 that he was unconcerned with the existing educational hierarchies:

> No it didn't worry particularly, I knew I was getting a very good education ... Oh I mean it was probably much better than they had in Glasgow University because we had this fantastic staff/student ratio, very well looked after, and generally the staff were pretty good people and *the students were good*. Several people in my class ended up being quite prominent academics.

For Sandilands, the student there in the mid-1960s included high-flyers who went on to stunning academic careers. A Strathclyde identity was already being formed:

> I do remember when, in my last year, there was a guy called Bill Scamell who is quite a well-known economist came round on a recruitment drive, he was at Simon Fraser University [in Canada]. He himself was Irish and a prominent international economist, and he came over from Simon Fraser to try and recruit people like me to go there to their graduate school and I remember him saying that he thought that of all the new universities, Strathclyde was the one that struck him as being more like a real university.

For students, study is not necessarily the happiest thing they could do. One interviewee,[8] retired now, recalls his years studying engineering at the Tech in the 1950s:

> I never studied for the joy of studying. Having said that I currently go to a French and an Italian class just to keep my brain active. Again do I

enjoy it? I wouldn't go if I didn't want to do it but I keep thinking 'Oh Christ don't tell me I have to do that homework', well it was a bit like that at the College as *well* with me. I mean I wasn't thinking every morning 'Oh gosh I'm going into the College this is going to be great'. I regarded it as a hurdle I had to get over to get involved in my career.

For women students, going to College in the 1950s and 1960s has produced a lasting sense of change. Pat Fraser recalls her small part in the vanguard of equal opportunities for women:

The business of working, that's another thing, once we finished. In my case my mother never worked because it was really frowned upon, she did one long *locum* for three weeks, but society would have pointed the finger at my father, 'He can't keep her', that was the kind of attitude then. And she said to us 'All of you keep your hand in'. So we did a fair wee bit of work. But you didn't really meet many people who did, in a way we were ahead of the times ... But there were some jobs that as soon as you got married you had to leave. The library was one, the police office was another. My father got great secretaries from the police office, frequently. A woman who, who had been working for years and years, and the minute she was a Mrs she didn't leave she was asked to go. Well I mean it was the rule. The library was another place.

**Table 7.1: Female proportion of graduate population,
by year of birth, Scotland, 1991**

	Female (%)
Born 1932–46	27.1
Born 1947–61	40.6
Born 1962–73	49.7

Source: Table adapted from data in Census of Scotland 1991, published in A. McIvor, 'Gender Apartheid?', in T. M. Devine and R. J. Finlay (eds), *Scotland in the Twentieth Century* (Edinburgh, Edinburgh University Press, 1996), p. 203.

As Table 7.1 shows, women made up little more than a quarter of the graduate population of Scottish people born in the mid-twentieth century, but those born in the 1960s and early 1970s enjoyed a far greater likelihood of graduation, making up a half of the total. University degrees for women changed women, changed employers' attitudes, and changed society too. What Strathclyde did especially was to open many of the technical and

scientific disciplines to women. John Paul recalls how women rose significantly in number in engineering, including his own daughter who joined a
class in our period and one of twelve women in a class of 107. Change,
diversification and the creation of new disciplines has brought women in
ever-increasing numbers into realms formerly exclusively male. John Paul
again:

> Well engineering was usually thought of as the muck and grime, heavy
> engineering which girls didn't go into in employment. They would have
> had a very rough time in the workshops within Clydeside, for instance.
> There were a few people, females working there, but usually on manual
> tasks and not on skills tasks. Now in bioengineering we're about equal
> males and females. They see somewhere to apply science and somewhere
> where they can maybe do something towards medical development.

Table 7.2 Sex of students in higher education, UK (thousands)

	Male	*Female*
1970–1	416	205
1980–1	526	301
1990–1	638	537
2000–1	940	1,128

Includes part-time, full-time and Open University.
Source: Department for Education and Skills; National Assembly for Wales; Scottish
Executive; Northern Ireland Department for Employment and Learning.

John Webster, emeritus professor of engineering, has seen a major impetus
by his discipline nationwide to open up the subject to women, to entice them
from those subjects like maths and even physics where they could find a
prominent part to play into an engineering profession made more conducive
to them philosophically as well as structurally:

> I think there were two girls in my, in my diploma class in 1946, but there
> was no great upsurge in number or indeed increase in numbers. And then
> in 1960 or thereafter, there was a move by the professional institutions to
> encourage women into engineering and nowadays there's an acronym for
> it WISE, Women In Science and Engineering. And they run courses and
> they run familiarisation events and so forth, to encourage girls from
> fifth/sixth year at school to investigate or think of the possibility of doing
> engineering and eh? that has; there's not enormous numbers, but where

Figure 7.2 Andersonian Library staff, 1975
The architects of the modern Andersonian Library in the 1960s and 1970s, when new technology was pioneered. Charles Wood, the University Librarian, is in the centre front. Other librarians include Dr Cargill-Thompson (to Wood's left), Hamish Good (tall figure in the back row), and Malcolm Allan (back row, far left), one of the interviewees. *Strathclyde University Archives.*

it was unusual to get a girl in a class, it's *highly unusual* to get a class without girls.

The University reflected rather than led the gender revolution in Scottish society. But it was still – and remains so to this day – a facilitator of those things that society wanted and desired to change. The opening of women's educational opportunity at degree, postgraduate and at staffing levels has fed back into society those things that were underway. In this sense, the University may not be a leader in all social change, but its co-operation is still an absolute necessity.

THE UNIVERSITY IN ITS SOCIETY

If the University has done fair by its staff and students, the society in which it is located has not always appreciated the products of its learning and research. In each year between 1949 and 1969, it was calculated that the Royal Technical College and University of Strathclyde produced 10 per cent of all technology graduates in the nation.[9] The status of science and especially engineering is seen by many to have gone down in British society since the 1950s. Even by 1969, it was clear that schools' science training was in decline in relative terms – though Lord Todd, the University Chancellor and a scientist, felt it was only a natural swing to redress the 1950s imbalance against arts.[10] But for engineers, feels James Brown (a postgraduate student in mechanical engineering), the consequences have been especially poor. He expresses a widespread feeling that they are just not appreciated:

> Well we knew it was very hard work but that was what you had to do to learn the amount of things you needed to know to be a competent engineer. Medicine was a hard subject, veterinary medicine was hard, engineering was hard. What we did resent was the poor remuneration at the end . . . All the years I've been getting the Institution of Mechanical Engineers magazines there have been letters complaining about poor pay and poor status of engineering of all branches in this country and the public confusion of what an engineer is. Recently there was a survey to find the best-known engineer in the UK and the overwhelming majority thought it was Phil Mitchell from *Eastenders*, you know, a motor mechanic . . . Whereas on the continent everyone respects an engineer and it's spelt differently meaning 'inventor', inventiveness . . .

As Dr Ronnie Simpson says:

> I think engineers tend to be their own *worst enemy*. I think engineers need to go out there and promote themselves and they're not good at selling themselves, they're good at working and producing and doing things. But if you ask them to stand up and promote themselves, *they're not very good* quite often, and I think that is bad.

The cultural gap between arts and engineering is greater than ever, thinks James Brown, recalling a recent joke sent by a colleague in the United States:

> It was about a group standing round looking at a piece of equipment. The physics graduate says 'Why does it work?', the engineering graduate

says '*How* does it work, how can I make one?', the accountancy graduate says 'How much would it cost?' and the Liberal Studies graduate says 'Would you like fries with those?' (*laughs*).

Former student Ronnie Scott recalls the 'turn' against his own liberal studies subject, sociology, in the 1980s:

I distinctly remember all through . . . the '80s, people would say 'Oh what did you do at university?' And I would say 'English and [*coughs intentionally*]'. And people would say 'What was that?' And I'd say 'Sociology – but we don't talk about it now'. And they'd say 'Hmmm, yes' [*laughing in background*]. So there was a kind of, at the least on the jokey level, there was a kind of feeling that sociology had been found out or it that it . . . wasn't a *social science*.

And yet some in arts and social studies have found that there is a convergence of research concept and method between applied sciences and applied social sciences. Professor Richard Rose, appointed to a chair in the University in the mid-1960s at the age of thirty-two, articulates the researching social scientist's appreciation of the value of the Strathclyde environment:

My approach in the study of politics and public policy is conceptual first of all, and attempt to apply ideas to real problems. In that sense there's an intellectual content, but it's not history because it's about recurring activities. While you can't collect the biographies of thirty million voters and so you need some sort of scientific data, and those we term in German *angewandte Sozialwissenschaft* – applied social science . . .

From the mid-1970s, Rose pursued one of the major trends in British universities in the last quarter of the twentieth century – the academic centre separate from the usual departmental structure:

When I came to Strathclyde in 1966 I thought of giving it seven years. By 1973 I was ready to move in to other things – and the big thing at that time was the development of interdisciplinary research in public policy. I spent part of 1974 in Washington researching the relation between social scientists and government. In 1976 I created the Centre for the Study of Public Policy as the first public policy research centre in a university in Europe. I then left the Politics Department and have spent the subsequent quarter-century as director of the CSPP.

245

The social sciences at Strathclyde quickly became well regarded in their different fields. In Psychology, Gustav Jahoda found that his department attracted scholars from many nations: 'It was quite a *cosmopolitan place* in that way and we managed to attract many distinguished visiting staff.' And as Strathclyde staff revolutionised their disciplines as researching scholars, so they revolutionised the discipline as teaching subjects for their students. In Politics, as Richard Rose recalls, 'the whole object was to help train students to give them skills so they could analyse problems in the real world which had a political dimension'. The result was students who became peculiarly in demand in the political process – as researchers, political reporters and as people skilled in quantitative method. With the arrival of the devolved Scottish parliament from 1999, Strathclyde graduates secured important positions in this process. As Richard Rose concludes: 'I was encouraging people in Strathclyde staff and students to be *confident* and get on with it. If you want an education we'll give it to you, if you're good you'll do well here, if you're no good, you're another mistake. That's true of students as well as staff.' In 1969, Samuel Curran stated his aim was to keep two-thirds of student places for science and engineering students, in reflection of the community's needs.[11] In this, Curran was facing both local and national difficulties. At national level in the 1960s, there was a definite and substantive swing on the part of school and university students away from science and technology towards arts and social science.[12] At local level, the decline of the staple industries of shipbuilding, engineering, textiles and deep-mining in the west of Scotland meant that the economic and educational needs of the community had changed, and student demand started an inexorable march away from science-based learning. On top of this, the increasing proportion of women amongst the student population, to the point where by 2002 they made up the majority of Scottish university students, emphasised the buoyancy of the humanities and social sciences.

A distinctive feature that Strathclyde inherited from the Royal College and from the College of Commerce was the link between the higher-education institution and private industry and trade. Part of this linkage was for teaching and educational purposes, but part has been for research and development. Andrew McGettrick in Computing and Information Sciences has had strong links all his time at Strathclyde with various outside bodies, including ICL and the National Engineering Laboratory. He still thinks this is important, but in his field especially there is a problem of globalisation removing out of the country corporate decision-making concerning partnerships with universities:

I would welcome stronger links with industry, but somehow or another many of the companies that are in the Scottish area aren't sort of in charge of their own destiny, you know, they do what they're told by the likes of America or something of that kind. What they do is they fulfil contracts that are passed to them from the States, and they're not necessarily in the business of driving forward some area of research [they] kind of think that might be of interest to the university. I think that's quite an issue for Scotland actually.

But in terms of teaching, subjects like computing science were producing graduates that were snapped up by industry: McGettrick again: 'Oh yes, some of the companies were taking more or less all the graduates out of particular degrees. I mean they were highly sought after and the companies were supportive in terms of industrial years and industrial placements and all of that, so there was a lot of that kind of thing going on.' Medical, government and charitable connections have also been extremely important in the Strathclyde tradition of innovation and applied research. For example, John Paul describes the birth of bioengineering in the 1960s in the context of the Vietnam war and the significant demands of the veterans for better artificial limbs. His work and international networking at that time led in 1970 to Strathclyde becoming the home of the new National Centre for Training and Education in Prosthetics and Orthotics.

The mid-1970s saw the consolidation of the University in all sorts of ways. One of these was the advent of national pay scales for most university staff. Whereas before pay scales were set on more local, and sometimes institutional, levels, the creation of a unified pay structure for the United Kingdom created a sense of the university network in Britain and confirmed the apparent democratisation of the university systems. This was widely appreciated. Ann Mair recalls the change in 1974:

Seventy-four was a big, big change because everyone in the University was moved off their little scales on to a set of nationally-negotiated scales and that confirmed whether people were clerical or technical or academic-related, or academic. And they put me on 'academic-related' because of the work I was doing and because I was paying FSU pension, and that was the way I was being treated. So they must have thought enough of me *then* to see that I wasn't just sitting doing what I was told, I was doing work, you know.

Above all, one of the big recollections is that the scale of the university was so much more compact in the 1960s and 1970s than at the beginning of the twenty-first century. People recall, as staff, support staff and as students, the intimacy of the environment, the close supervision in teaching, the lower case-loads, and the smaller classes. As Karen Morrison recalls of chemical engineering, it was a 'much slower pace I think, of life and much fewer students. Even when we were down here, which we came in '71, even in the Seventies, I can remember a final year of thirteen, now we've got nearly pushing seventy now. We had an intake of eighty-plus this year, we used to have intakes of maybe fifteen to twenty and that was kind of the norm.' Since then, the university has grown some tenfold in numbers of staff and students, site area, and significance to the city centre. Its subjects have diversified, its functions in research, instruction and consultancy vastly grown. It is a different animal now.

An important feature, not unique to Strathclyde by any means, is the way in which non-academic staff come to have a close affinity with not just the institution as a whole, but their part of it. Those who have belonged for as much as three or four decades become almost as qualified as the lecturing staff. Karen Morrison would never presume to know all the technicalities of her subject, but since the 1960s she has acquired considerable engineering knowledge:

> I think you get immersed in it to be honest. Although I'm a layman, I'm not a chemical engineer, my background's in education and environment, I can read an exam paper because I'm responsible for our distance-learning course and I run the distance-learning course for part-time students in industry, that's my baby. I do it from start to finish, from advertising, getting the bodies in, to getting them out the door and graduating. I can read the exam paper and know when something is not right – not necessarily the formula because some of them I might recognise but they're just a – but, I can recognise if something's not right so, yes, I guess you do.

Yet, for non-academic staff as well as for teachers, not all in the academic world is rosy. The new world of administrative paperwork that developed since the 1960s has changed the nature of work itself. Alan Riley from Estates Management remarks how as an apprentice in the university in the 1960s, he was answerable to only 'two charge-hands, one foreman and one assistant master of works as he was called then and that was all we answered to.' All the work to be done was marked up by them. In the early twenty-first century, by contrast, 'There's more paperwork now and there's more dodges in the place, but the place is a lot bigger. But there again, what you've got to remember is the place is a lot bigger.' Professor Andrew McGettrick in Computing and Information Sciences reflects the mood of

Figure 7.3 State-of-the-art lecture theatre, 1971
Pictured not long after opening, this 455-seat lecture theatre in the John Anderson Building was (and remains today) the University's largest. Lecture theatres today include multi-media and interactive facilities. *Courtesy of* The Herald.

many, we suspect, when he notes that the speed of email communication causes a sloth in decision-making:

> Whereas in the old days you could write a letter and fire it off and then wait for a week or so before the reply comes in, you get it back before it's gone, sort of thing, you know. And to me that's the big change that people, all of a sudden things are going an awful lot faster than they did before. But also there's a lot of bureaucracy around that's also part of it which is horrendous actually, you'll know what I mean!

Change has itself become a legacy of the 1960s and early 1970s. In architecture, Professor Thomas Maver opines that there is a constant inner drive for change in modern higher education which, if not linear, can be a tad circular at times:

In architecture, teaching tries to reinvent itself every semester. So it was the same as now, all bloody change, everything turned upside down but there was more resistance to it then. I think it's taken for granted now. I think we don't know how to teach architecture so we have endless experiments. And if you've been in the game as long as I have you see we're on a third lap changing the balance between science and art and between formal teaching and studio-design projects and it comes and goes. My colleagues are fed up with me saying 'Yeah but we did that twelve years ago and it didn't work.'

But at the same time, there is no gainsaying the very real leap in concept that new technology has brought to architecture where computer-aided architecture, in which Strathclyde has been a world leader, has constituted a massive paradigmatic shift:

My own view is that the use of information technologies, computer-aided design and multimedia and virtual reality, we've got a big specialism here, is having a significantly beneficial effect and certainly our ability; *mainly* because it allows experimentation so there's a huge variety in new building forms but also a huge contribution to being able to design and build buildings which work better environmentally and use significantly less amounts of energy, and therefore reduce the amount of pollution produced by energy production. So, yes, I remain optimistic about it and I think the profession has now got the tools that it has needed all along (*laughs*) and just never had.

That optimism lies at the heart of the Strathclyde experience. From the student perspective, Bill Speirs regards his years at Strathclyde with unalloyed praise: 'as for anybody who goes to university but certainly for me it was a life-shaping and altering experience and, I think probably the thing that *was really good* was that it was, in my experience, it was an academically *very good institution*. It was self-confident.' From the staff point of view, their arrival at a new university with poor facilities and little more than embryonic good ideas has meant opportunities for large-scale development – though they could take some time. It was in the 1990s that Pharmacy designed and moved into a building that was not perfect, but still a major development. This brings to long-term staff a sense of immense excitement, a life-changing event – and one not without stress, as Brian Furman describes:

I saw it from an embryonic project to a completed building, which was exciting. You know, to be involved in that programme was tremendously exciting – starting from one day when we the project was going ahead and we sat in an office in Estates Management with a whole pile of yellow stickers and the project manager had a blank wall and we took these yellow stickies, *post-its*, and labelled them and we started constructing the building on the wall with these *post-its*. That was trying to decide what the geographical relationships were between one part of the building and another. And to think of how we started from that point, then developing through architects' plans, and then through detailed room design and room planning through to the construction phase and seeing the building develop and then *moving into* the building as a functional building, *was a really exciting thing*. I mean, not many people have. Well it's got a *huge amount* of stress associated with it and heartache and particularly as head of department it was very hard. But it was a tremendously exciting project to be involved in, and every time I look at the building now I think 'Well, I played an integral part in the development of that building'. And walking round it you think it's incredible to think that this just started off as a load of *post-its* on a wall of somebody in Estates Management.

What for a university may be no more than the opening of yet another new building amidst a score or more of others over forty years, may be for some staff an absolutely identity-shaking event – an experience that, if it went awry, could have major adverse impact on morale and longevity in the profession. On the other hand, the prize if it is pulled off is immense.

The saddest change has been the biggest – the demise of the heavy industrial base of Glasgow and the west of Scotland. This has been a lasting transition through which the University has had to navigate. The institution was created in the early 1960s when the industry was still vibrant if not booming, and was critical to the economy of the city and its hinterland for miles around. Its disappearance has made a heavy impact upon the industrial side of the university. Professor John Webster speaks of what happened to engineering:

There was *a shift*, it wasn't a total decline. There was a shift from, what you might call the smoke-stack heavy engineering stuff across [to] the light work, and electronics and so forth, and *it*, has prospered and it continued to prosper, but it employs fewer people and it employs people of a different type. Employs a very much higher graduate population, are required for it, and that's a good thing from the point of view of universities and colleges but many of the others, opportunities which previously existed, have gone.

251

In the early 1960s, a new degree in textiles was being planned, and it started prior to the chartering of the University, but suffered from the collapse of the textile industry. Ever adaptable, though, the unit (part of the Department of Pure and Applied Chemistry) switched its emphasis and name to Fibre Science and recruited students from Hong Kong, Bangladesh, India and mainland China before it succumbed in the 1980s.[13] With such economic change at home, some disciplines have all but disappeared from the University. Mining, Petroleum Engineering and Applied Geology, departments whose subjects had fed off the coal-mining tradition of the Scottish coalfields, have gone with the end of deep-mining in the 1980s and 1990s. But most disciplines have modernised, developing new techniques for export, or developing what were minor sub-disciplines in the 1950s and 1960s into major areas of research expertise; such was the case with bioengineering. If training and research in the making of things has declined somewhat in importance, there has been a shift into the making of the abstract and the conceptual. Whatever has an applicability has tended to find a place in the Strathclyde tradition of academic research and teaching.

The teaching legacy of Strathclyde is an area of distinctiveness and one resulting in institutional pride. A devotion to the useful and practical has directly implied an impulse to imparting knowledge and skills, to teaching as a *sine qua non* of the institutional purpose. Such a drive to teach is not always to be found at the forefront of every academic stable, but it is at Strathclyde. This is nowhere more apparent than in engineering, a discipline whose traditional economic base in the surrounding community was devastated between 1960 and 1990 and had to be rebuilt. Computers implied a new character to the discipline – new knowledge, new outcomes, new economic products, and new methods of organising, storing and imparting knowledge. Professor John Webster recalls:

> We had to teach in smaller groups simply because of the fact that you know there was, a limit to the number you can get to operate on a single desk-top any time (*laughs*). So we had to adopt different teaching methods and different systems but we were still face to face with the fact that so much of what we had been trained to do, or trained our students to do, they could now achieve by the push, by pushing the appropriate buttons ... You know, the whole design process of analysis, synthesis and so forth, done on the computer ... You had to sort of buy a number [of computers], a small number, and then use them in groups, group teaching. But it was, it was not a problem otherwise. And once you understood and appreciated what the computer was doing in relation to what you had been doing, it was, it was very *sad*, to realise that all of the

background you had built up and the information you had built up and *your memory bank* had been replaced. It was all in there, you didn't need to bother remembering it. Press the right button, it was there. And the same was true of decision-making – you know the sort of, the decision trees and so forth, which we'd taught very successfully, I think and which people learned to use and understood in relation to their thought processes, decision tree was in there [in the computer].

The effects of the revolution in the nature of knowledge are to be found across the university community. This is not merely, or even primarily, a computer-driven thing, but a product of complex conceptual change in the understanding of information, perception and the imagination.

The sense of pride in the institution is something that has lasted also over many decades amongst former students. Dr Diana Henderson, Foundation Director at Fettes College in Edinburgh, writes: 'I am very proud of being a Strathclyder. I owe a lot to the University, to my Strathclyde degree and to the terrific people with who I shared my student days. I did not enjoy every bit of the four years, but I would not change any of it.' David Paterson confesses to having spent too much time on student politics in his finals year in the mid-1960s, and not performing to his full potential in his Economics examinations. However, he went on to complete a Masters at the University of Birmingham, proving to himself that he could do it. But David bears no grudge against Strathclyde:

Now I think if you look around all the so-called new universities in Britain I would say that Strathclyde was pre-eminent amongst them. I don't think there's another one that really challenges it, in the length of time it's been around and that's partly because there was a long pre-history of teaching in these institutions before the University became into being. But I think, I mean comparisons are always invidious, but I think Strathclyde *has* established itself as a very major university in Britain and there's not many of the new universities just now can really make this their claim.

The University has changed with the city in which it is located. Bashir Maan described in Chapter 1 the sights that greeted him on arrival from Pakistan in the city of Glasgow on 28 February 1953 – a city he described as composed of 'people shabbily dressed, poor people, drunk people standing at every corner', and a city of slums with manifest 'mess and poverty and deprivation'. He was asked fifty years later, in 2003, to describe his impressions of the city:

Q And has Glasgow changed more than you thought it would?

A It has changed very much so, very much so. I can remember Glasgow, the dirtiest town in the country. Now Glasgow's a different city. As I said, twelve people used to live in one single end, one room, sleeping packed like sardines. And now everything is different. The city is very clean, the city is bright and the housing is very good, facilities are there, of course there's poverty in certain cases, but not as much poverty and deprivation as that time.

When John Davies first came in 1969, he was less than enthusiastic about the quality of the city or its urban hinterland, but more than three decades later he celebrates the transformation: 'I think it's far better now; as an environment it's nicer than Manchester or Liverpool which I think have gone backwards.' In the metamorphosis of the city from poverty to relative prosperity, the University has in a major sense been agent of the change. The University campus was created at the western end of the poorest part of the city – the east end. It was located beside the Royal Maternity Hospital which itself had been placed there in the 1880s to transform the high mortality rates for infants amongst the poor and working-class women of the city, and to which they still came until the Hospital's closure in 2002. The University's very location was a message, a beacon of change and transformation in the very heart of the poorest areas. It transformed directly through its expertise in applied technical and science subjects (in architecture, building science, the law, and the social-science subjects that have been part of the Strathclyde experience in the later twentieth century) – subjects that investigated and explored new ways to build buildings of high quality, to transform old tenements into modern places of living, how modern sewage systems might be installed, and how the legal system could be responsive to the vulnerable and poor in our society. In the mid and late 1960s, Professor Thomas Markus of Architecture and Building Science was the chairman of the staff-student Strathclyde University Housing for Glasgow Trust which channelled the department's expertise into rehousing the homeless of Glasgow. Tenement housing was refurbished, with Glasgow Corporation paying half the cost.[14] There has also been the transformative power of the increasingly entrepreneurial role of the university, in counselling and initiating wealth creation through invention, innovation and advice to the private (and public) sectors on how new systems could be inaugurated, new production facilities formed, and jobs created. The University has been a wealth creator, and still is, in the heart of the city.

One of the features this book has sought to illuminate is the way that the University – perhaps any university – is defined by its constituents. The

Figure 7.4 The McCance Building and the Livingstone Tower
Strathclyde University Archives.

common culture is not a product of mission statements and Research Assessment Exercises and Quality Assurance Exercises and Academic Audits. It is the staff and the students. Barbara Graham is eloquent on the way the academic staff make the place tick:

I have just a growing respect for the commitment of most staff that I meet. I think that it is now becoming *very* difficult for academic staff with the pressures upon them to maintain that across all areas of their work. So for them to turn out internationally renowned research whilst remembering the names of every student in first year whatever, that I think is just getting very, very difficult . . . But I think for the most part that sort of commitment to make students' experience at Strathclyde a good one is there with *virtually* every member of staff that I care to meet. Obviously I see that at first hand most in the student services. I love when we go to the hand-in-hand events where the parents come and the various staff say how they will look after your students and then at the very, very end current students talk a bit about what being at Strathclyde has been like for them and naturally to some extent they are hand-picked but they are not a minority, they are not a minority. And I love it if I am on a train or in a café in the city centre and somebody says 'You were my careers advisor' oh that's really nice. So I suppose . It's just that opportunity to make a difference with somebody and that may sound a bit sort of corny but for that's what it's about, it is. And I especially like the fact that in the careers service although a good deal of our work is with groups, the heart for me is with individuals. And in a kind of world where everything is rush, rush, rush there is still an opportunity to sit down with people and say 'OK, let's hear a bit about you and then we'll talk together about what might be happening for you in the future'. I mean that . . . it's a privilege for me to be able to work in that way. And I hope it is something which does literally make a difference for people for you know who are students and graduates today.

One of the lasting attributes of Strathclyde is that it lies at not just the geographical or literal heart of Glasgow. The University lies at the city's *metaphorical heart*, at the intersection between intellect, morality and sociability. It is a moral city in which to not socialise is somehow to reject one of the moral imperatives of life, where to miss the buzz of the city is to miss out on life. Learning and life intersect at Strathclyde. In his time as a student between 1969 and 1974, Noel Cochrane found it an eye-opener commuting from the rather different city of Edinburgh: 'to be in Glasgow, to commute to Glasgow to get the opportunity, limited *though it was*, to go to Glasgow pubs, listen to Glasgow craic, just walk the street and see the architecture, that was all good experience.' That city culture rubs off on the University. The legacy of the mid-twentieth-century University of Strathclyde lingers long because it was made by thousands of students and hundreds of staff who created a learning and researching institution of dynamism, innovation and quality. The experience of those who participated in those years may not conform to the stereotypes of radical students and drop-out youth. The experience was a more subtle blend of the new with the very traditional. The University today is itself a legacy of its members. This is perhaps best summed up by Richard Rose when he says that Samuel Curran came back to Scotland and founded the country's first university in 400 years:

256

It was an honourable challenge to an honourable man and he was a big man. If you say it in those terms to a Scotsman, you couldn't say no and they were lucky to get him. And the Chancellor was from Hillhead, Alec Todd, who ended up Lord Todd of Trumpington. A university doesn't find a pair like that very often!

Glasgow was notoriously 'no mean city'. Curran's modelling of the University of Strathclyde was no mean feat.

NOTES

1. BPP 1963, Cmnd 2154, Robbins Report on Higher Education, pp. 82–3.
2. Brian Pullan refers to 1967–70 as the period of 'crisis' at Manchester; B. Pullan with M. Abendstern, *A History of the University of Manchester 1951–73* (Manchester, Manchester University Press, 2000), p. 207. J. C. Holt describes the period 1957–71 at Reading as 'cataclysmic'; J. C. Holt, *The University of Reading: The First Fifty Years* (Reading, Reading University Press,1977), p. 155.
3. Michael Sanderson calls this period the 'time of troubles' at UEA; M. Sanderson, *The History of the University of East Anglia Norwich* (London, Hambledon and London, 2002), pp. 187–222.
4. Testimony of Barrie Walters.
5. Such as J. Green, *Days in the Life: Voices from the English Underground 1961–1971* (London, Pimlico, 1998); J. Green, *All Dressed Up: The Sixties and the Counter Culture* (London, Pimlico, 1999).
6. Testimony of Anonymous Interviewee 6.
7. Written testimony of emeritus professor Eric L. Furness.
8. Testimony of Anonymous Interviewee 6.
9. John Butt, 'Education for all was his aim', special supplement, *The Times*, 11 February 1969, p. 11.
10. Ibid.
11. Ibid.
12. M. Sanderson, *The Missing Stratum: Technical School Education in England 1900–1990s* (London, Athlone Press, 1994), p. 155.
13. Testimony of Anonymous Interviewee 5.
14. *The Times*, 11 February 1969.

The Oral History Project

NOTES ON METHOD

The oral history in this book has been used in a way that has sought to allow, as much as possible, the testimony to generate its own agenda. It is never the case that research in any field can be free from the existing research protocols, issues and agendas in the field, as mediated through the researchers. In this volume, the agenda that has emerged from testimony – both from students and from staff – has led the authors in directions that have appeared little in the literature on university education or in experiential analysis of the 1950s and 1960s in British culture. The optimism, the regard for the university and for the university experience, the validation that interviewees gave to the institution during the 1950s and 1960s, was a powerful feature of the testimony. This we have sought to reflect throughout the book.

The task of collecting oral testimony for any oral-history study demands time and patience, with an appreciation of participants' experience and where their place belongs in any projected history. The aim here was not to produce a representative sample of staff and students who attended Strathclyde and its antecedent colleges, but to get a good cross-section of people who could express and illustrate the diversity of experiences during this vital period of post-war education.

The archive of material was collected by recruiting interviewees through university publications (such as the magazine *PRISM*), through talks to the Tech Club, by word of mouth, and by reference from university officers. Hundreds of emails were sent out and possible interested parties approached in other ways. We offered interviews or sought written memories from all who approached us. Several former staff and students submitted written material to us. Some people whom we approached declined to be interviewed, and some did not reply. Once we had received positive responses from those willing to be interviewed, we sent out a very brief questionnaire and then the process began. Interviewees were interviewed in a variety of locations (including their offices, in the Department of History, or in their homes). The interviewees were made aware in advance of the nature and purpose of the interview to ensure that theirs was an informed consent to proceed. The interviews were all conducted by Dr Neil Rafeek, except those by Hilary Young B.A. (the interviews with Robin Alpine, Pat Fraser and Elizabeth McCudden, and Barbara Graham). The interviews were recorded, transcribed, and a copy of the transcription sent to the interviewee for scrutiny and suggestions for change; interviewees then signed a consent form for the interview to be published and archived. Interviewees were asked if they would allow their name to be used. In seven cases, permission to use was granted only on an anonymous or (in one case) partially-anonymous basis.

The interviewers operated to a basic set of headings concerning experience of Strathclyde University and its antecedent colleges (teaching, research, community, home life, and the city), and from these detailed questions were developed by the interviewer in the light of the background and experiences of each interviewee. Discussions were designed to be open-ended, and the material as little formally-structured as possible. Each interview lasted from around fifty to around 170 minutes. The material produced is by no means limited to the history of the two colleges and the Universities, but covers childhood memories, some prescient descriptions of war, and often emotional occurrences in people's lives. It is important to observe, therefore, that the testimony is important not merely for educational history, but because it places educational experience in the wider context of people's complex and diverse lives.

In all, consent was achieved with forty-six interviews involving forty-eight individuals – eight women and forty men. Written memories came from a further one woman and five men. Some further manuscript personal testimony came into our hands, but it was without consent to use or without contact details, and has sadly had to be omitted. Some individuals were interviewed in more than one capacity (i.e. some were students and staff, and some attended more than one institution). The range of experiences broke down as follows:

Table App. 1

	Royal College	College of Commerce	University
Academic staff	7	2 (1)	26 (2)
Academic-related & non-academic staff	1	1	8
Students	8 (2)	3 (1)	7 (1)

(Written testimony in brackets)

The total of the tape/disc recordings comes to approximately sixty-five hours, and transcripts to 360,000 words. A complete set has been deposited in the University Archives and in the Archive of the Scottish Oral History Centre in the Department of History.

Select Bibliography

ORAL HISTORY TESTIMONY

See Appendix and footnotes.

UNIVERSITY OF STRATHCLYDE AND ITS ANTECEDENTS

Primary sources

(SUA denotes Strathclyde University Archives)

Royal College of Science and Technology, *Students' Representative Council/Union, Dance Committee (later Entertainment Committee) Minutes*, 1950–9 (SUA JA 6).

Mask: Journal of the Royal Technical College Students' Representative Council (SUA, JD 1).

Pivot: Magazine of the Commercial College, session 1950–1 (SUA, JB/12).

Strathclyde Telegraph: Journal of the University of Strathclyde Students' Union (SUA, JD 3).

CRUST (SUA, JD 2).

The Pitt, March 1959 (SUA, JB/13).

Secondary sources

J. Butt, *John Anderson's Legacy: The University of Strathclyde and its Antecedents 1796–1996* (East Linton, Tuckwell, 1996).

J. Graham, *One Hundred and Twenty-Five Years: The Evolution of Commercial Education in Glasgow* (Glasgow, n.pub., 1964).

J. A. Rae (ed.), *The History of Allan Glen's School, 1853–1953* (Glasgow, Aird and Coghill, 1953).

Sarah Smith, 'Retaking the register: women's higher education in Glasgow and beyond, c.1796–1845', *Gender & History* vol. 12 (2000), pp. 310–35.

HIGHER EDUCATION

T. Ali, *1968 and After: Inside the Revolution* (London, Blond and Briggs, 1978).

R. D. Anderson, *Education and Opportunity in Victorian Scotland: Schools and Universities* (Oxford, Clarendon Press, 1983).

R. D. Anderson, 'In search of the "lad of parts": the mythical history of Scottish education', *History Workshop* vol. 19 (1985).

R. D. Anderson, *The Student Community at Aberdeen, 1860–1939* (Aberdeen, Aberdeen University Press, 1988).

R. D. Anderson, *Universities and Elites in Britain since 1800* (Basingstoke, Macmillan, 1992).

R. D. Anderson, *Education and the Scottish People 1750–1918* (Oxford, Clarendon, 1995).

R. D. Anderson, M. Lynch and N. Phillipson, *The University of Edinburgh: An Illustrated History* (Edinburgh, Edinburgh University Press, 2003).

H. Bourges, *The Student Revolt: The Activists Speak* (London, Pantheon, 1968).

BPP 1963, Cmnd 2154, Robbins Report on Higher Education.

H. Corr, 'An exploration into Scottish education', in W. H. Fraser and R. J. Morris (eds), *People and Society in Scotland vol. II 1830–1914* (Edinburgh, John Donald, 1990).

C. Crouch, *The Student Revolt* (London, Bodley Head, 1970).

G. Davie, *The Democratic Intellect: Scotland and her Universities in the Nineteenth Century* (Edinburgh, Edinburgh University Press, 1961).

J. C. Holt, *The University of Reading: The First Fifty Years* (Reading, Reading University Press, 1977).

D. Jacks, *Student Politics and Higher Education* (London, Lawrence and Wishart, 1975).

M. Moss, J. F. Munro and R. H. Trainor, *University, City and State: The University of Glasgow since 1870* (Edinburgh, Edinburgh University Press, 2000).

B. Pullan with M. Abendstern, *A History of the University of Manchester 1951–73* (Manchester, Manchester University Press, 2000).

K. A. Reader, *The May 1968 Events in France: reproductions and Interpretations* (New York, St Martin's Press, 1993).

M. Sanderson, *The Missing Stratum: Technical School Education in England 1900–1990s* (London, Athlone Press, 1994).

M. Sanderson, *The History of the University of East Anglia Norwich* (London, Hambledon and London, 2002).

E. P. Thomson et al., *Warwick University Ltd* (Harmondsworth, Penguin, 1970).

W. Thompson and C. McCallum, *Glasgow Caledonian University: Its Origins and Evolution* (East Linton, Tuckwell, 1998).

G. Walford, *Restructuring Universities: Politics and Power in the Management of Change* (London, Croom Helm, 1987).

GLASGOW

C. G. Brown, 'Urbanization and living conditions', in R. Pope (ed.), *Atlas of British Social and Economic History since c. 1700* (London, Routledge, 1989).

S. Bruce, *No Pope of Rome: Anti-Catholicism in Modern Scotland* (Edinburgh, Mainstream, 1985).

D. Daiches, *Glasgow* (London, Grafton, 1982).

S. Damer, *Glasgow: Going for A Song* (London, Lawrence & Wishart, 1990).

T. C. Ferguson and J. Cunnison, *The Young Wage Earner: A Study of Glasgow Boys* (Oxford, Oxford University Press, 1951).

T. C. Ferguson and J. Cunnison, *In Their Early Twenties: A Study of Glasgow Youth* (London, Nuffield/Oxford University Press, 1956).

T. Gallagher, 'Protestant extremism in urban Scotland 1930–1939: its growth and contraction', *Scottish Historical Review* vol. lxix (1985).

T. Gallagher, *Glasgow: The Uneasy Peace: Religious Tension in Modern Scotland* (Manchester, Manchester University Press, 1987).

I. Maver, *Glasgow* (Edinburgh, Edinburgh University Press, 2000).

SOCIAL AND CULTURAL HISTORY

B. R. o'G. Anderson, *Imagined Communities: Reflections on the Origin and Spread of Nationalism* (London, Verso, 1991).

C. G. Brown, *Religion and Society in Scotland since 1707* (Edinburgh, Edinburgh University Press, 1997).

C. G. Brown, 'Religion and secularisation', in A. Dickson and J. H. Treble (eds), *People and Society in Scotland vol. III 1914–1990* (Edinburgh, John Donald, 1992).

A. H. Halsey (ed.), *Trends in British Society since 1900* (London, Macmillan, 1972).

L. Heron (ed.), *Truth, Dare or Promise: Girls Growing up in the Fifties* (London, Virago, 1985).

S. G. E. Lythe and J. Butt, *An Economic History of Scotland 1100–1939* (Glasgow and London, Blackie, 1975).

D. McCrone, *Understanding Scotland: The Sociology of a Stateless Nation* (London, Routledge, 1992).

I. Macdonald, *Revolution in the Head: The Beatles' Records and the Sixties* (London, Pimlico, 1995).

A. J. McIvor, 'Women and work in twentieth-century Scotland', in A. Dickson and J. H. Treble (eds), *People and Society in Scotland, vol. III 1914–1990* (Edinburgh, John Donald, 1992).

A. Marwick, *The Sixties: Cultural Revolution in Britain, France, Italy and the United States c. 1958–c. 1974* (Oxford, Oxford University Press, 1998).

B. Osgerby, *Youth in Britain since 1945* (Oxford, Blackwell, 1998).

S. Rowbotham, *A Century of Women: The History of Women in Britain and the United States* (London, Viking, 1997).

P. Summerfield, *Women Workers in The Second World War* (London, Croom Helm, 1984).

P. Summerfield, *Reconstructing Women's Wartime Lives: Discourse and Subjectivity in Oral Histories of the Second World War* (Manchester, Manchester University Press, 1998).

ORAL HISTORY

B. Miles, *Paul McCartney: Many Years from Now* (London, Vintage, 1998).

J. Green, *Days in the Life: Voices from the English Underground 1961–1971* (London, Pimlico, 1998).

J. Green, *All Dressed Up: The Sixties and the Counter Culture* (London, Pimlico, 1999).

R. Johnston and A. McIvor, *Lethal Work* (East Linton, Tuckwell, 2000).

T. Lummis, *Listening to History: The Authenticity of Oral Evidence* (London, Hutchison, 1987).

R. Perks and A. Thomson (eds), *The Oral History Reader* (London, Routledge, 1998).

P. Thompson, *The Voice of the Past: Oral History*, third edition (Oxford, Oxford University Press, 2000).

Index